Politics as Usual

To Albert Hirschman
Courageous Cosmopolitan

Politics as Usual

What Lies Behind the Pro-Poor Rhetoric

Thomas Pogge

polity

First published in 2010 by Polity Press

Polity Press
65 Bridge Street
Cambridge CB2 1UR, UK

Polity Press
350 Main Street
Malden, MA 02148, USA

ISBN-13: 978-0-7456-3892-8
ISBN-13: 978-0-7456-3893-5(pb)

A catalogue record for this book is available from the British Library.

Typeset in 10.5 on 12 pt Times New Roman
by Toppan Best-set Premedia Limited
Printed and bound in Great Britain by MPG Books Group Limited, Bodmin, Cornwall

The publisher has used its best endeavours to ensure that the URLs for external websites referred to in this book are correct and active at the time of going to press. However, the publisher has no responsibility for the websites and can make no guarantee that a site will remain live or that the content is or will remain appropriate.

Every effort has been made to trace all copyright holders, but if any have been inadvertently overlooked the publisher will be pleased to include any necessary credits in any subsequent reprint or edition.

For further information on Polity, visit our website: www.politybooks.com

Contents

Acknowledgments

This book owes much to Matt Peterson who has not only critically supported my work on chapters 4, 5, and 7, but has also played a major role in selecting, adapting, and updating all the component essays and in weaving them together into a coherent volume. We also have Matt to thank for the bibliography and the index.

Chapter 1 originally appeared as an essay under the same title in Andreas Follesdal and Thomas Pogge, eds., *Real World Justice* (Dordrecht: Springer, 2005). It has also appeared in Chinese and Spanish, and has been heavily revised for this book.

Chapter 2 is an updated version of an essay first published under the same title in the *Leiden Journal of International Law* 18/4 (2005): 717–45, as part of a Symposium on Cosmopolitism, Global Justice, and International Law. It has also appeared in Portuguese, Spanish, French, German, and Czech. Many thanks to Roland Pierik for very helpful comments and suggestions.

Chapter 3 was first presented at the University of Oslo as the first Oslo Lecture in Moral Philosophy on September 11, 2003, and then published, under its present title, in the *Journal of Human Development* 5 (2004): 377–97. It has also appeared in German and Spanish. Based on a new set of purchasing power parities (PPPs), the World Bank, in the summer of 2008, unveiled a new international poverty line (IPL), which the UN is now using to track progress toward the first Millennium Development Goal (MDG-1). In order to take account of this new IPL and of the new poverty figures the Bank is generating with it, I have thoroughly rewritten the whole essay. I have also abridged it somewhat to avoid overlap with chapter 4.

Chapter 4 was first published, under its present title, in *Philosophical Topics* 37/2 (2009): 199–221. It has also appeared in Spanish, and is here only lightly revised. Many thanks to Kieran Donaghue, Alison Jaggar, Justine Kolata, Matt Peterson, and Elizabeth Weissberg for their good comments and suggestions.

Chapter 5 was first published, under its present title, in *Dissent* 55/1 (2008): 66–75. It has also appeared in German, Italian, Chinese, and Spanish. The facts and figures have been updated.

Chapter 6 first appeared, under the title "Dworkin, the Abortion Battle, and World Hunger," in Steffen Wesche and Veronique Zanetti, eds., *Dworkin* (Brussels: Ousia, 1999). It has also appeared in Spanish. The facts and figures have been updated. Many thanks to Christian Barry, Rüdiger Bittner, Bonnie Kent, Jens Saugstad, Ser-Min Shei, Judith Thomson, and Ling Tong for very helpful comments and criticisms. The question of moral priorities addressed in this essay is further discussed in my "Moral Priorities for International Human Rights NGOs," in Daniel A. Bell and Jean-Marc Coicaud, eds., *Ethics in Action: The Ethical Challenges of International Human Rights Nongovernmental Organizations* (Tokyo: United Nations University Press; Cambridge: Cambridge University Press, 2007).

Chapter 7 was first presented on February 24, 2006, under its present title, in Oxford's Sheldonian Theater as an Amnesty International Lecture. It then appeared in the *Journal of Political Philosophy* 16/1 (2008): 1–25 and in Chris Miller, ed., *War on Terror* (Manchester: Manchester University Press, 2009). I am grateful for written comments and suggestions I received from Jeff McMahan, Chris Miller, Rekha Nath, Matt Peterson, Michael Ravvin, Ling Tong, Leif Wenar, and Andrew Williams.

Chapter 8 was first presented at the August 2002 Convention of the American Political Science Association in Boston, as a response to a paper by the late Thomas Franck. The exchange took place against the background of the then impending invasion of Iraq and was subsequently published, with excessive delay, in Terry Nardin and Melissa Williams, eds., *Humanitarian Intervention*, NOMOS vol. 47 (New York: New York University Press, 2005). Many thanks for very helpful criticisms and suggestions are due to Jerry Gaus, Seumas Miller, Terry Nardin, Dwight Newman, David Rodin, John Tasioulas, John Weckert, Leif Wenar and Melissa Williams. This paper, which has also appeared in Spanish, is complementary to my essay "Preempting Humanitarian Interventions," in Ian Carter and Mario Ricciardi, eds., *Freedom, Power and Political Morality: Essays for Felix Oppenheim* (London: Palgrave, 2001).

Chapter 9 first appeared in the *Journal of Political Philosophy* 5/2 (1997): 163–82. Many thanks to Dagfinn Follesdal for the kind invitation to join him at the Centre for Advanced Study in Oslo, where this essay was written, to Sverker Gustavsson for essential materials, and to Robert Goodin for valuable comments. This essay is complementary to two others not included in this book: "Cosmopolitanism and Sovereignty," *Ethics* 103 (1992): 48–75, explores the desirability of a multilayered global scheme of vertically dispersed sovereignty in which governmental authority and citizen loyalties would be widely distributed over a plurality of nested territorial units. "Self Constituting Constituencies to Enhance Freedom, Equality, and Participation in Democratic Procedures," *Theoria* 99 (2002): 26–54, describes a system of large-scale democratic governance that, while preserving political parties, would afford citizens vastly more meaningful opportunities for substantive political participation.

General Introduction

As a child, I made a remarkable discovery. I found out that the country into which I had been born had, a few years earlier, unleashed a horrendous war on its neighbors and, during this war, had interned, enslaved and murdered unimaginably many Jewish and other civilians in camps. Every adult I knew had played a part in these events, in one way or another.

This discovery turned my world on its head. It was not a mere updating of information or a learning of new facts. It shattered what rudimentary order of the world I had begun to map out. In the world of my emergent understanding, it was inconceivable that the people around me could do such things to other human beings. My discovery of the Nazi crimes was the experience that I had misunderstood the world – completely.

Rebuilding involved much questioning: What then is the world like? How can I form reliable judgments about it when adult guidance is not trustworthy? Are flowers experiencing great sadness and pain when we cut them and sell them in shops? How would I be thinking about the war, the Jews, and the Slavic peoples, if Germany had won?

Children growing up in the affluent countries today may have a similar experience when they discover world poverty or one of its manifestations. They may learn about children elsewhere going hungry, chained to a loom, forced to be soldiers, sold into prostitution, dying of treatable diseases. And they may be stunned to find that the adults around them don't care.

I imagine few children in today's affluent countries have their emerging view of the world shattered by such discoveries. Being on the winning side makes a difference. With reassurance from all sides, it is easy to set aside nascent doubts and to join one of the reigning narratives on how these problems are intractable or disappearing, and on how our noble and advanced countries are doing all they can (or, at worst, a tiny bit less).

Being on the winning side also makes one wonder what the point would be of looking more closely. What do we have to fear from leaving the world's poor to their fate? They can do us no harm. They cannot confront us, ask us uncomfortable questions, hold us to account. They won't even get space in the history books – much less than the American Indians or the Australian Aboriginals. There will never be a monument to their suffering. A monument to the unknown child killed by the IMF, or by the *WTO Treaty*? It will not exist.[1]

This book is for those who want to look more closely, who want to understand our world and their own role within it. My account is not flattering: the global economic regime that our countries designed and impose kills more efficiently than the Nazi extermination camps; the daily suffering from poverty and disease greatly exceeds that caused by World War II in its darkest years. World poverty is actively perpetuated by our governments and officials, and knowingly so. We citizens, too, have enough information to know what is going on, or at least to find out easily, if we care. Our politicians celebrate themselves, and us, for our selfless "development assistance," and we like to listen to these stories. But if we don't shut our eyes, we also know that our efforts against poverty abroad are tiny compared to our means and tiny also relative to the poverty we systematically produce through unjust policies and social institutions. Still, the stories are useful for the children, as they would not understand why we act the way we do.

So don't feel safe with the title. This book is not only about our politicians, about their corruption and their crimes against humanity. It is also about citizens, who are disregarding, trivializing, and condoning these crimes in the vague belief that we are benefiting from them. In this we get plenty of help from academia and the media, from people who know better but have more to gain by flattering us and serving our political elites than by seeking and speaking the truth. And the book is then also about the lies and deceptions, the hypocrisy, the carefully made-up statistics that keep us comfortably ignorant of what we are doing.

The central lie, the foundation of the others, is that we are moral people, who care about our moral responsibilities. If we were, we would take morality seriously in shaping foreign policy and in nego-tiating transnational institutional arrangements, especially those that affect the evolution of severe poverty. We would seek to develop a full understanding of morality's demands on our conduct in these areas, and we would try to live up to these demands. In fact, we do no such thing even while we traffic heavily in moral language.

A few experts eschew moral language, holding that morality does not apply beyond our national borders. This is wrong. But these "realists" at least can provide an accurate analysis of what is driving our policies toward impoverished populations and an accurate view also of the deceptions and hypocrisies of their more ideological col-leagues. Reading them is a relief from the usual deceptions and self-deceptions.

I have sketched the two main themes of the book: the monumental crime we are committing against the world's poor and the monumental deception we are visiting upon ourselves and our children to cover up this crime. If you rank comfort above truth, you have reason not to read on. If you are a minimally moral person, one committed to work out what morality demands concretely, you can find here a second opinion about our culture and times. Think for yourself, read criti-cally, accept nothing on faith from either side.

The book proceeds through a series of case studies. After a brief first chapter on the current global justice debate, chapter 2 explicates and supports my central claim: the dominant Western countries are designing and upholding global institutional arrangements, geared to their domestic economic elites, that foreseeably and avoidably produce massive deprivations in most of the much poorer regions of Asia, Africa, and Latin America.

Chapter 3 looks at how the situation of the world's poor is officially presented and tracked by the United Nations and the World Bank. What I document is appalling. While earnestly admonishing govern-ments to live up to their commitment to halving world poverty by 2015, the UN has surreptitiously revised this goal twice to make it dramatically less ambitious. Turning a promised 50 percent reduction of the number of poor into a 20 percent reduction, the UN has added nearly half a billion to the number of those whose extreme poverty in 2015 will be deemed acceptable – indeed, will be celebrated as our achievement of the first Millennium Development Goal.

Half a billion more condemned to life-threatening poverty by our politicians – this corresponds to about 6 million additional premature

deaths *each year* from poverty-related causes. One is reminded of the
Wannsee Conference, where senior Nazi officials planned the deaths
of millions as part of their "final solution." Of course, there is an
important difference. The German bureaucrats of 1942, and the Führer
whom they sought to please, intended to get rid of the Jews and other
people they deemed inferior. The UN bureaucrats of 2001, and the
national politicians on whom they depend, harbor no ill will toward
the world's poor. Concerned for their careers and hence eager for our
support, they merely do not care. This is a fine moral difference on the
side of the agents. But it does not make the suffering and dying of the
victims any less real.

The UN Food and Agriculture Organization reports that the
number of chronically undernourished people now exceeds 1 billion,
for the first time in human history. Yet the World Bank (henceforth
"the Bank") reports impressive progress from the poverty front.
Chapter 4 examines how the Bank is producing its figures. It shows
that the Bank's happy news depends decisively on fixing the international poverty line at an absurdly low level. It also shows that the
Bank's method is internally unreliable because it is excessively sensitive
to the prices of commodities that are irrelevant for poverty avoidance
and excessively sensitive also to the Bank's arbitrary choice of base
year for comparing the purchasing power of currencies. Chapter 4 also
analyzes other, "multidimensional" measures of development, such as
the UNDP's Human Development Index. It concludes that a morally
and empirically plausible measure of the extent and depth of human
deprivation remains to be devised, offering some initial ideas toward
the formulation of such a measure.

Chapter 5 looks at the stunning growth of global inequality, which
in recent years has been driven by rapid intra-national polarization.
Inequality is doubly related to poverty: empirically and mathematically. Empirically, the economic prospects of persons and groups are
greatly affected by the institutional rules of their society and (increasingly) also by transnational, including global, institutional arrangements. All these institutional schemes are shaped and reshaped through
political struggles that – democratic rhetoric notwithstanding – more
closely approximate a "one dollar, one vote" principle. Large economic inequalities are then self-reinforcing: the more affluent corporations and states can bring their much greater power to bear in order
to shape the rules so as to entrench and expand their advantage.

Mathematically, globalization's compression of the relative position of the poor aggravates their deprivation. The bottom half of
humankind has seen its share of global private wealth shrink to 1.1

percent and its share of global household income to 3 percent, while the corresponding shares of the top decile (tenth) of humankind have risen to 85.1 and 71.1 percent, respectively.[2] So the top decile has 387 times the per capita wealth and 119 times the per capita income of the bottom half. Had the design of global institutional arrangements involved a little more concern for poverty avoidance, the share of the poorest half in global household income might well have sunk no lower than to 5 percent – high enough to avoid life-threatening poverty. Even if this protection of the poor had come entirely at the expense of the top decile, our share of global household income would still be 69.1 percent – and 69.1 times the per capita income of the poorest half. Would this not have been good enough for us? And are we leading better, happier lives with those extra 2 percent of global household income?

Chapter 6 raises an obvious yet neglected question to those who hold that abortion is wrong and believe that we all have a responsibility to prevent abortions (for instance, through the law): why not also accept an at least equally weighty responsibility to protect children who are dying at the rate of 25,000 daily from poverty-related causes? After refuting various defenses of the view that it makes sense to be more concerned with potential future citizens as yet unborn than with foreign children living in life-threatening poverty, I present several weighty reasons for the opposite conclusion: even those who believe that abortion is murder have much stronger reasons to join the battle against world poverty than to devote themselves to the cause of outlawing abortion. Being moral is not a matter of adopting some good cause we like. Rather, being serious about morality requires that we reflect carefully about our moral priorities and support the cause that matters most. In our world, this cause is the eradication of severe poverty.

Having lived through the terrorist attacks of September 11, 2001 in New York City, I witnessed and shared the moral outrage that this mass murder of innocent people evoked. Chapter 7 explicates this moral response by explaining in detail why these attacks were such a horrendous wrong: the attackers either aimed to kill many innocent people or, at least, failed to make reasonable efforts to pursue their aims with a minimum loss of innocent lives. Moreover, the attackers perpetrated their attacks in the name of God without taking reasonable care to assure themselves that what they did really accords with His will.

Encouraged by legitimate moral outrage over these terrorist attacks, the United States and its allies unleashed a massive "war on terror" that copied the two great moral failings of the terrorists: they systematically refused to take reasonable care to exclude the innocent from the massive violence they saw fit to inflict in our name, thus subjecting thousands of wholly innocent people to grievous harm, including horrendous tortures. And they prosecuted this war with heavy appeals to morality without taking reasonable care to assure themselves that what they did was really morally justifiable. They acted under color of morality much like the terrorists had acted under color of religion. Widely condoned by the public while it was going on, the war on terror shows once more that we are interested in morality only insofar as it serves our interests – that we are not committed to constraining our own conduct, or that of our governments, by reference to the moral values we otherwise like to invoke.

Chapter 8 discusses another stand-out in the pantheon of hypocrisy: Kofi Annan's appeal to the Rwandan genocide to support the view that the UN Charter's tight constraints on military intervention should not be taken too seriously. Making it easier for the world's sole remaining superpower to disregard the tedious requirement of UN Security Council authorization, and thus paving the way for the 2003 US invasion of Iraq, this appeal is remarkable for two reasons. First, the suggestion that the Rwandan genocide was in any way facilitated by constraints of the UN Charter is a complete fantasy: there was no state willing to help stop the slaughter and, a fortiori, no state discouraged from doing so by legal concerns. Second, as head of UN Peacekeeping Operations, and again acting in behalf of the US (without consulting the Secretary-General of the UN), Kofi Annan was himself a main cause of the genocide by doing what he could to prevent UN peacekeepers in Rwanda from taking action to prevent the slaughter – action that, well within the authorized mission parameters, the commander on the ground, General Romeo Dallaire, was eager to take. We learn from the story how horrendously morality is abused by those in power, and how completely indifferent they are to its demands.

Chapter 9 relates the failures of our foreign policies back to the flaws of our domestic democratic institutions. Many accept that, as citizens of affluent and globally dominant countries, we share responsibility for the rules and policies that our governments are devising and pursuing in our name. But this responsibility seems thin and theoretical. For what can we really do to make a difference? To be sure, our countries call themselves democracies and have regular elections. But, really, legislative and executive decisions – especially with regard to foreign policy and international rule-making – are made by a tiny politico-economic elite trading favors and concessions through the intermediation of lobbyists and revolving doors. Despite the flattering slogans about all political power emanating from the people, in fact the people have very little say and many are disillusioned with politics and unwilling to make the effort to try to form, defend, and implement well-founded views on important political issues. Given the way our political systems have been organized, and given widespread resignation and active acceptance among other citizens, there is then no realistic prospect for us to moralize the foreign policies of our countries. We are thus not responsible for these policies in more than a nominal sense.

Such views are widely held among citizens of the more powerful Western countries in regard to their domestic politics. And these views indeed contain much truth. But they cannot relieve us of responsibility in the way suggested. To see this, consider that the situation of those pleading powerlessness is relevantly similar to the situation of a large majority of citizens. Each of them is powerless to affect foreign policy given that the other citizens are reluctant to support such efforts. So if any one is to be acquitted of responsibility, then all of them must be acquitted. And then we arrive at the absurd conclusion that a large majority of citizens are cleared of responsibility for their government's foreign policies because they were unable to affect these policies. This conclusion is absurd because it is obviously possible for a large majority of citizens to affect, very fundamentally, both the foreign policies prosecuted by their government and also the way their country's political process is structured. To be sure, to achieve such change these citizens must join together. But asking this of them is not asking too much, given the great harms at stake and given the comparatively low costs and negligible risk of political organization.

Again, this thought has a close analogue in the Nazi case. After the war, many Germans said that they had been opposed to Nazi violence but, given the willing collaboration of so many others, had been unable to do anything about the crimes their country was committing. If we suppose that most of these people were lying, we may perhaps excuse a few truthful Germans on the ground that they really could do nothing to mitigate the violence.[3] But if we suppose that many millions were opposed to the Nazis, it is hard to excuse them on the ground that there was nothing they could do. This is reflected in how the Germans were judged after the war. And if Germans then were responsible for their country's policies, then surely we are responsible now for our country's policies: we are much more affluent than those Germans, have much better sources of information as well as means of communication and of political organization at our disposal, and are much better protected through a set of civil rights that are enforced effectively by an independent judiciary.

But how can we make politics more responsive to the citizens' judgment and will? One great obstacle here is the widespread sense – nurtured by the elites – that such responsiveness is simply impossible. Modern societies are too large, too complex, too sophisticated for ordinary citizens to have a meaningful role in governing them; periodic input into who makes the decisions, that's about as much as ordinary people can reasonably handle. If we are to discharge our responsibility to take on a more meaningful role in the political process, then we need to break through this supposed impossibility by imaginatively conceiving how our politics could be organized differently. Chapter 9 does this by focusing concretely on the example of the European Union and its much-lamented democratic deficit – showing how the EU could have been shaped to be more democratic and, more importantly, how it could have been shaped more democratically.

A philosopher by trade, I am often confronted by colleagues who, somewhat disdainfully, give me to understand that work like that presented in this book – and like that of specifying the Health Impact Fund proposal – is not really philosophy, that is, not something that academic philosophers ought to be doing. My response begins by pointing out that my work is perhaps more true to the historical roots of philosophy than much of what is done today in philosophy departments. "Philosophy" means "love of wisdom"; and wisdom, one might say, is understanding what matters. For many contemporaries, including many philosophers, the question what matters boils down to what we care about. This is a paradoxical reduction, because people – initially, certainly, when we begin our adult lives – care deeply that what we care about should be important: *worth* caring about.

Philosophers have not been much help, lately, in giving us ways of evaluating and critically modifying what we care about. Many have rejected the very search for such standards as inseparably tied to an outdated metaphysics or as incompatible with the pluralism of multicultural societies. And some have then seen it as their task to cure us of the ambition that their reductionism presents as incapable of fulfillment. These are fascinating views that deserve discussion. But I continue to believe that philosophers can illuminate what really matters. The best support for this belief comes not from abstract argument. It comes from showing by doing: from working through a problem so as to make evident its importance.

This book is devoted to one such problem: world poverty, the unjust global institutional arrangements that contribute to it, and our responsibility, as affluent countries' citizens, for this injustice. An adequate treatment of this problem involves work not merely in moral or even political philosophy proper, but also in economics, health policy, political science, history, and the law – fields that produce ample data about the condition of our world as well as about causal relationships and historical-political possibilities. I do not claim to be an expert in these other fields. But I try to understand their relevant areas well enough to be able to analyze pertinent work there for errors and distortions and competently to collaborate with willing experts on the interdisciplinary work that is needed to show what progress toward global justice would look like and how it is possible.

Philosophical or not, this work is far too neglected and needs to be done. When the poorer half of humankind have been squeezed down below 3 percent of global household income, living in dire poverty and dying therefrom at the rate of 2,000 every hour, we cannot all just look the other way. As Albert Hirschman said to me, breaking into German in a conversation about the Spanish Civil War: "Da musste man dabeisein" – one just had to get involved. Our children should not grow up among killers.

* * * * * *

In 1999–2000, I had the humbling experience of working alongside Albert Hirschman (*1915). Fatherless and a refugee at eighteen, Hirschman fought fascism by serving in the Spanish Civil War and in the French and U.S. Armies, and he also worked with Varian Fry to help victims of Nazi persecution escape. He later lived in Latin America, where he analyzed the links among underdevelopment, oppression, and poverty in search of new ways for farmers and governments to overcome these evils. His amazing intellectual legacy, his fertile, illuminating, and wide-ranging scholarship, and his courageous opposition to injustice anywhere will always remain an inspiration for me.

1

What Is Global Justice?

1.0 Introduction

A literature search on "global justice" finds this to be a newly prominent expression. There were more books and essays on global justice in the first few years of the new millennium than in the preceding one, at least as far as computers can tell. Of course, some of the broad topics currently debated under the heading of "global justice" have been discussed for centuries, back to the beginnings of civilization. But they were discussed under different labels, such as "international justice," "international ethics," and "the law of nations." This chapter explores the significance of this shift in terminology. Having been involved in this shift for more than three decades, I realize that there is likely to be a personal element in my account of it, which is due to the specific motives and ideas that have animated my thinking and writing. This is not an objective scholarly report from a distance, which, in any case, would be hard to write at this early time.

For centuries, moral reflection on international relations was focused on matters of war and peace. These issues are still important and much discussed. Since World War II, however, other themes have become more prominent due to increasing global interdependence and an erosion of sovereignty. The United Nations and the *Universal Declaration of Human Rights* reflect efforts to establish globally uniform minimum standards for the treatment of citizens within their own countries. The Bretton Woods institutions and later the World Trade Organization powerfully shape the economic prospects of countries and their citizens. Global and regional organizations, most notably the UN Security Council and the European Union, have acquired political functions and powers that were traditionally thought to belong to national governments.

These developments are in part a response to the horrors of World War II. But they are also fueled by technological innovations that limit the control governments can exert within their jurisdictions. Thus, industrialization has massive effects that no country can avoid – effects on culture and expectations, on biodiversity, climate, oceans, and atmosphere. New communication technologies make it much harder to control the information available to a national population. And many of the goods demanded by more affluent consumers everywhere require ingredients imported from foreign lands. The traditional concerns with the just internal organization of societies and the moral rules governing warfare leave out some highly consequential features of the modern world.

1.1 The extent of global poverty

After some delay, academic moral reflection has responded to these developments. Beginning in the early 1970s, philosophers and others have asked probing questions about how the emergence of a post-Westphalian world modifies and enlarges the moral responsibilities of governments, corporations, and individuals. These debates were driven also by the realization that world poverty has overtaken war as the greatest source of avoidable human misery. Many more people – some 360 million – have died from hunger and remediable diseases in peacetime in the 20 years since the end of the Cold War than perished from wars, civil wars, and government repression over the entire twentieth century.[4] And poverty continues unabated, as the official statistics amply confirm: 1,020 million human beings are chronically undernourished, 884 million lack access to safe water, and 2,500 million lack access to basic sanitation;[5] 2,000 million lack access to essential drugs;[6] 924 million lack adequate shelter and 1,600 million lack electricity;[7] 774 million adults are illiterate;[8] and 218 million children are child laborers.[9]

Roughly one third of all human deaths, 18 million annually, are due to poverty-related causes, easily preventable through better nutrition, safe drinking water, cheap rehydration packs, vaccines, antibiotics, and other medicines.[10] People of color, females, and the very young are heavily overrepresented among the global poor, and hence also among those suffering the staggering effects of severe poverty. Children under the age of 5 account for over half, or 9.2 million, of the annual death toll from poverty-related causes.[11] The overrepresentation of females is clearly documented.[12]

Such severe deficits in the fulfillment of social and economic human rights also bring further deficits in civil and political human rights in their wake. Very poor people – often physically and mentally stunted as a result of malnutrition in infancy, illiterate due to lack of schooling, and much preoccupied with their family's survival – can cause little harm or benefit to the politicians and officials who rule them. Such rulers have far greater incentives to attend to the interests of agents more capable of reciprocation: the interests of affluent compatriots and foreigners, of domestic and multinational corporations, and of foreign governments.

1.2 The moral significance of global poverty

Three facts make the great ongoing catastrophe of human poverty deeply problematic, morally.

First, it occurs in the context of unprecedented global affluence that is easily sufficient to eradicate all life-threatening poverty. Suppose we think of the very poor narrowly as those who suffer the deprivations detailed above – lack of access to safe food and water, clothing, shelter, basic medical care, and basic education. This narrow and absolute definition of severe poverty corresponds roughly to the World Bank's "$2.50 per day" poverty line, according to which a household is poor just in case the local cost of its entire consumption, per person per day, has less purchasing power than $2.50 had in the United States in 2005. Although 48 percent of the world's population, 3,085 million human beings, were reportedly living below this poverty line in 2005[13] – on average, 45 percent below it – their collective shortfall from this line amounts to only 2 percent of global household income.[14] A 2 percent shift in the distribution of global household income could wholly eradicate the severe poverty that currently blights the lives of nearly half the human population.

While the income ratio between the top and bottom decile of the human population is a staggering 273:1,[15] their wealth ratio is ten times greater still. In 2000 the bottom half of the world's adults together owned 1.1 percent of global wealth, with the bottom 10 percent having only 0.03 percent, while the top 10 percent had 85.1 percent and the top 1 percent had 39.9 percent.[16] Severe poverty today is avoidable at a cost that is tiny in relation to the incomes and fortunes of the affluent – vastly smaller, for instance, than the Allies' sacrifice in blood and treasure for victory in World War II.

Second, the unprecedented global inequalities just described are still increasing relentlessly. For the 1988–98 period, Branko Milanovic finds that, assessed in terms of purchasing power parities (PPPs), the Gini measure of inequality among persons worldwide increased from 62.2 to 64.1, and the Theil from 72.7 to 78.9.[17] He adds that real incomes among the poorest 5 percent of world population (identified by PPP comparison) *declined* 20 percent during 1988–93 and another 23 percent during 1993–8, even while real global per capita income rose 5.2 percent and 4.8 percent respectively.[18] I confirm and update his findings with other, more intuitive data below.[19] There is a clear pattern: global inequality is increasing as the global poor are not participating proportionately in global economic growth.

Third, conditions of life anywhere on earth are today deeply affected by international interactions of many kinds and thus by the elaborate regime of treaties and conventions that profoundly and increasingly shape such interactions. Those who participate in this regime, especially in its design or imposition, are morally implicated in any contribution it makes to ever-increasing global economic inequality and to the consequent persistence of severe poverty.

1.3 From international to global justice

These plain facts about the contemporary world render obsolete the traditional sharp distinction between *intra*-national and *interna*-tional relations. Until the twentieth century, these were seen as constituting distinct worlds, the former inhabited by persons, households, corporations, and associations within one territorially bounded society, the latter inhabited by a small number of actors: sovereign states. National governments provided the link between these two worlds. On the inside, such a government was a uniquely important actor within the state, interacting with persons, households, corporations, and associations, and typically dominating these other actors by virtue of its special power and authority – its *internal sovereignty*. On the outside, the government *was* the state, recognized as entitled to act in its name, to make binding agreements on its behalf, and so on – its *external sovereignty*. Though linked in this way, the two worlds were seen as separate, and normative assessments unquestioningly took this separation for granted, sharply distinguishing two separate domains of moral theorizing.

Today, very much more is happening across national borders than merely interactions and relations among governments. For one thing, there are many additional important actors on the international scene: international agencies, such as the United Nations, the European Union, the World Trade Organization, the World Bank, and the International Monetary Fund, as well as multinational corporations and international non-governmental organizations (NGOs).[20] Interactions and relations among states and these new actors are structured through highly complex systems of rules and practices, some with associated adjudication and enforcement mechanisms. Those actors and these rules powerfully influence the domestic life of national societies: through their impact on pollution and climate change, invasive diseases, conflict and violence, culture and information, technology, and (most profoundly) through market forces that condition access to capital and raw materials, export opportunities, domestic tax bases and tax rates, prices, wages, labor standards, and much else.

This double transformation of the traditional realm of international relations – the proliferation of international, supranational, and multinational actors, and the profound influence of transnational rules and of the systematic activities of these actors deep into the domestic life of national societies – is part of what is often meant by the vague term *globalization*. It helps explain why "global" is displacing "international" in both explanatory and moral theorizing. This terminological shift reflects that much more is happening across national borders than before. It also reflects that the very distinction between the national and international realms is dissolving. With national borders losing their causal and explanatory significance, it appears increasingly incongruous and dogmatic to insist on their traditional role as moral watersheds.

1.4 Interactional and institutional moral analysis

The emergence of global-justice talk is closely related to the increasing explanatory importance of social institutions. There are two distinct ways of looking at the events of our social world. On the one hand, we can see such events interactionally: as actions, and effects of actions performed by individual and collective agents. On the other hand, we

can see them institutionally: as effects of how our social world is structured and organized – of our laws and conventions, practices and
social institutions. These two ways of viewing entail different descrip-
tions and explanations of social phenomena, and they also lead to two
distinct kinds of moral analysis or moral diagnostics.

Take some morally salient event – for example, the fact that some
particular child suffers from malnutrition, that some woman is unemployed, or that a man was hurt in a traffic accident. We can causally
trace such events back to the conduct of individual and collective
agents, including the person who is suffering the harm. Doing so
involves making counterfactual statements about how things would or
might have gone differently if this or that agent had acted in some
other way. We can then sort through these counterfactual statements
in order to determine whether any of the causally relevant agents ought
to have acted differently and thus is partly or wholly at fault for the
regrettable event. This will involve us in examining whether any such
agents could have foreseen that their conduct would lead to the regrettable event and could also reasonably have averted the harm without
causing substantial costs to themselves or to third parties. Inquiries of
this kind might be referred to as *interactional* moral analysis or *interactional* moral diagnostics.

Often, regrettable events can also be traced back to standing features of the social system in which they occur: to its culture, for
example, or to its institutional order. In this vein, one might causally
trace child malnutrition back to high import duties on foodstuffs,
unemployment to a restrictive monetary policy, and traffic accidents
to the lack of regular motor vehicle safety inspections. Doing so
involves making counterfactual statements about how things would or
might have gone differently if this or that set of social rules had been
different. We can then sort through these counterfactual statements in
order to determine whether the causally relevant rules ought to have
been different and whether anyone is responsible for defects in these
rules that are partly or wholly to blame for the regrettable events. This
will involve us in examining whether those responsible for the design
of the relevant rules – for instance, Members of Parliament – could
have foreseen that these rules would lead to harm and could reasonably have formulated them differently without causing substantial
harm elsewhere. We might refer to inquiries of this kind as *institutional*
moral analysis or *institutional* moral diagnostics.

Interactional moral analysis emerged quite early in the evolution of
moral thought. Institutional moral analysis is more demanding, pre-
supposing an understanding of the conventional (rather than natural

or divine) nature of social rules as well as of their – often statistical – comparative effects. Even a mere 80 years ago, the poor and unemployed were still often seen as lazy and delinquent merely on the ground that others of equally humble origins had risen from dishwasher to millionaire. Many people then did not understand the *structural* constraints on social mobility: that the pathways to riches are limited and that the structure of prevailing markets for capital and labor unavoidably produce certain basic rates of ("structural") unemployment and poverty. Nor did they understand that existing rates of unemployment and poverty could be influenced through intelligent redesign of the rules. Today, after Keynes, the US New Deal, and various similar national transformations that also include the Bolsa Família program in Brazil, these matters are well understood, and governments are held responsible for their decisions regarding institutional design and for the effects of such decisions on the fulfillment or frustration of human needs.

This understanding has been – belatedly, yet admirably – articulated in philosophy through John Rawls's classic *A Theory of Justice*. Through this grand work, Rawls has firmly established social institutions as a distinct domain of moral assessment and has marked this domain terminologically by associating it with the term *(social) justice*. This terminological innovation has taken hold, by and large, at least in Anglophone philosophy. So the term *justice* is now predominant in the moral assessment of social rules (laws, practices, social conventions and institutions) and used only rarely in the moral assessment of the conduct and character of individual and collective agents. In the wake of Rawls the distinction between institutional and interactional moral analysis has come to be marked as a distinction between *justice* and *ethics*.

1.5 Global institutional analysis

We are quite familiar today with the focus of Rawls's book: with institutional moral analysis applied to the internal organization of one state. Still in its infancy, however, is institutional moral analysis applied beyond the state. This time lag is hardly surprising, seeing that the realm of international relations is traditionally conceived as so much smaller and more surveyable than the vast and highly complex inner workings of a modern national society. We don't need institutional moral analysis, it seems, for a world of a few dozen relevant actors in which, when bad things happen, it is usually pretty clear whose conduct is at fault. And Rawls himself, in his late work *The Law of Peoples*, explicitly shunned such analysis and confined himself to developing and defending a set of rules of good conduct for states.[21]

The phenomena of globalization, described above, show such an account to be deeply and increasingly inadequate to the world in which we live. It ignores the rising importance of transnational actors other than states as well as the increasingly profound effects international rules, practices, and actors have on the domestic life of national societies. Shaping the environment (e.g., global markets) in which national societies exist, such international rules and practices deeply shape these societies themselves: how they govern and tax themselves, how they organize education, health care, agriculture, and defense, and how they regulate foreign investment, intellectual property rights, and foreign trade.

Some of this influence is due to competitive pressures and transnational bargaining. Some of it works by affecting domestic incentives and power distributions: international rules that recognize any person or group exercising effective power in a less developed country as entitled to sell this country's natural resources and to borrow and to import weapons in its name make it extremely tempting, especially in resource-rich such countries, to attempt to take power by force. These countries are therefore especially likely to experience coup attempts, civil wars, and repressive (often military) rule.

Such foreseeable effects of transnational institutional arrangements are surely relevant to their moral assessment. But other factors may be relevant as well: the (typically highly opaque and undemocratic) way such arrangements were created or emerged, for example, and also the extent to which those affected by them either accept them or seek their reform. The discourse about global justice is about this question, how to assess global (and, more broadly, transnational) institutional arrangements.

Reflecting the crumbling of the traditional separation of intranational and international relations, the shift to the language of global justice extends institutional moral analysis to the whole field. We have already seen how this shift is fueled by the realization that the traditional conception of the world of international relations as inhabited only by states is rapidly losing its *explanatory* adequacy – through the emergence and increasing importance of transnational rules and through the creation and increasing stature on the international stage of non-state actors, such as multinational corporations, international agencies, regional organizations, and NGOs. As this traditional conception of international relations loses its grip, we should also realize, however, that its *moral* adequacy has always been lacking. It has never been plausible that the interests of states – that is, of governments – should furnish the only considerations that are morally relevant in international relations.[22]

Consider, for example, a long-term contract concerning the exportation of natural resources, which the government of some African country concludes with a rich Western state or one of its corporations. Within the traditional philosophical framework, it is self-evident that such an agreement must be honored: "People are to observe treaties and undertakings," says Rawls's second principle of state conduct, and the third one adds: "Peoples are equal and are parties to the agreements that bind them."[23] But here is the reality. The African government is corrupt and oppressive, and its continuation in power depends on the military. The sales it conducts impose severe environmental harms and hazards on the indigenous population. Yet, most of these people do not benefit, because the revenues are either embezzled by the small political elite or else spent on arms needed for political repression (arms mostly supplied by affluent Western states in accordance with other contracts executed, without coercion, between them and the African government.)

There is an obvious question here: by what right can a free and fair agreement between a military junta or strongman in Africa and some foreign government or corporation entitle these two parties to deprive the inhabitants of that African country of their natural resources and to despoil their environment?

This question is invisible so long as we think of international relations as a separate realm in which each state is identified with its government. Conversely, once we see the question, the old philosophical framework becomes manifestly untenable. We must then ask ourselves whether it is morally acceptable that the existing international order recognizes rulers – merely because they exercise effective power within a country and regardless of how they acquired or exercise such power – as entitled to confer legally valid property rights in this country's resources and to dispose of the proceeds of such sales, to borrow in the country's name and thereby to impose debt service obligations upon it, to sign treaties on the country's behalf and thus to bind its present and future population, and to use state revenues to buy the means of internal repression. Such recognition accords international resource, borrowing, treaty, and arms privileges to many governments that are plainly illegitimate. These privileges are *impoverishing*, because their exercise often dispossesses a country's people who are excluded from political participation as well as from the benefits of their government's borrowing or resource sales. These privileges are moreover *oppressive*, because they often give illegitimate rulers access to the funds they need to keep themselves in power even against the will of the majority. And these privileges are *disruptive*, because they provide strong incentives toward the undemocratic acquisition and exercise of political power, resulting in the kinds of coups and civil wars that are so common in countries with a large resource sector.[24]

By breaking down the traditional separation of intra-national and international relations and extending institutional moral analysis to the whole field, the concept of global justice also makes visible how citizens of affluent countries are potentially implicated in the horrors so many must endure in the so-called less developed countries: how global institutional arrangements they uphold are implicated in the violence and hunger that are inflicted upon the global poor.

The old framework was comfortable: citizens of affluent countries share responsibility for the institutional order of their own society and for any harms this order may inflict upon their fellow citizens. They also share responsibility for their government's acting honorably abroad by complying with reasonable international laws and conventions, especially those relating to warfare, and by honoring its contracts and treaties. In this traditional framework, such citizens generally bear no responsibility for the violence and poverty inflicted upon foreigners within the black box of their own state.

The new philosophical framework, associated with the expression "global justice," is considerably less comfortable. Central to this framework is the causal impact of the design of the transnational institutional arrangements upon the conditions of life experienced by human beings worldwide. Since the end of the Cold War, major components of the global order – such as the global trading system and the rules governing military interventions – have been substantially redesigned, while other components – such as the international resource, borrowing, treaty, and arms privileges just discussed – have been left in place. There were many alternative ways in which such transnational institutional arrangements could have been shaped and reshaped when, after the end of the Cold War, the North Atlantic powers found themselves in full control. And the question is, then: How would other paths of globalization have been different in their effects upon people worldwide, in their effects upon the incidence of violence, oppression, extreme poverty, and human trafficking for example? And how, in light of such a comparative-impact assessment, is the existing global order to be judged in moral terms?

1.6 The global institutional order contributes to severe poverty

The global institutional order is causally related to the incidence of morally significant harms in two main ways. First, its rules may affect individuals indirectly, by co-shaping the national institutional order under which they live. The four international privileges accorded even to highly illegitimate rulers provide an obvious example. By enabling despotic rulers and juntas to entrench themselves in power and by giving potential such oppressors strong incentives to try to take power by force, these privileges facilitate and foster oppressive and corrupt government in many less developed countries where the resource sector is a large part of the national economy and where ordinary citizens have few means to resist their oppression.

Secondly, the rules of the global institutional order may affect people more directly. Consider, for example, the current WTO treaty system, which permits the affluent countries to protect their markets against cheap imports (agricultural products, textiles and apparel, steel, and much else) through tariffs, anti-dumping duties, quotas, export credits, and huge subsidies to domestic producers. Such protectionist measures reduce the export opportunities from poor countries by constraining their exports into the affluent countries and also, in the case of subsidies, by allowing less efficient rich-country producers to undersell more efficient poor-country producers in world markets.[25] In the absence of these constraints, poor countries would realize welfare gains in excess of $100 billion annually (comparable to current official development assistance or ODA)[26] and reductions of several hundred million in the number of poor.[27] The magnitude of this amount suggests that the *WTO Treaty's* high tolerance for rich-country protectionism greatly aggravates severe poverty in the less developed countries. If the WTO treaty system did not allow the protectionist measures in question, there would be much less poverty in the world today.

Another important example of the direct impact of the global institutional order is the globalization of intellectual property rights through the TRIPS (Trade-Related Aspects of Intellectual Property Rights) component of the *WTO Treaty*. Under TRIPS, WTO members are required to adjust their domestic laws so as to grant 20-year monopoly patents on a wide range of innovations, which, most importantly, include advanced seeds and medicines. In this way, TRIPS has dramatically curtailed the access poor people have to cheap generic versions of advanced medicines. The absence of generic competition multiplies the prices of advanced medicines – often 10- to 15-fold – and thereby effectively excludes the poor.[28] In addition, this globalized monopoly patent regime strongly discourages pharmaceutical innovators from doing any research and development focused on the diseases concentrated among the global poor – diseases that kill millions each year. It is obvious that pharmaceutical research could be incentivized differently: governments could reward any newly developed medicine in proportion to its impact on the global disease burden on condition that this medicine is sold at the (competitively determined) lowest feasible cost of production and distribution. Under this alternative regime, both deadly defects of the TRIPS regimes would be avoided: the price of advanced medicines would be vastly lower, which would greatly expand access to such medicines by the world's poor, and there would be many new medicines developed for the neglected diseases that continue to ravage the world's poorest populations.[29]

Much more could and should be said about these three examples: about the four privileges that fuel and perpetuate oppression and civil war in many poor countries, about the rules that shelter the protectionism practiced by the affluent countries, and about the rules that exclude the global poor from the benefits of pharmaceutical innovation. But the point here is not to demonstrate injustice, but merely to illustrate what institutional moral analysis applied to the global institutional order would look like. In the next chapter, I will take a closer look at the ways in which the global institutional order contributes to severe poverty.

1.7 Global poverty is foreseeable and avoidable

Insofar as the current design of the global institutional order does turn out to entail substantial excesses of violence and severe poverty with consequent excesses of mortality and morbidity (relative to some alternative design), we might go on to ask who bears responsibility for the existing design and whether these responsible parties could have foreseen and could reasonably have avoided these excesses.

The governments of the more powerful developed countries, especially the so-called G-7, have played the dominant role in designing the post-Cold War global institutional order. In shaping this order, those governments have given much weight to the interests of their domestic business and finance elites and rather little weight to the interests of the poor and vulnerable populations of the less developed countries. The resulting global institutional order is arguably unjust insofar as the incidence of violence and severe poverty occurring under it is much greater than would have been the case under an alternative order whose design would have given greater weight to the interests of the poor and vulnerable. As the G-7 countries are reasonably democratic, their citizens share responsibility for the global order their governments have built as well as for the comparative impact of this order upon human lives. At least this is the kind of moral diagnosis that moves center-stage as normative debates about international relations shift from the *international ethics* to the *global justice* paradigm by extending institutional moral analysis beyond the state.

Two objections are often advanced against this moral diagnosis by defenders of the adequacy of the international-ethics paradigm. Objection One asserts that the global institutional framework cannot be unjust because its participants have consented to it – *volenti non fit iniuria*. Objection Two asserts that it cannot be wrong for the affluent countries' governments to design and impose the present global order because their primary responsibility is to their own people, not to foreigners. Let me conclude by briefly responding to these two objections in turn.

Objection One holds that the global institutional order is immune from moral criticism insofar as it has been freely consented to also by the poorer and less powerful states. The objector would allow that, in some cases, the consent given – to the WTO treaty system, for example – was perhaps problematic. He would be willing to entertain the possibility that some weak states were negotiating under considerable duress and also lacked the expertise to work out whether the asymmetrical market access rules they were being offered were better or worse for them than remaining outside the WTO. Our objector might even be willing to consider that perhaps the bargaining power of states entering the negotiations was inappropriately affected by historical crimes, such as colonialism. Still, the objector would insist, insofar as states have freely and competently consented to common rules, these rules are morally unobjectionable.

A proponent of the new global-justice paradigm would reject this reasoning as question-begging. The objection *assumes* what needs to be shown: namely that the only morally relevant question about a global institutional order is whether it does wrong to any of its member states. This is precisely the point challenged by the global-justice paradigm, with the claim that it is relevant for the moral assessment of a global institutional order how it treats individual human beings. As I argue in the next chapter (section 2.4.2), insofar as the present design of the global institutional order foreseeably produces a large excess of avoidable mortality and morbidity, it cannot be justified through even the unanimous consent of the world's governments.

Objection Two holds that it is the very point and purpose of governments to represent and promote the interests of their people. It is therefore entirely appropriate and permissible for affluent countries' governments to do their utmost to shape the global institutional order in the best interest of their citizens.[30]

There is evidently some truth in this objection. Surely a government is not required to give equal weight to the interests of all human beings worldwide. Rather, it is permitted to be partial by showing special concern for the interests of its own people, present, and future. But there are obvious ethical limits to a government's partiality; for example, insofar as it is impermissible for a country's citizens to kill innocent foreigners in order to advance their economic interests, it is likewise impermissible for these citizens' government to do so on their behalf.

The limits on permissible government partiality with regard to the shaping of the global institutional order are less familiar but no less compelling. Quite generally, partiality is legitimate only in the context of a "level playing field," broadly conceived as including fair rules impartially administered. This idea is familiar and widely accepted in many contexts: it is permissible for persons to concentrate on promoting their own interests, or those of their group, sports team, or relatives, provided they do so in the context of a fair competition. Because such a fair setting is a moral precondition for permissible partiality, such partiality cannot extend to the subversion of the level playing field. To the contrary, those who are *partial* in favor of their own group must, as a condition of the permissibility of such partiality, also be *im*partially concerned for preserving the fairness of the larger social setting.

In a domestic setting, for example, it is entirely permissible for you to concentrate your time and money on securing a good education for your own children, at the expense of other children whose education you could also promote. Yet it would be morally wrong for you to seek to promote your children's prospects by using your political influence to oppose equal access to education for children whose gender, color, religion, or class differs from that of your own children. In short: partiality of concern is alright within a minimally fair setting, but not alright when it seeks to undermine the minimal fairness of this setting itself. The minimal fairness of the terms of the competition must not itself become an object of this competition. And the justice limit to a government's partiality in favor of its own citizens forbids, then, partial conduct that undermines the minimal fairness of the global institutional order. An appeal to permissible partiality cannot justify the imposition, by the most powerful governments on the rest of the world, of an unjust global institutional order under which a majority of humankind is foreseeably and avoidably deprived of anything resembling a fair start in life.

1.8 Conclusion

This chapter has sketched the philosophical framework associated with the increasingly prominent expression "global justice." Distinctive of this framework is the focus on the causal and moral analysis of the global institutional order against the background of its feasible and reachable alternatives. Within this general global-justice approach, distinct conceptions of global justice will differ in the specific criteria of global justice they propose. But such criteria will coincide in their emphasis on the question of how well our global institutional order is doing, compared to its feasible and reachable alternatives, in regard to the fundamental human interests that matter from a moral point of view. Extending institutional moral analysis beyond the state, this question focuses attention on how today's massive incidence of violence and severe poverty, and the huge excesses of mortality and morbidity they cause, might be avoided not merely through better government behavior, domestically and internationally, but also, and much more effectively, through global institutional reforms that would, among other things, elevate such government behavior by modifying the options governments have and the incentives they face.

The importance of this global-justice approach reaches well beyond philosophy. It is crucial for enabling ordinary citizens – in the developed countries especially – to come to an adequate understanding of their moral situation and responsibilities. And it is very helpful also for pushing social scientists, and development economists especially, to overcome their bias toward explanatory nationalism, their tendency to explain poverty and hunger exclusively in terms of causal factors that are domestic to the societies in which they occur. However valid and useful, such nationalist explanations must be complemented by substantial inquiries into the comparative effects of global institutional factors on the incidence of severe poverty and (more generally) unfulfilled human rights worldwide.

It is gratifying that the development of the global-justice approach for once shows the owl of Minerva spreading its wings well *before* the falling of dusk: that philosophy has been giving an important conceptual impulse to economics, political science, and politics. What effect this impulse will have, however, remains to be seen.

2

Recognized and Violated by International Law: The Human Rights of the Global Poor

2.0 Introduction

This chapter will substantiate in more detail what was suggested in the first. While codified and customary international law recognizes various human rights that promise all human beings protection against specific severe harms that might be inflicted on them domestically or by foreigners, international law also establishes and maintains institutional structures that greatly contribute to violations of these human rights. Fundamental components of international law systematically obstruct the aspirations of poor populations for democratic self-government, civil rights, and minimal economic sufficiency. And central international organizations, like the World Trade Organization (WTO), the International Monetary Fund (IMF), and the World Bank, are designed so that they systematically contribute to the persistence of severe poverty.

2.1 Human rights and correlative duties

Supranational, national, and sub-national systems of law create various human rights. The content of these rights and of any corresponding legal obligations and burdens depends on the legislative, judicial, and executive bodies that maintain and interpret the laws in question. In the aftermath of World War II, it has come to be widely acknowledged that there are also moral human rights, whose validity is independent of any and all such governmental bodies. In their case, in fact, the dependence is thought to run the other way: only if they respect moral human rights do governmental bodies have legitimacy, that is, the capacity to create moral obligations to comply with, and the moral authority to enforce, their laws and orders.

Human rights of both kinds can coexist in harmony. Whoever cares about moral human rights will grant that laws can greatly facilitate their realization. And human-rights lawyers can acknowledge that the legal rights and obligations they draft and interpret are meant to give effect to pre-existing moral rights. In fact, this acknowledgment seems implicit in the common phrase "internationally recognized human rights." It is clearly expressed in the Preamble of the *Universal Declaration of Human Rights* (*UDHR*), which presents this *Declaration* as stating moral human rights that exist independently of itself. This acknowledgement bears stressing because the distinction between moral and legal human rights is rarely drawn clearly. Many are therefore inclined to believe that our human rights are whatever governments declare them to be. This may be true of legal human rights. But it is false, as these governments have themselves acknowledged, of moral human rights. Governments may have views on what moral human rights there are – their endorsement of the *UDHR* and various subsequent human-rights covenants and treaties expresses one such view. But even all governments together cannot legislate such rights out of existence.

The widespread recognition of moral human rights is important because it makes room for an independent critical assessment of existing international law. A more limited form of such assessment is possible even within the law itself – one can investigate how well international law complies with the human rights it itself recognizes. But such a purely internal assessment is vulnerable to legal change. The critical potential of legal human rights can be sapped through revisions of the law – through explicit reformulation or amendment ("anti-terrorism" legislation), through adjudications that render other parts of the law coherent with human rights by enfeebling the latter, or through precedents that modify customary international law (recognizing preemptive occupations or the status of "enemy combatants").[31] Dependent as they are on good arguments rather than the good will of those in power, moral human rights provide more solid grounds for critical assessment, and I base my case upon them. In doing so, I conceive human rights and their correlative duties quite narrowly to ensure that the moral premises I invoke are widely acceptable. I do not contend that human rights are exhausted by what I invoke – only that human rights require at least this much.

I focus on the human rights of the global poor because the great human-rights deficits persisting today are heavily concentrated among them. Socioeconomic human rights, such as that "to a standard of living adequate for the health and well-being of himself and his family, including food, clothing, housing, and medical care" (*UDHR*, Article 25) are currently, and by far, the most frequently violated human rights. Their widespread violation also plays a decisive role in explaining the global deficit in civil and political human rights, which demand physical security, due process, political participation, and the rule of law. As described in the previous chapter (section 1.1), the human costs of poverty – including some 18 million avoidable deaths each year – are grossly disproportionate to the economic magnitude of the problem. Although 48 percent of all human beings live below $2.50 per day (2005 purchasing power in the US), and, on average, 45 percent below this level, a 2 percent shift in the distribution of global household income would suffice entirely to erase this poverty gap.

Despite the undisputed great importance of basic necessities for human life, the existence of social and economic human rights is controversial, especially in the United States, which never ratified the *International Covenant on Social, Economic, and Cultural Rights.* Much of this controversy is due to the false assumption that a human right to freedom from poverty must entail correlative positive duties. Such human-rights-imposed positive duties to aid and protect any human beings who would otherwise suffer severe deprivations are widely rejected in the US and in other affluent countries. But what is rejected here is not a specific class of rights, but a specific class of duties: *positive* duties. Those who deny that very poor foreigners have a human-rights-based moral claim to economic assistance typically also deny that foreigners have any other human-rights-based moral claims to aid or protection – against genocide, enslavement, torture, tyranny, or religious persecution. What these people actually reject are not human rights as such, or any particular category of human rights. They reject human-rights-imposed positive duties and therefore *any* human rights specified so that they entail correlative general positive duties.

While some passionately reject such human-rights-imposed positive duties and others passionately endorse them, I simply leave them aside here, without prejudice. To keep my argument widely acceptable, I conceive human rights narrowly as imposing only negative duties.

This way, my argument can be acceptable to those who reject human-rights-imposed positive duties, because they generally endorse only stringent negative duties (not to torture, not to rape, not to destroy crops and livestock needed for survival, etc.). And my argument can also be acceptable to those who endorse human-rights-imposed positive duties, because, by failing to invoke such duties, I am not denying them.

Negative duties are of two main kinds: interactional and institutional.[32] The human right not to be tortured is violated interactionally by torturers and physicians assisting them as well as by politicians and officials who order or approve their conduct. The same human right is violated institutionally by those who make an uncompensated contribution to the imposition of social institutions that foreseeably give rise to substantially more torture than would be avoidable through a better institutional design. More generally, human rights are violated institutionally by those who make an uncompensated contribution to the imposition of social institutions that foreseeably give rise to an avoidable human-rights deficit.[33] Citizens often feel that they are not implicated in any human-rights violations committed by their country's military or security officials or by its politicians. This may be true when such violations are individual cases that cannot reasonably be avoided through appropriate institutional protections. But citizens may be implicated when social institutions they uphold foreseeably produce an avoidable human-rights deficit on a regular basis. For example, through their uncompensated support of the grievously unjust Nazi regime, many German officials and citizens facilitated the human-rights violations this regime foreseeably gave rise to – thereby participating in a collective crime and violating the human rights of its victims, even if they never personally killed or tortured or otherwise harmed anyone directly.

A similar distinction among negative duties can be drawn in the domain of social and economic human rights. Those who, through pillage and plunder, deprive others of their livelihood violate negative duties interactionally, and those who collaborate in the imposition of an institutional order under which, foreseeably and avoidably, many cannot meet their basic needs are violating negative duties of the institutional kind. Even conservatives and libertarians, who often present themselves as rejecting subsistence rights altogether, recognize such cases. In particular, they classify as human-rights-violating some institutional arrangements that foreseeably and avoidably produce life-threatening poverty – the feudal systems of France's Ancien Régime or tsarist Russia, for instance, or Stalin's economic policies during

1930–3, which caused some 7–10 million famine deaths among peas-
ants, mostly in the Ukraine, whom he considered hostile to his regime.
Even if they reject any positive duty to intervene in behalf of the
victims of such a regime, conservatives and libertarians recognize
a negative duty to refrain from helping to impose such a human-
rights-violating regime.

In what follows, I leave interactional negative duties aside and
base my argument entirely on institutional negative duties correlative
to human rights. I contend that most of the vast human-rights deficits
regularly persisting in today's world can be traced back to institutional
factors – to the national institutional arrangements in many so-called
less developed countries, for which their political and economic
elites bear primary responsibility, as well as to present global institutional arrangements, for which the governments and citizens of the
affluent countries bear primary responsibility. Focusing on the latter
subject, I argue that current global institutional arrangements as codified in international law constitute a massive human-rights violation
to which most of the world's affluent are making uncompensated
contributions.

The *moral* component of my argument was concisely stated more
than 60 years ago:

> Everyone is entitled to a social and international order in which the
> rights and freedoms set forth in this Declaration can be fully realized.
> (*UDHR*, Article 28, see also Article 22)

I read this Article in light of four interpretive conjectures:

1 Alternative institutional designs that do not satisfy the requirement
   of Article 28 can be ranked by how close they come to enabling the
   full realization of human rights: any social system ought to be structured so that it enables human rights to be realized as fully as is
   reasonably possible.[34]
2 How fully human rights *can* be realized by some institutional design
   is indicated by how fully these human rights generally are, or (in the
   case of a hypothetical design) generally would be, realized by it.
3 A human right is *realized* in a population insofar as (and fully if and
   only if) this human right is *fulfilled* for all members of this
   population.
4 A human right is fulfilled for some person if and only if this person
   enjoys *secure access to the object of this human right*.

Taking these four conjectures together, Article 28 should be read as holding that the moral assessment of any institutional order turns primarily on the extent to which it facilitates, insofar as is reasonably feasible, secure access to the objects of human rights: any institutional design is to be assessed and reformed principally by reference to its relative impact on the realization of human rights. I call this "relative" impact, because a comparative judgment is required about how well the existing institutional design does in terms of realizing human rights relative to its best feasible alternative. An institutional order and its imposition are human-rights-violating if and insofar as this order foreseeably gives rise to a substantial *and reasonably avoidable* human-rights deficit.

The *empirical* component of my argument begins from the basic facts about poverty previously reviewed. Half of all human beings live in severe poverty, and about one third of all human deaths are from poverty-related causes: lack of nutrients, clean water, sanitation, medical care, clothing, shelter, rest, or basic education. This continuous global death toll of about 50,000 human beings per day – disproportionately including children, females, and people of color – matches that of four major airplane disasters every hour, and it matches, every three years, the entire death toll of World War II, concentration camps and gulags included.

I believe that most of this death toll and of the much larger poverty problem it epitomizes are avoidable through comparatively minor modifications in the global order that would entail only slight reductions in the incomes of the affluent. Such reforms have been blocked by the governments of the affluent countries which, advancing their own interests and those of their corporations and citizens, are designing and imposing a global institutional order that, continually and foreseeably, produces vast excesses of severe deprivation and premature poverty-related deaths.

There are three main strategies for denying this charge. One can deny that variations in the design of the global order have any significant impact on the evolution of severe poverty worldwide. Failing this, one can claim that the present global order is close to optimal in terms of poverty avoidance. Should this strategy fail as well, one can still contend that the present global order, insofar as it is suboptimal in terms of poverty avoidance, is not *causing* severe poverty but merely failing to alleviate such poverty (caused by other factors) as much as it could. I will defend the charge by discussing these three strategies in order.[35]

2.2 The purely domestic poverty thesis

Those who wish to deny that variations in the design of the global institutional order have a significant impact on the evolution of severe poverty explain such poverty by reference to national or local factors alone. John Rawls is a prominent example. He claims that, when societies fail to thrive, "the problem is commonly the nature of the public political culture and the religious and philosophical traditions that underlie its institutions. The great social evils in poorer societies are likely to be oppressive government and corrupt elites."[36] He adds:

> [T]he causes of the wealth of a people and the forms it takes lie in their political culture and in the religious, philosophical and moral traditions that support the basic structure of their political and social institutions, as well as in the industriousness and cooperative talents of its members, all supported by their political virtues . . . the political culture of a burdened society is all-important. . . . Crucial also is the country's population policy.[37]

Accordingly, Rawls holds that our moral responsibility with regard to severe poverty abroad can be fully described as a "duty of assistance."[38]

It is well to recall briefly that existing peoples have arrived at their present levels of social, economic, and cultural development through a historical process that was pervaded by enslavement, colonialism, even genocide. Though these monumental crimes are now in the past, they have left a legacy of great inequalities which would be unacceptable even if national populations were now masters of their own development. In response, it is often said that colonialism happened too long ago to contribute to the explanation of poverty and inequality today. But consider the 30:1 inequality in per capita income in 1960, when Europe released Africa from the colonial yoke. Even if Africa had consistently enjoyed annual growth in per capita income one full percentage point above Europe's, this inequality ratio would still be 18:1 today. At this rate, Africa would be catching up with Europe at the beginning of the twenty-fourth century.

Consider also how such a huge economic inequality entails inequalities in the expertise and bargaining power that Africans and Europeans can bring to bear in negotiations about the terms of their interactions. Relations structured under so unequal conditions are likely to be more beneficial to the stronger party and thus tend to reinforce the initial economic inequality. This phenomenon surely plays some role in explaining why the inequality in per capita income has actually *increased* since 1960. In 2007, gross national income (GNI) per capita was $952 in sub-Saharan Africa as opposed to $37,566 in the high-income countries – a 39:1 ratio.[39] Rawls (implausibly) finds such entrenched economic inequality morally acceptable when it originates in choices freely made by earlier generations within each people. But his justification is irrelevant to this world, in which our enormous economic advantage is deeply tainted by how it accumulated over the course of *one* historical process that has devastated the societies and cultures of four continents.

Let us leave aside the continuing legacies of historical crimes and focus on the empirical view that, at least in the postcolonial era, which brought impressive growth in global per capita income, the causes of the *persistence* of severe poverty, and hence the key to its eradication, lie within the poor countries themselves.

Many find this view compelling in light of the great variation in how the former colonies have evolved over the past 50 years. Some of them have achieved solid economic growth and poverty reduction, while others exhibit worsening poverty and declining per capita incomes. Is it not obvious that such strongly divergent national trajectories must be due to differing *domestic* causal factors in the countries concerned? And is it not clear, then, that the persistence of severe poverty is due to local causes?

However oft-repeated and well received, this reasoning is fallacious. When national economic trajectories diverge, then there must indeed be local (country-specific) factors at work that explain the divergence. But it does not follow that global factors play no role. We can see this by considering a parallel case. There may be great variations in the performance of students in one class. These must be due to student-specific factors. Still, it does not follow that these "local" factors fully explain the performance of a class. Teacher and classroom quality, teaching times, reading materials, libraries, and other "global" factors may also play an important role. Dramatic contrasts of success and failure, among students or among less developed countries, do not then show global factors to be causally inert. In the former case, such global factors can greatly influence the overall progress of a class; they can influence the distribution of this progress by being differentially appropriate to the needs and interests of different students; and they can affect the student-specific factors, as when a racist or sexist teacher causes or aggravates motivational deficits in his black or female students. Analogous to these three possibilities, global institutional factors may greatly influence the evolution of severe poverty worldwide.

Exposure of this popular fallacy does not, however, settle the issue. We have seen that dramatic divergences in national poverty trajectories do not prove that decisions about the design of global institutional arrangements exert no powerful influence on the evolution of severe poverty worldwide. But it does not follow that such an influence exists.

Still, once the popular fallacy is exposed, it is hard to doubt that there is such an influence. In the modern world, the traffic of transnational and even intra-national economic transactions is profoundly shaped by an elaborate system of treaties and conventions about trade, investments, loans, patents, copyrights, trademarks, double taxation, labor standards, environmental protection, use of seabed resources, production and marketing of weapons, maintenance of public security, and much else. Structuring and enabling, permitting and constraining, these different parts of the present global institutional order realize highly specific design decisions within a vast space of alternative design possibilities. It is incredible on its face that all these alternative ways of organizing global interaction would have produced the same evolution in the overall incidence and geographical distribution of severe poverty. I will discuss such effects of global institutional design decisions more concretely in sections 2.3 and 2.4.3.

2.3 The Panglossian view of the present global order

How does the design of the global institutional order affect the evolution of severe poverty worldwide? It is often suggested that we live, in this regard, in the best of all possible worlds: that the present global order is close to optimal in terms of poverty avoidance.

A commonsense way of questioning this claim might develop a counter-hypothesis in four steps. First, the interest in avoiding severe poverty is not the only interest to which those who negotiate the design of particular aspects of the global institutional order are sensitive. Such negotiators are likely to care also about their home government's political success and, partly as a consequence of this, about their compatriots' interest in economic prosperity. Second, at least with negotiators for the more affluent states, these "nationalist" interests are not (to put it mildly) perfectly aligned with the interest in global poverty avoidance. In negotiations about the design of the global order, particular decisions that are best for the governments, corporations, or citizens of the affluent countries are sometimes not best in terms of avoiding severe poverty in the less developed countries. Third, when faced with such conflicts, negotiators for the affluent states generally (are instructed to) give precedence to the interests of their own country's government, corporations, and citizens over the interests of the global poor. Fourth, with only 16 percent of the world's population, the high-income countries have over 75 percent of the global product.[40] Able to exact a high price for access to their capital, technology, and gigantic markets, the affluent states enjoy great advantages in bargaining power which, compounded by advantages in expertise, enable their negotiators to deflect the design of the global order from what would be best for poverty avoidance toward a better accommodation of the interests of the governments, corporations, and citizens of the affluent countries they represent. These four steps lead to the commonsensical counter-hypothesis: we should expect that the design of the global institutional order reflects the shared interests of the governments, corporations, and citizens of the affluent countries more than the interest in global poverty avoidance, insofar as these interests conflict.

There is much evidence that this counter-hypothesis is true. The present rules favor the affluent countries by allowing them to continue protecting their markets through tariffs, anti-dumping duties, quotas, export credits, and huge subsidies to domestic producers in ways that poor countries are not permitted, or cannot afford, to match.[41] Other important examples include the WTO regulations on cross-border investment and intellectual property rights, such as the TRIPS Agreement of 1995.

Such skewed rules increase the share of global economic growth going to the affluent and decrease the share going to the poor relative to what these shares would be if poor populations had less inferior opportunities to compete in world markets. The existing design of global institutional arrangements thus reinforces the very inequality that enables the governments of the affluent countries to impose such a skewed design in the first place. As I document in sections 1.2 and 5.4, the already grotesquely large global inequality of incomes continues to increase.

Falling further and further behind, the global poor become ever more marginalized, with their interests ignored in both national and international decision-making. Annual spending power of less than $200 per person does not command much attention from international negotiators when per capita incomes in the affluent countries are some 200 times higher. And the interests of poor African countries do not carry much weight when the combined GNI of 26 of them, representing more than 400 million people, falls short of the annual sales volumes of the world's largest corporations.

These data should suffice to refute the Panglossian view: the present design of the global order is nowhere near optimal in terms of poverty avoidance. It is clear in many cases how this value could be better served. International negotiations might include experts representing the interest of poverty avoidance and reporting on how alternative design proposals would affect poor people worldwide. The poorest countries might be entitled to expert advice on how to defend their interests in WTO negotiations, toward maintaining missions at WTO headquarters in Geneva, toward bringing cases before the WTO, and toward coping with all the regulations they are required to implement. Exports from poor countries might not face protectionist barriers, nor have to compete with heavily subsidized products from affluent countries (see endnote 25). Poor countries might not be required to collect billions in economic rents for "intellectual property" or be required to prevent their own citizens from buying essential medicines and seeds at competitive market prices.[42] The *WTO Treaty* might specify a global minimum wage and minimal global constraints on working hours and working conditions in order to halt the current "race to the bottom" where poor countries competing for foreign investment must outbid one another by offering ever more exploitable workforces.[43] Affluent countries might be required to make up for the negative externalities we impose on the poor, such as the effects on their environment and climate or the pollution we have produced over many decades. Poverty avoidance would also be better served in the future, if the *Law of the Sea Treaty* guaranteed the poor countries some share of the value of harvested seabed resources,[44] and if the affluent states and their banks and corporations were barred from facilitating the flow of illicit funds from poor to affluent countries, which is estimated at between $850 billion and $1 trillion annually.[45]

Examples could be multiplied. But I think it is clear that there are feasible variations to the present global order that would dramatically reduce severe poverty worldwide, far below the current, staggering figures. This order is *not* optimal in terms of poverty avoidance.

2.4 Is the present global order merely less beneficial than it might be?

As the first two possible lines of defense have turned out to be indefensible, attention turns to the third: can one say that the global institutional order, though clearly and greatly suboptimal in terms of poverty avoidance, is nonetheless not harming the global poor, not violating their human rights? Let us turn to this last challenge to my view.

This challenge is especially important if one leaves undisputed, as I have here done, the narrow account of human-rights violations according to which agents can be condemned as human-rights violators only if they *actively* cause human rights to be unfulfilled, in violation of a *negative* duty. Appealing to this narrow account, the countries shaping and imposing the present global order could argue as follows. It is true that the incidence of severe poverty is greater under the present regime than it would be under some of the outlined variations thereof that would reduce oppression, corruption, and deprivation in the poor countries. But it does not follow that the existing global order *causes* excess poverty or excess poverty deaths, that it *harms* or *kills* anyone, or that it *violates* human rights. The design of this order is merely failing to benefit people, failing to be as protective of human life as it might be. And the same should then be said about our decision to impose the existing global institutional order rather than a more poverty-avoiding alternative: this decision does not cause excess poverty or excess poverty deaths, is not violating human rights by harming and killing people. It is merely failing to benefit people and failing to prevent human deaths. Collectively (just as individually), we are at most failing to do all we can to fulfill human rights.

This third defense strategy appeals to something like the distinction between acts and omissions. It seeks to diminish the moral significance of the affluent states' decision to impose the present design of the global order rather than a foreseeably more poverty-avoiding alternative by assigning this decision the status of a mere omission. Now the affluent countries are clearly active in formulating the global economic rules they want, in pressing for their acceptance, and in pursuing their enforcement. The defense strategy must then apply the act/omission distinction at another place: not to how the relevant governments are related to the global rules, but to how these global rules are related to avoidable poverty. The idea must be that the rules governing the world economy are not actively causing excess poverty, thus harming and killing people, but merely passively failing to prevent such poverty, failing to protect people from harm.

The distinction between acts and omissions is difficult enough when applied to individual and collective agents.[46] Its application to social institutions and rules is at first baffling. When more premature deaths occur under a system of rules than would occur under some feasible alternative, we might say that there are excess deaths under the existing regime. But how can we distinguish between those excess deaths that the existing rules *bring about* and those that these rules merely *fail to prevent*? Let us examine three ideas for how this defense strategy can be made to work.

2.4.1 First Idea: invoking baseline comparisons

There is much debate about the apparently empirical question of whether WTO globalization is harming or benefiting the global poor.[47] Harm and benefit are comparative notions, involving the idea of people being worse or better off. But what is the implied baseline here – the alternative fate in comparison to which the global poor are either worse off (and therefore harmed) or better off (and therefore benefited by globalization)?

In most cases, it turns out, the popular debate is about whether poverty worldwide has been rising or falling since the latest globalization push began in the 1980s. This question is hotly debated, with considerable career prizes awarded to any economists with a good story of declining poverty.[48] Yet, this debate is largely irrelevant to the charge under discussion: that governments, by imposing a global institutional order under which great excesses of severe poverty and poverty deaths persist, are violating the human rights of many poor people. This is the moral charge before us. The plausibility of this charge is unaffected by whether severe poverty is rising or falling. To see this, consider the parallel charges that slaveholding societies harmed and violated the human rights of those they enslaved, or that the Nazis violated the human rights of those they confined and killed in their concentration camps. These charges can certainly not be defeated by showing that the rate of victimization declined.

To be sure, the words "harm" and "benefit" are sometimes appropriately used with implicit reference to an earlier state of affairs. But such a historical baseline is irrelevant here. For even if there were less severe poverty today than there was 20 years ago, we could not infer that the present global order is (in a morally significant sense) *benefiting* the global poor. This inference would beg the whole question by simply assuming the incidence of severe poverty 15 years ago as the appropriate no-harm baseline. Just as the claim that the US violated the human rights of black slaves in the 1850s cannot be refuted by showing that such slaves were better off than in earlier decades, so the claim that the imposition of the present global order violates the human rights of poor people cannot be refuted by showing that their numbers are falling.[49]

No less inconclusive than such *diachronic* comparisons are *subjunctive* comparisons with a historical baseline. Even if severe poverty were below what it now would be if the preceding regime had continued, we cannot infer that the present regime is benefiting the poor. This inference would again beg the question by assuming the incidence of severe poverty as it would have evolved under the old rules as the appropriate no-harm baseline. By the same reasoning, the current military junta under Than Shwe could be said to be benefiting the Burmese people provided that they are better off than they would now be if the earlier junta under Ne Win were still in power. And by the same reasoning we could argue that the regime of Jim Crow laws[50] did not harm African Americans in the US South because they were better off than they would have been had slavery continued.

Sometimes subjunctive comparisons are presented with a historical baseline defined by reference to a much earlier time. Thus it is said that Africans today are no worse off than they would now be if there had never been significant contacts with outsiders. In response, we should question whether there are knowable facts about such a remote alternate history. We should also, once again, question the moral relevance of this hypothetical baseline involving continued mutual isolation: if world history had transpired without colonization and enslavement, then there would – *perhaps* – now be affluent people in Europe and very poor ones in Africa. But these would be persons and populations entirely different from those now actually living there, who in fact are very deeply shaped and scarred by their continent's involuntary encounter with European invaders. So we cannot tell starving Africans that *they* would be starving and *we* would be affluent even if the crimes of colonialism had never occurred. Without these crimes, there would not be the actually existing radical inequality which consists in *these* persons being affluent and *those* being extremely poor.

Similar considerations refute the moral relevance of subjunctive comparison with a *hypothetical* baseline – the claim, for instance, that even more people would live and die even more miserably in some fictional state of nature than in this world as we have made it. Many such states have been described, and it is unclear how one can be singled out as the uniquely appropriate specification. Moreover, it is doubtful that *any* coherently describable state of nature on this planet would be able to match our globalized civilization's record of sustaining a stable death toll of 18 million premature deaths per year from poverty-related causes.[51] If no such state of nature can be described, then the present global order cannot be said to benefit the global poor by reducing severe poverty below a state-of-nature baseline. Finally,

how can the claim that some people are being harmed now be undermined by pointing out that people in a state of nature would be even
worse off? If such an argument succeeded, would it not show that
anything done to another counts as harm only if it reduces the latter
below the state-of-nature baseline? If we are not harming the 3 billion
we are keeping in severe poverty, then enslavement did not harm the
slaves either, if only they were no worse off than people would be in
the relevant state of nature.

I conclude that baseline comparisons of the three kinds we have
considered are unsuitable for defending any institutional scheme from
the charge that it harms or violates human rights. Severe burdens and
disadvantages that people suffer under some institutional scheme
cannot be justified by any diachronic comparison with how such
people had fared before or by any subjunctive comparison with how
such people would have been faring under some preceding regime or
in a state of nature. What matters is whether the institutional order in
question foreseeably leads to severe burdens that are reasonably
avoidable.[52]

2.4.2 Second Idea: invoking the consent of the global poor

In the preceding chapter, we briefly encountered another common way
of denying that the present global order is harming the poor, violating
their human rights: the appeal to the venerable precept of *volenti non
fit iniuria* – no injustice is done to the consenting. Global institutional
arrangements cannot be harming the poor when participation, in the
WTO for example, is voluntary.

This line of argument is refuted by four mutually independent considerations. First, appeal to consent cannot defeat a charge of human-
rights violation given that, on the usual understanding of moral and
legal human rights, they are inalienable and thus cannot be waived by
consent. Persons can promise, through a religious vow perhaps, to
serve another, to refrain from voting, or to keep silent. But, wherever
human rights are respected, such promises are legally unenforceable
and thus do not succeed in waiving the person's human rights to personal freedom, political participation, and freedom of expression.
There are various reasons for conceiving human rights in this way: a
person changes over time, and her later self has a vital interest in being
able to avoid truly horrific burdens that her earlier self had risked or
incurred. Moreover, the option of placing such burdens on one's future

self is likely to be disadvantageous even to the earlier self by encouraging predators seeking to elicit a waiver from this earlier self through manipulation of her or of her circumstances – for instance, by getting her into a life-threatening situation from which one then offers to rescue her at the price of her permanent enslavement.[53] Finally, waivers of human rights impose considerable burdens on third parties who will be (more or less directly) confronted with the resulting distress of people enslaved or tortured or starving.

Second, an appeal to consent cannot justify the severe impoverishment of children who are greatly overrepresented among those suffering severe poverty and its effects.[54] Insofar as the present global order is, foreseeably, greatly suboptimal in terms of avoiding severe poverty of children, the claim that this order violates their human rights cannot be blocked by any plausible appeal to consent.

Third, most of the severely impoverished live in countries that lack meaningful democracy. Thus, Nigeria's accession to the WTO was effected by its military dictator Sani Abacha, for example, Myanmar's by the notorious SLORC junta, Indonesia's by Suharto, Zimbabwe's by Robert Mugabe, and the Congo's by dictator Mobutu Sese Seko. These rulers' success in subjecting people to their rule does not give them the moral authority to consent on behalf of those whom they are oppressing – nor does such success entitle us to treat the populations of these countries as if they had consented through their rulers' signatures.

Fourth, insofar as very poor people do consent, through a meaningfully democratic process, to some global institutional arrangements, the justificatory force of such consent is typically weakened by their having no other tolerable option, and often weakened even further by the fact that their calamitous circumstances are partly due to those whose conduct this consent is meant to justify. Poor countries need trade for development. They do not get fair trading opportunities under the WTO regime; but a country that failed to sign up would find its trading opportunities even more severely curtailed. Any poor country must decide about whether to accept the WTO rules against the background of other rules that it cannot escape and that make it extremely costly to decline.

One such background rule entitles countries selectively to exclude foreigners from their markets and thereby enables the affluent countries to exact a price for whatever access to their markets they are prepared to offer – for instance, in the form of intellectual-property rents for the use of advanced medicines, seeds, and technologies. This background rule may seem so natural and obvious that any calamity it may entail cannot be attributed to those who are imposing it: surely, any country is entitled to restrict access to its territory and markets as it pleases, regardless of the economic consequences for foreigners. Well, not too long ago, the world's most affluent countries proclaimed the opposite to be natural and obvious, when they forcefully insisted on their right to sell opium in China for example.[55] And the claimed right of the US, Canada, Australia, and New Zealand to exclude outsiders from their territories and markets is further undermined by the historical path on which their present occupants have come to possess these territories.

It is worth mentioning in this context another popular fallacy often adduced in defense of the status quo. As empirical research shows, poor countries that embrace the new global rules tend to perform better, economically, than countries that don't. This is taken to prove that the new global rules benefit the poor countries. To see the fallacy, consider this parallel reasoning. Suppose empirical research had shown that, around 1940, smaller European states collaborating with the fascist alliance performed better than the rest. Would this have proved that the new dominance of this fascist alliance was good for small European states? – Surely not. Drawing this conclusion, one would be conflating two separate claims. First, *given* the dominance of fascism in continental Europe, it is better for a small state to cooperate. Second, the fascist dominance in continental Europe is better for small European states than, say, the hypothetical dominance of parliamentary democracies. The inference from the first claim to the second is plainly fallacious. Nonetheless, its analogue is frequently adduced in contemporary globalization debates. Evidence is produced to show that, *given* the dominance of the affluent countries and of their rules and organizations, it is better for a poor country to cooperate. And it is then concluded that the dominance of these rich countries' rules and organizations is better for the poor countries than alternative institutional arrangements. Once these two claims are properly distinguished, it is obvious that the latter does not follow from the former.

2.4.3 Third Idea: invoking the flaws of the poor countries' social institutions and rulers

A further, popular way of denying that the present global institutional order is harming the poor invokes the success stories – such as the Asian tigers (Hong Kong, Taiwan, Singapore, and South Korea) and

China – to show that any poor country can defeat severe poverty under the existing global order.

This reasoning involves a "some–all" fallacy. The fact that *some* individuals born into poverty become millionaires does not show that *all* such persons can do likewise.[56] The reason is that the pathways to riches are sparse. They are not rigidly limited, to be sure, but it is clearly impossible to achieve the kind of economic growth rates needed for everyone to become a millionaire (holding fixed the value of the currency and the real income millionaires can now enjoy). The same holds for formerly poor countries. The Asian tigers achieved impressive rates of economic growth and poverty reduction through a state-sponsored build-up of industries that mass-produce low-tech consumer products. These industries were globally successful by using their considerable labor-cost advantage to beat competitors in the developed countries and by drawing on greater state support and/or a better-educated workforce to beat competitors in other poor countries. It also helped that the US, eager to establish healthy capitalist economies as a counterweight to Soviet influence in the region, allowed the tigers free access to its market even while they maintained high tariffs to protect their own. Building such industries was hugely profitable for the Asian tigers. But if many more poor countries had adopted this same developmental strategy, competition among them would have rendered it much less profitable.

Over the past two decades, China has been the great success story, achieving phenomenal growth in exports and per capita income. So China's example is now often used to argue that the rules of the world economy are favorable to the poor countries and conducive to poverty eradication. This argument commits the same some–all fallacy. Exporters in the poorer countries compete over the same heavily protected markets of the rich countries. Thanks to its extraordinary ability to deliver quality products cheaply in large quantities, China has done very well in this competition. But this success has greatly reduced market share and export prices for firms in many poorer countries. To be sure, the world economy as presently structured is not a constant-sum game, where one player's gain must be another's loss. Yet, outcomes are strongly interdependent. We cannot conclude, therefore, that the present global institutional order, though less favorable to the poor countries than it might be, is still favorable enough for all of them to do as well as the Asian tigers and then China have done in fact. Moreover, China's success story deserves closer scrutiny than proponents of the current global institutional order have given it, as my discussion of growth and inequality in China will show (section 5.3).

Still, could the poor countries on the whole not do much better under the present global order than they are doing in fact? And must the present global order then not be acquitted of responsibility for any excess poverty that would have been avoided if the political elites in the poor countries were competent and uncorrupt?

Suppose the two sets of relevant causal factors – the global institutional order and the economic regimes and policies of the countries in which severe poverty persists – were symmetrically related so that each set of factors is necessary for the current reproduction of severe poverty worldwide. Then, if we insist that the global factors must be absolved on the ground that modification of national factors would suffice to eradicate world poverty, defenders of national factors could insist, symmetrically, that these national factors must be absolved on the ground that modification of global factors would suffice to eradicate world poverty. Acquitting both sets of factors on these grounds, we would place their cooperative production of huge harms beyond moral criticism.

The implausibility of such an assessment can be illustrated through a more straightforward interactional case. Suppose two upstream tribes release pollutants into a river on which people downstream depend for their survival. And suppose that each of the pollutants causes only minor harm, but that, when mixed, they react to form a lethal poison that kills many people downstream. In this case, both upstream tribes could deny responsibility, each insisting that the severe harm would not exist if the other upstream tribe stopped its polluting activity. Acceding to this denial would be absurd, as neither tribe would then have an appropriately strong moral reason to alter its practice.

The example suggests, more generally, that synergistic harm must not be left unassigned. The synergistic harm here is the harm produced by two interacting causal factors, HAB, insofar as it exceeds the sum of the harm (HA) that factor A would produce without B's contribution plus the harm (HB) that factor B would produce without A's contribution. In such cases, if we held each factor responsible for only the harm that would still occur even without the other's contribution, then the synergistic harm (= HAB − HA − HB) would be the responsibility of neither.

This is not the place to develop a full theory of synergistic harm.[57] But it seems clear that such harm should be assigned to the contributing factors, and perhaps even be assigned fully to each in the case

under discussion. On this account, the mutually aggravating cooperation of causal factors would not merely fail to decrease, but would
increase total responsibility. This is analogous to how two criminals,
if both make a necessary contribution to a homicide, are each held
legally and morally fully responsible for that single death (rather than
for half a death). Each of the two is required to desist on pains of
becoming guilty of homicide. And likewise with the two tribes: each is
required to stop – cooperatively or unilaterally – the severe harm they
cause together.[58]

The persistence of severe poverty worldwide is analogous to the
harms suffered by the people downstream. It is true – as the defenders
of the affluent countries and of their present globalization project
point out – that most severe poverty would be avoided, despite the
current unfair global order, if the national governments and elites of
the poor countries were genuinely committed to "good governance"
and poverty eradication. It is also true – as the defenders of governments and elites in the poor countries insist – that much severe poverty
would be avoided, despite the corrupt and oppressive regimes holding
sway in so many poor countries, if the global institutional order were
designed to achieve this purpose. Much of the harm thus is synergistic.
But this fact cannot negate the responsibility of the citizens and governments of the affluent countries: given our contribution, we may
bear responsibility for the severe poverty of even those people who
would not be poor if their countries were better governed.

By assuming symmetry between the two sets of causal factors, my
response is still too generous to the affluent countries, failing fully to
expose their responsibility and that of their globalization project.
There is an important asymmetry. While domestic institutional
arrangements and policies in the poor countries have little influence
on the design of the global order, the latter has a great deal of influence
on the former. The global institutional order exerts its pernicious influence on the evolution of world poverty not only directly, in the ways
already discussed, but also indirectly through its influence on the
domestic institutions and policies of the poorer countries. Oppression
and corruption, so prevalent in many poor countries today, are themselves very substantially produced and sustained by central features of
the present global order.

It was only in 1999, for example, that the developed countries finally
agreed to curb their firms' bribery of foreign officials by adopting the
OECD *Convention on Combating Bribery of Foreign Public Officials
in International Business Transactions*.[59] Until then, most developed
states did not merely legally authorize their firms to bribe foreign

officials, but even allowed them to deduct such bribes from their taxable revenues, thereby providing financial incentives and moral support for the practice of bribing politicians and officials in the poor countries.[60] This practice diverts the loyalties of officials in these countries and also makes a great difference to which persons are motivated to scramble for public office in the first place. Poor countries have suffered staggering losses as a result, most clearly in the awarding of public contracts. These losses arise in part from the fact that bribes are priced in: bidders on contracts must raise their price in order to get paid enough to pay the bribes. Additional losses arise as bidders can afford to be non-competitive, knowing that the success of their bid will depend on their bribes more than on the substance of their offer. Even greater losses arise from the fact that officials focused on bribes pay little attention to whether the goods and services they purchase on their country's behalf are of good quality or even needed at all. Much of what poor countries have imported over the decades has been of no use to them – or even harmful, by promoting environmental degradation or violence (bribery is especially pervasive in the arms trade).

The new anti-bribery convention has been "difficult to enforce in practice."[61] And banks in the affluent countries continue to invite corrupt rulers and officials in the poorer countries to move and invest their earnings from bribery and embezzlement abroad. Illicit transfers from poor to rich countries are estimated to total up to $1 trillion annually (see endnote 45) – vastly more than would be needed to eradicate severe poverty everywhere. International rules and practices are sustaining a pervasive culture of corruption that has become deeply entrenched in many poor countries.

Bribery and embezzlement are part of a larger problem. The political and economic elites of poor countries interact with their domestic inferiors, on the one hand, and with foreign governments and corporations, on the other. These two constituencies differ enormously in wealth and power. The former are mostly poorly educated and heavily preoccupied with the daily struggle to survive. The latter have vastly greater rewards and penalties at their disposal. Politicians with a normal interest in their own political and economic success thus cater to the interests of foreign governments and corporations rather than to competing interests of their much poorer compatriots. There are plenty of poor-country governments that have come to power or remained in office solely thanks to foreign support. And there are many poor-country politicians and bureaucrats who, induced or even bribed by foreigners, work against the interests of their people: *for* the development of a tourist-friendly sex industry (with forced exploitation of children and women), *for* the importation of unnecessary, obsolete, or overpriced products at public expense, *for* the permission to import hazardous products, wastes, or factories, *against* laws protecting employees or the environment, and so on.

In most poor countries, these incentive asymmetries are aggravated by the lack of genuine democracy. This democratic deficit also has global roots. It is a central feature of our global institutional order that any group controlling a preponderance of the means of coercion within a country is internationally recognized as the legitimate government of the country's territory and people – regardless of how this group came to power, of how it exercises power and of how much popular support it has. International recognition means not merely that we engage such a group in negotiations, but also that we accept its right to act for the people it rules and thereby authorize it to sell the country's resources and to dispose of the proceeds of such sales, to borrow in the country's name and thereby to impose debt service obligations upon it, to sign treaties on the country's behalf and thus to bind its present and future population, and to use state revenues to buy the means of internal repression. This global practice goes a long way toward explaining why so many countries are so badly governed.

The *resource privilege* we confer upon de facto rulers includes the power to effect legally valid transfers of ownership rights over resources. A corporation that has purchased resources from a tyrant thereby becomes entitled to be – and actually *is* – recognized anywhere as their legitimate owner. This is a remarkable feature of our global order. A group that overpowers the guards and takes control of a warehouse may be able to give some of the merchandise to others, accepting money in exchange. But the fence who pays them becomes merely the possessor, not the owner, of the loot. Contrast this with a group that overpowers an elected government and takes control of a country. Such a group, too, can give away some of the country's natural resources, accepting money in exchange. In this case, however, the purchaser acquires not merely possession, but all the rights and liberties of ownership, which are supposed to be – and actually *are* – protected and enforced by all other states' courts and police forces.

This international resource privilege has disastrous effects in poor countries whose resource sector constitutes a large segment of the national economy. Whoever can take power in such a country by whatever means can maintain his rule, even against broad popular opposition, by buying the arms and soldiers he needs with revenues from the export of natural resources and with funds borrowed against future resource sales. The resource privilege thus gives insiders strong incentives toward the violent acquisition and exercise of political power, thereby causing coup attempts and civil wars. And it gives outsiders strong incentives to corrupt the officials of such countries who, no matter how badly they rule, continue to have resources to sell and money to spend.

Nigeria is a case in point. Its oil exports of more than two million barrels per day generate a revenue stream that enables any de facto ruler to buy enough weapons and soldiers to keep himself in power regardless of what the population may think of him. And as long as he succeeds in doing so, his purse will be continuously replenished with new funds with which he can cement his rule and live in opulence. With such a powerful incentive, it cannot be surprising that, during most of its history, Nigeria has been ruled by military strongmen who took power and ruled by force. Nor can it be surprising that corruption is endemic: no politician can end corruption without risking a military coup that – thanks to the international resource privilege – would restore the customary perks of military officers.

The incentives arising from the international resource privilege help explain the significant *negative* correlation between resource wealth (relative to gross domestic product, or GDP) and economic performance. This "resource curse" is exemplified by many less developed countries, which, despite great natural wealth, have achieved little economic growth or poverty reduction.[62] This explanation has been confirmed by two Yale economists who demonstrate by regression analysis that the causal link from resource wealth to poor economic performance is mediated through reduced chances for democracy: "All petrostates or resource-dependent countries in Africa fail to initiate meaningful political reforms. . . . [B]esides South Africa, transition to democracy has been successful only in resource-poor countries."[63] "Our cross-country regression confirms our theoretical insights. We find that a one percentage increase in the size of the natural resource sector [relative to GDP] generates a decrease by a half percentage point in the probability of survival of democratic regimes."[64] Holding the global order fixed as a given background, the authors do not consider how the causal link they analyze itself depends on global rules that grant the resource privilege to any ruling group, regardless of its domestic illegitimacy.

The *borrowing privilege* we confer upon de facto rulers includes the power to impose internationally valid legal obligations upon the whole country. Any successor government that refuses to honor debts incurred by an ever so corrupt, brutal, undemocratic, unconstitutional, repressive, unpopular predecessor will be severely punished by the banks and governments of other countries. At a minimum, it will lose its own borrowing privilege by being excluded from the international financial markets. Such refusals are therefore very rare, as governments, even when newly elected after a dramatic break with the past, are compelled to pay the debts of their ever so awful predecessors.

The international borrowing privilege makes three important contributions to the high incidence of oppressive and corrupt rulers in the less developed countries. First, it facilitates borrowing by destructive rulers who can borrow more money and can do so more cheaply than they could do if they alone, rather than the whole country, were obliged to repay, and thereby helps such rulers maintain themselves in power even against near-universal popular opposition. Because they have collateral to offer, the rulers of resource-rich less developed countries have enjoyed greater freedom than their peers to supplement their income from resource sales by imposing huge debt service burdens on their countries.[65] Needless to say, little of the borrowed funds were channeled into productive investments, for example in education and infrastructure, which would augment economic growth and generate additional tax revenues that could help meet interest and repayment obligations. Much was taken for personal use or expended on "internal security" and the military. Second, the international borrowing privilege imposes upon democratic successor regimes the often huge debts of their corrupt predecessors. It thereby saps the capacity of democratic governments to implement structural reforms and other political programs, thus rendering such governments less successful and less stable than they would otherwise be. (It is small consolation that putschists are sometimes weakened by being held liable for the debts of their democratic predecessors.) Third, the international borrowing privilege strengthens incentives toward coup attempts: whoever succeeds in bringing a preponderance of the means of coercion under his control gets the borrowing privilege as an additional reward.

The ongoing international resource and borrowing privileges are complemented by the international treaty privilege, which recognizes any person or group in effective control of a country as entitled to undertake binding treaty obligations on behalf of its population, and the international arms privilege, which recognizes such a person or group as entitled to use state funds to import the arms needed to stay in power. Like the formerly tax-deductible bribery of poor-country officials and the complicity by banks in the embezzlement of public funds, the four privileges are significant features of our global order, greatly benefiting the governments, corporations, and citizens of affluent countries and the political-military elites of poor countries at the expense of the vast majority of ordinary people in poor countries. Thus, while the present global order indeed does not make it strictly impossible for poor countries to achieve genuine democracy and sustained economic growth, central features of this order greatly contribute to poor countries' failures on both counts. These features are crucial for explaining the inability, and especially the unwillingness, of these countries' leaders to eradicate poverty more effectively. And they are crucial therefore for explaining why global inequality is increasing so rapidly that substantial global economic growth since the end of the Cold War has not reduced income poverty and malnutrition – *despite* substantial technological progress and global economic growth, *despite* a huge reported poverty reduction in China,[66] *despite* the post-Cold-War "peace dividend,"[67] *despite* substantial declines in real food prices,[68] *despite* official development assistance, and *despite* the efforts of international humanitarian and development organizations.

2.5 The present global order massively violates human rights

In just 20 years since the end of the Cold War, some 360 million human beings have died prematurely from poverty-related causes, with some 18 million more added each year. Much larger numbers must live in conditions of life-threatening poverty that make it very difficult for them to articulate their interests and effectively to fend for themselves and their families. This catastrophe was and is happening, foreseeably, under a global institutional order designed for the benefit of the affluent countries' governments, corporations, and citizens and of the poor countries' political and military elites. There are feasible alternative designs of the global institutional order, feasible alternative paths of globalization, under which this catastrophe would have been largely avoided. Even now, severe poverty could be rapidly reduced through feasible reforms that would modify the more harmful features of this global order or mitigate their impact.

Take the unconditional international resource privilege, for example. It is beneficial to the affluent countries by giving us access to a larger, cheaper, and more reliable supply of foreign natural resources, because we can acquire ownership of them from anyone who happens to exercise effective power without regard to whether the country's population either approves the sale or benefits from the proceeds. Unconditional international resource and borrowing privileges are also highly advantageous to many a putschist or tyrant in the poor countries, for whom they secure the funds he needs to maintain himself in power even against the will of a large majority of his compatriots. Such privileges are, however, an unmitigated disaster for the global poor, who are being dispossessed through loan and resource agreements over which they have no say and from which they do not benefit.[69]

The example illustrates the clear-cut injustice of the present global institutional order. It also illustrates that this injustice does not consist in too little aid being dispensed to the poor. There is still so much severe poverty, and so much need for aid, only because the poor are systematically impoverished by present institutional arrangements and have been so impoverished for a long time during which our advantage and their disadvantage have been compounded. It is true that eradicating severe poverty at a morally acceptable speed would impose costs and opportunity costs on the affluent countries – just as the end of slavery imposed costs and opportunity costs on slaveholders. But acceptance of such costs is not generous charity, but required compensation for the harms continuously produced by unjust global institutional arrangements whose past and present imposition by the affluent countries brings great benefits to their citizens.[70]

Given that the present global institutional order is foreseeably associated with such massive incidence of avoidable severe poverty, its (uncompensated) imposition manifests an ongoing human-rights violation – arguably the largest such violation ever committed in human history. It is not the *gravest* human-rights violation, in my view, because those who commit it do not intend the death and suffering they inflict either as an end or as a means. They merely act with willful indifference to the enormous harms they cause in the course of advancing their own ends, while going to great lengths to deceive the world (and often themselves) about the impact of their conduct. But it is still the *largest* such human-rights violation.

To be sure, massive poverty caused by human agency is not unprecedented. British colonial institutions and policies are blamed for up to a million poverty deaths in the Irish Potato Famine of 1846–9 and for about 3 million poverty deaths in the Great Bengal Famine of 1943–4. Around 30 million poverty deaths in China during 1959–62 are attributed to Mao Tse-Tung's insistence on continuing the policies of his "Great Leap Forward" even when their disastrous effects became apparent. Still, these historical catastrophes were of more limited duration and even at their height did not reach the present and ongoing rate of 18 million poverty deaths per annum.

The continuing imposition of this global order, essentially unmodified, constitutes a massive violation of the human right to basic necessities – a violation for which the governments and electorates of the more powerful countries bear primary responsibility. This charge cannot be defeated through appeal to baseline comparisons, by appeal to the consent by the victims themselves, or by appeal to other detrimental causal factors that the present global order may merely do too little to counteract.

2.6 The promise of global institutional reform

Human rights impose on us a negative duty not to contribute to the imposition of an institutional order that foreseeably gives rise to an avoidable human-rights deficit without making compensating protection and reform efforts for its victims. Analogous to the negative duties not to break a promise or contract and not to make emergency use of another's property without compensation, this negative institutional duty may impose positive obligations on advantaged participants: obligations to compensate for their contribution to the harm. Such compensation can take the form of individual efforts (donations to effective NGOs) or of bilateral or multilateral government aid programs. Or it can focus on institutional reform. I close with some comments on this latter option.

In the modern world, the rules governing economic transactions – both nationally and internationally – are the most important causal determinants of the extent and depth of severe poverty and other human-rights deficits. They are most important because of their great impact on the economic distribution within the jurisdiction to which they apply. Thus, even relatively minor variations in a country's laws about tax rates, labor relations, social security, and access to health care and education can have a much greater impact on poverty than even large changes in consumer habits or in the policies of a major corporation. This point applies to the global institutional order as well. Even small changes in the rules governing transnational trade, lending, investment, resource use, or intellectual property can have a huge impact on the global incidence of life-threatening poverty.

Rules governing economic transactions are important also for their greater visibility. To be sure, like particular conduct decisions, rule changes can have unintended and even unforeseeable effects. But with rules it is much easier to diagnose such effects and to make corrections. Assessing adjustments of the rules within some particular jurisdiction is relatively straightforward: one can try to estimate how a rise in the minimum wage, say, has affected the unemployment rate and per capita income in the bottom quintile or fifth of the population. (Other things are happening in the economy besides the change in the minimum wage, so the exercise is complex and imprecise. Still, exercises of this sort can be done, and *are* done, sufficiently well in many countries.) It is more difficult, by contrast, to assess the relative impact of variations in the conduct of individual or collective agents. Such an assessment can be confined to the persons immediately affected – for example, to the employees of a corporation or to the inhabitants of a town in which an aid agency is running a project. But such a confined assessment is always vulnerable to the charge of ignoring indirect effects upon outsiders or future persons.

A further point is that morally successful rules are much easier to sustain than morally successful conduct. This is so because individual and collective agents are under continuous counter-moral pressures not merely from their ordinary self-interested concerns, but also from their competitive situation as well as from considerations of fairness. These phenomena are illustrated by the case of competing corporations, each of which may judge that it cannot afford to pass up immoral opportunities to take advantage of its employees and customers because such unilateral self-restraint would place it at an unfair competitive disadvantage vis-à-vis its less scrupulous competitors. Domestically, this sort of problem can be solved through changes in the legal rules that require all corporations, on pain of substantial penalties, to observe common standards in their treatment of customers and employees. Corporations are often willing to support such legislation even while they are unwilling to risk their competitive position through unilateral good conduct.

Similar considerations apply in the international arena, where corporations and governments compete economically. Given their concern not to fall behind in this competition and not to be unfairly handicapped through unilateral moral efforts and restraints, it is perhaps not surprising (though still appalling) that individuals, corporations, and governments have been so reluctant to make meaningful efforts toward eradicating global poverty.[71] Again, it is possible that affluent governments and corporations could be brought to do much more by accepting and complying with legal rules that apply to them all and thereby relieve each of the fear that its own good conduct will unfairly disadvantage it and cause it to lose ground against its competitors. Successful efforts to reduce poverty within states exemplify this model of structural reform rather than individual moral effort.

To be sure, this thought is not new, and governments have been very reluctant to commit themselves, even jointly, to serious global anti-poverty measures. Their solemn promise to halve global poverty by 2015 has been reiterated – in cleverly weakened formulations – but has yet to result in serious implementation efforts.[72] Official development assistance (ODA) from the affluent countries, once supposed to reach 1 percent, then 0.7 percent of their combined gross national incomes, actually shrank throughout the 1990s, from 0.33 percent in 1990 to 0.22 percent in 2000.[73] With the "war on terror," ODA is reported to have grown back to 0.30 percent (2008) of the affluent countries' combined GNI thanks to dramatic growth in aid to occupied Iraq and Afghanistan.[74] Yet, even this new $120 billion level is only 40 percent of what is needed to eradicate severe poverty – and only a tiny fraction of ODA is actually spent for this purpose (see endnote 71).

This discouraging evidence suggests that improvements in the global institutional order are difficult to achieve and difficult to sustain. However, this fact does not undermine my hypothesis that such structural improvements are *easier* to achieve and much *easier* to sustain than equally significant unilateral improvements in the conduct of individual and collective agents. We know how much money individuals, corporations, and the governments of the affluent countries are now willing to spend on global poverty eradication. This amount is very small in comparison to the harms inflicted on the global poor by evident injustices in the present global order. It is also very small in comparison to what would be required to achieve substantial progress: the amount needed in the first few years of a serious offensive against poverty is closer to $300 billion annually.[75] It is not realistic to hope that we can achieve such a large increase in available funds through appeals to the morality of the relevant agents: affluent individuals, corporations, and the governments of affluent countries. It is *more* realistic – though admittedly still rather unrealistic – to achieve substantial progress on the poverty front through institutional reforms that make the global order less burdensome on the global poor. Accepting such reforms, affluent countries would bear some opportunity costs of making the international trade, lending, investment, and intellectual-property regimes fairer to the global poor as well as some costs of compensating for harms done – for example, by helping to fund basic health facilities, vaccination programs, basic schooling, school lunches, safe water and sewage systems, basic housing, power plants and networks, banks and microlending, road, rail, and communication links where these do not yet exist. If such a reform program is to gain and maintain support from citizens and governments of affluent countries, it must distribute such costs and opportunity costs fairly among them. Transparency will be required in order to assure each of these actors that their competitive position will not be eroded by the non-compliance of others.

The path of global institutional reform is far more realistic and sustainable for three obvious reasons. First, the costs and opportunity costs each affluent citizen imposes on herself by supporting structural reform is extremely small relative to the contribution this reform makes to avoiding severe poverty. The reform lowers an affluent family's standard of living by $900 annually, say, while improving by $300 annually the standard of living of hundreds of millions of poor families. By contrast, a unilateral donation in the same amount would lower the affluent family's standard of living by $900 annually while improving by $300 annually the standard of living of only three poor families. Given such pay-offs, rational agents with some moral concern for the avoidance of severe poverty will be far more willing to support structural reform than to sustain donations.[76] Second, structural reform assures citizens that costs and opportunity costs are fairly shared among the more affluent, as discussed. And third, structural reform, once in place, need not be repeated, year after year, through painful personal decisions. Continual alleviation of poverty leads to fatigue, aversion, even contempt. It requires affluent citizens to rally to the cause again and again while knowing that most others similarly situated contribute nothing or very little, that their own contributions are legally optional and that, no matter how much they give, they could for just a little more always save yet further children from sickness or starvation. Today, such fatigue, aversion, and contempt are widespread attitudes among citizens and officials of affluent countries toward the "aid" they dispense and its recipients.

For these reasons, I believe that today's vast human-rights deficit, especially among the global poor, is best addressed through efforts at global (and national) institutional reform. Relatively small reforms of little consequence for the world's affluent would suffice to eliminate most of this human-rights deficit, whose magnitude makes such reforms our most important moral task.

3

The First UN Millennium Development Goal: A Cause for Celebration?

3.0 Introduction

In the *UN Millennium Declaration* of the year 2000, the 191 member states of the UN committed themselves to the goal "to halve, by the year 2015, the proportion of the world's people whose income is less than one dollar a day and the proportion of people who suffer from hunger."[77] This is the first and most prominent of what have come to be known as the eight UN Millennium Development Goals (MDGs).

The commitment to this goal, in such a prominent text, has been widely celebrated. The governments of the world have finally united behind the goal of eradicating hunger and extreme poverty, defined as the inability to afford "a minimum, nutritionally adequate diet plus essential non-food requirements."[78] And they have not merely endorsed this goal in a vague and general way, but have committed themselves to a concrete path with a precise intermediate target. Given the abject poverty in which so many human beings subsist today, this highly official and highly visible commitment is surely reason for celebration. – Isn't it?

I am not so sure. In any case, I want to offer some skeptical reflections that we might ponder before judging the goal our governments have set in our names.

3.1 Reflection one – on halving world poverty

The goal of halving extreme poverty and hunger by 2015 is not new. It was very prominently affirmed, for instance, four years earlier, at the World Food Summit in Rome, where the 186 participating governments declared: "We pledge our political will and our common and national commitment to achieving food security for all and to an ongoing effort to eradicate hunger in all countries, with an immediate view to reducing the number of undernourished people to half their present level no later than 2015."[79] An "immediate" view that budgets 19 years to solve merely half a problem is not especially ambitious, to be sure, but at least the pledge seemed definite and firm.

Is the first MDG then merely a reaffirmation of a commitment made earlier? Well, not exactly. Looking closely at the two texts, we find a subtle but important shift. While the earlier *Rome Declaration* spoke of halving by 2015 the *number* of undernourished, the later *Millennium Declaration* speaks of halving by 2015 the *proportion* of people suffering from hunger and extreme poverty.

Substituting "proportion" for "number" makes a considerable difference. The relevant proportion is a fraction consisting of the number of poor people in the numerator and "the world's people" in the denominator. With world population expected to increase by 2015 to about 120 percent of what it was in 2000,[80] a reduction in the number of poor to 60 percent of what it was in 2000 suffices to cut the proportion in half. The *Rome Declaration* promised a 50 percent reduction in the number of poor by 2015. The *Millennium Declaration* promised only a 40 percent reduction in this number.

In highlighting this revision, I attach no importance to whether governments focus on the number of poor people or their proportion. My concern is with the dilution of the 2015 goal and with the effort to obscure this dilution. The dilution can be expressed in either idiom: the number of poor is to be reduced by 50 percent according to the *Rome Declaration* and by only 40 percent according to the *Millennium Declaration*. Or: the proportion of poor is to be reduced by 58.33 percent according to the *Rome Declaration* and by only 50 percent according to the *Millennium Declaration*. Either formulation makes apparent that the goalposts were moved.

The significance of the dilution can be gauged in terms of the World Bank's current poverty statistics. These figures show 1,656 million extremely poor people in 1996,[81] and the *Rome Declaration* thus promised that this number will be no more than 828 million in 2015.

The same figures show that there were 1,665 million extremely poor people in 2000[82] – 27.2 percent of world population then. And the *Millennium Declaration* thus promised that this number will be no more than 993 million in 2015 – 13.6 percent of the expected world population in 2015.[83] The subtle shift in language quietly adds 165 million to the number of those whose extreme poverty in 2015 will be deemed morally acceptable – an extra 165 million human beings for whom "a minimum, nutritionally adequate diet plus essential non-food requirements" will be out of reach. This dilution was successfully obscured from the public, and kept out of the media, by opaquely switching from "number" to "proportion" while retaining the language of "halving poverty by 2015."

Since its celebrated adoption by the UN General Assembly, the poverty promise has undergone further revision, in two respects. The current UN statement and tracking of MDG-1 express the poor not as a "proportion of the world's people,"[84] but as a "proportion of people in the developing world."[85] This change is significant because the population of the developing world grows faster than that of the world at large. Because such faster population growth accelerates the rise in the denominator of the proportion, a smaller reduction in the numerator suffices to halve the proportion.

The other change is that the current UN statement of MDG-1 backdates the baseline to 1990, thus envisioning that the halving should take place "between 1990 and 2015"[86] rather than between 2000 and 2015. This change is significant because, lengthening the period in which population growth occurs, it further inflates the denominator and thereby diminishes even more the needed reduction in the number of poor. The population of the developing countries in 2015 is expected to be 146 percent of what it was in 1990.[87] Therefore a reduction of the number of poor to 73 percent of what it was in 1990 suffices to cut that proportion in half.

It is worth noting that the creative accounting is not confined to MDG-1. The most recent MDG report states quite generally that "the baseline for the assessment is 1990, but data for 2000 are also presented, whenever possible, to provide a more detailed picture of progress since the Declaration was signed."[88] The year "1990" occurs 62 times in the *Report 2008* and not even once in the *UN Millennium Declaration*. As the UN is now phrasing MDG-4 and MDG-5, they require us to "reduce by two thirds, between 1990 and 2015, the under-five mortality rate" and to "reduce by three quarters, between 1990 and 2015, the maternal mortality ratio."[89] What the UN General Assembly had actually agreed to promise is rather different: "By the same date [2015], to have reduced maternal mortality by three quarters, and under-five child mortality by two thirds, of their *current* rates."[90]

One remarkable consequence of the UN's backdating of the MDG baselines is that China's massive poverty reduction in the 1990s – the number of Chinese living in extreme poverty reportedly declined by 264 million during that decade[91] – can now be counted as progress toward achieving the MDGs. The revision of MDG-1 thus led UN Secretary-General Kofi Annan tragicomically to report to the General Assembly[92] that for the world's most populous region – East Asia and the Pacific – the 2015 poverty target was met already in 1999, a full year before this goal had even been adopted.

How does the dual revision of MDG-1 affect the allowable number of extremely poor people in 2015? According to the current World Bank statistics, there were 1,813.4 million extremely poor people in 1990 (43.8 percent of the 1990 population of the developing countries).[93] The new target for 2015 is therefore to reduce the number of extremely poor persons to 1,324 million (21.9 percent of the 2015 population of the developing countries). By revising MDG-1, the UN has thus raised the number of those whose extreme poverty in 2015 will be deemed morally acceptable by 331 million (from 993 to 1,324 million). Relative to the *Rome Declaration*, the target was raised by 496 million and the promised reduction in the number of extremely poor people correspondingly lowered by nearly three-fifths: from 828 to 332 million. How are Kofi Annan and the rest of us going to explain to those 496 million people that we changed our minds and that consequently they shall not have a minimum, nutritionally adequate diet plus essential non-food requirements?

Let me sum up my first reflection. MDG-1 is taken to supersede a commitment the world's governments had made years earlier, notably in the 1996 *Rome Declaration*. There they promised to reduce, by 2015, the *number* of extremely poor people to half its *present* (1996) level. The current statement of MDG-1 retains the language of halving world poverty by 2015 but also deforms this goal through three highly deliberate dilutions. First, it aims to halve the *proportion* of extremely poor people, not their number, thus taking advantage of population growth. Second, it redefines this proportion, replacing "the world's people" by "the population of the developing world," thereby taking advantage of faster growth in the latter population (and also detracting from the global moral responsibility of the affluent countries). Third, it extends the plan period backward in time, having it start in 1990 rather than at the time the commitment was made, thereby

Table 3.1: A promise diluted

	Baseline year	Baseline number of poor (millions)	Promised reduction by 2015	Target for 2015 (millions)	Required annual rate of reduction	Target for 2005 (millions)
World Food Summit	1996	1,656	50.0%	828	3.58%	1,193
MDG-1 as adopted	2000	1,665	40.4%	993	3.39%	1,401
MDG-1 as revised	1990	1,813	27.0%	1,324	1.25%	1,501

increasing population growth in the denominator and taking advantage of a reported massive poverty reduction in China.

Drawing on the currently official World Bank figures, table 3.1 summarizes what the dilutions mean in human terms. Compared to the 1996 World Food Summit commitment, MDG-1 as now stated by the UN *raises* the number of extremely poor people deemed morally acceptable in 2015 by 496 million (from 828 to 1,324 million) and thereby *shrinks* by more than half (from 837 to 341 million) the reduction in this number which governments pledge to achieve during the 2000–15 period. Had we stuck to the promise of Rome, our task for 2000–15 would have been to reduce the extremely poor by 837 million or 50.3 percent. MDG-1 as revised envisages a reduction by only one-fifth or only 341 million: from 1,665 million in the year 2000 to 1,324 million in 2015.

With the World Bank's 2005 figure already down to 1,376.7 million,[94] there is little doubt that the UN will be able to announce in 2015 that the goal of halving world poverty has been achieved. But this success will depend decisively on having replaced the promise of the *Rome Declaration* – to halve between 1996 and 2015 the number of people in extreme poverty – with the promise of MDG-1 as subsequently diluted: to halve between 1990 and 2015 the proportion of people in the developing world who live in extreme poverty.

The story of the sly revisions of the grand commitment of Rome and, more generally, of how the world's governments are managing the "halving of world poverty by 2015" illustrates one main reason for the persistence of massive poverty: the poor have no friends among the global elite. Hundreds of officials in many governments and international agencies were involved in shifting the goalposts to the detriment of the poor. Thousands of economists, statisticians, and other academics understood what was happening. So did thousands of people in the media, who had been reporting on the Rome Summit and the MDGs – with some of them expressly denying that the revisions were worth reporting.[95] Most of these privileged harbor no ill will toward poor people. They merely have other priorities. And they don't care how their pursuit of these other priorities is affecting the global poor.

3.2 Reflection two – on tracking poverty by counting the poor

My first reflection may have been a little discomforting. But are the clever revisions really such a big deal? Should we not also appreciate that poverty is declining, albeit not at the once envisioned rate?

Before answering this question, let us think a little more about whether poverty really is declining, that is, whether the Bank's figures provide an accurate portrait of the evolution of extreme poverty.

The Bank's portrait centrally involves counting the poor. It thereby relies on a binary criterion that categorizes each person as either poor or non-poor according to the per capita cost of the consumption of the household to which she or he belongs. This criterion is an international poverty line (IPL), which the Bank currently defines in terms of average daily consumption whose cost in local currency has the same purchasing power as $1.25 had in the US in 2005 (henceforth $1.25 PPP 2005).[96] Persons whose average daily consumption (of all goods and services) costs less than $1.25 PPP 2005 are poor; persons whose average daily consumption costs $1.25 PPP 2005 or more are non-poor.

This method of tracking world poverty is problematic insofar as it wholly disregards information about how far above or below the IPL particular persons are living. Intuitively, the world poverty problem is alleviated when people manage to raise their average daily consumption from $1.00 to $1.20 PPP 2005, say, or from $1.30 to $1.60 PPP 2005 – and such gains constitute more significant progress, actually, than gains from $1.24 to $1.25 PPP 2005.

It may be said in response that this is just a technicality. In the real world (in contrast to worlds imagined by philosophers), counting the number of poor people relative to *any* reasonable poverty line is going to give us an adequate picture of the global poverty problem and its evolution over time.

This response can be rebutted in two ways. One rebuttal points out that the Bank's poverty index serves not merely as a passive instrument of observation, but also as a guide for the policies of governments, international agencies, and NGOs. Insofar as such agents care about their perceived performance in regard to poverty, they will take account of how their policies are likely to affect future poverty figures reported by the Bank. Doing so, they will focus their efforts on people living just below the poverty line because such efforts produce the most cost-effective reductions in the poverty count. Such incentives are obviously undesirable; and their effects may cause the Bank's poverty statistics to deliver an overly rosy picture of the evolution of world poverty.

The other rebuttal points out that the response fails empirically. Thanks to Chen and Ravallion, the key World Bank researchers in charge of the poverty count, we know exactly how sensitive the Bank's portrait of the evolution of poverty is to the level at which the IPL is set. Chen and Ravallion provide headcounts not only for their own chosen IPL of $1.25 PPP 2005 (average daily consumption), but also for three other poverty lines likewise denominated in 2005 international dollars.[97] Table 3.2 displays, for each of these four poverty lines (leftmost column) the headcount change for various time periods all ending with the year 2005 (top row).[98] The highlighted column shows how the actual change in the number of poor people during 1990–2005 compares to the 17.2 percent reduction in this number that would put the world exactly "on track" for achieving the 27 percent reduction that the diluted MDG-1 promises for the 1990–2015 period.

Table 3.2 shows how heavily the reportable headcount progress depends on the chosen IPL level. No matter what time period one may wish to examine, the change in the poverty count during this period looks better the lower the IPL is set. Choosing the UN's newly favored 1990 benchmark, for instance, the number of poor people has, in the 1990–2005 period, fallen *86 percent more than required* to be "on track" for meeting MDG-1 as diluted – when poverty is defined in terms of average daily consumption of $1.00 PPP 2005. On this definition, the world had already in 2005 exceeded the 2015 target of a 27 percent reduction from the 1990 baseline. Yet, if poverty is defined in terms of average daily consumption of $2.50 PPP 2005, then there has been *no reduction at all*, during 1990–2005, in the number of poor people; on

Table 3.2: How success against poverty depends on the level of the IPL

Period:	1981–2005	1984–2005	1987–2005	1990–2005	Relative to path of diluted MDG-1	1993–2005	1996–2005	1999–2005
Poverty line								
$1.00 PPP 2005	–42%	–34%	–29%	–32%	**86% ahead**	–29%	–21%	–24%
$1.25 PPP 2005	–27%	–24%	–20%	–24%	**40% ahead**	–23%	–17%	–19%
$2.00 PPP 2005	1%	–2%	–3%	–7%	**59% behind**	–9%	–9%	–11%
$2.50 PPP 2005	13%	8%	5%	0%	**103% behind**	–3%	–5%	–7%

the contrary, this number has actually increased very slightly. More generally, if one of the two lower poverty lines is chosen, we are well on schedule for realizing the 27 percent headcount reduction required for reaching the diluted MDG-1. If one of the two higher poverty lines is chosen, we are very far behind schedule for realizing that 27 percent reduction by 2015.

In the preceding reflection we saw that MDG-1 will probably be achieved, but that this achievement depends decisively on the promise of the *Rome Declaration* – to halve between 1996 and 2015 the number of extremely poor people – having been replaced at the UN with the promise of MDG-1 as diluted: to halve between 1990 and 2015 the proportion of people in the developing world who are living in extreme poverty. The present reflection shows that even the achievement of this greatly diluted goal depends decisively on fixing the IPL at a sufficiently low level. The steady stream of happy news the World Bank delivers from the poverty front – worked into the titles lest anyone miss the point – is not robust with respect to the level at which the IPL is set. This discredits the method the Bank and the UN are using to track world poverty by counting the poor. It also raises with urgency the question how the Bank decides to fix the level of the IPL where it does.

3.3 Reflection three – on where the line is drawn

How then does the World Bank decide the level of its IPL? It is widely accepted that the IPL should express a narrow conception of absolute poverty that is closely tied to hunger. The UNDP, for instance, affirms that people should be counted as poor only if they fall short of "the income or expenditure level below which a minimum, nutritionally adequate diet plus essential non-food requirements are not affordable."[99] It is only on this minimalist understanding that the world's governments have agreed that poverty is to be eradicated.[100]

How does the Bank convert this shared minimalist understanding of poverty into a specific level for its IPL? We have a rich historical record for answering this question, because the Bank has in fact successively employed and defended four distinct IPLs denominated in international dollars of three different base years: 1985, 1993, and 2005. The Bank has done so while contending that it is desirable to change the poverty line from time to time to keep it up to date. It is indeed true that an IPL denominated in international dollars of a recent base year leads to a more accurate picture of poverty around that year – but it is also true that such an updated poverty line gives us a less accurate picture of poverty in earlier years. So periodic switching of IPLs is not needed for the sake of attaining a more accurate picture of the long-term poverty trend.[101]

The Bank has defended all four of its successive IPLs as "anchored to what 'poverty' means in the poorest countries."[102] How do they know what "poverty" means in the poorest countries? The Bank infers its answer from one single piece of information: from the official domestic poverty lines used in poor countries. Thus, its latest IPL of $1.25 PPP 2005 is calculated as the mean of the official poverty lines – converted at 2005 PPPs into 2005 international dollars – used in the world's 15 poorest countries: Malawi, Mali, Ethiopia, Sierra Leone, Niger, Uganda, Gambia, Rwanda, Guinea-Bissau, Tanzania, Tajikistan, Mozambique, Chad, Nepal, and Ghana. It is unclear why political decisions made by rulers or bureaucrats in these 15 countries – 9 of which have very small populations and 13 of which are located in sub-Saharan Africa – should be thought a reliable indicator of what "poverty" means to poor people all over the world. Nor can the Bank's involvement in setting domestic poverty lines for many poor countries[103] increase confidence in the exercise: mere consistency of the Bank's judgments is no substitute for their justification.

To make matters worse, the most recent anchoring exercise – using the mean of the domestic poverty lines of the world's 15 poorest countries – is at variance with previous anchoring exercises. In 2000, the Bank introduced a revised IPL of $1.08 PPP 1993 while defending this level as the median of the 10 lowest official poverty lines – converted at 1993 PPPs into 1993 international dollars.[104] And in 1990 the Bank had unveiled its first IPL of $1.02 PPP 1985 while defending this level with the argument that eight poor countries had official poverty lines that, converted at 1985 PPPs into 1985 international dollars, were close to this amount.[105] This first IPL was then, by the way, quickly "rounded off" to the more memorable $1.00 PPP 1985 figure[106] which, also enshrined in the text of the *Millennium Declaration*, survives in the still frequent colloquial associations of extreme poverty with living below a dollar a day.

The Bank's successive substitutions have resulted in a tightening of the poverty criterion in most countries and a broadening in a few.[107] The case of the US is not atypical. If we use the US consumer price index[108] to convert the Bank's four successive IPLs into 2005 international dollars, we get the figures displayed in table 3.3. The last and now exclusively used IPL comes to roughly $9.69 per person per

Table 3.3: Historical IPLs and their 2005 US$ equivalents

$1.02 PPP 1985	=	$1.85 (2005)
$1.00 PPP 1985	=	$1.82 (2005)
$1.08 PPP 1993	=	$1.46 (2005)
$1.25 PPP 2005	=	$1.25 (2005)

week in 2009 – or $42 per month or $506 per year.[109] A US household would count as poor by the Bank's new standard only if the cost of its entire 2009 consumption of goods and services had been below $506 per person.

Perhaps it is obvious that the Bank's latest IPL is absurdly low. But we should confirm this judgment. The US Department of Agriculture has for many decades published data about what it costs to adhere to an elaborately designed low-cost food plan that has variously been called the "Restricted Food Plan for Emergency Use," the "Economy Food Plan . . . developed as a nutritionally adequate diet for short-term or emergency use," and the "Thrifty Food Plan."[110] In 2005, the cost of purchasing this minimal diet for a household of two to four people was (depending on household size and children's ages) between $3.59 and $4.97 per person per day.[111] If this was the cost of a minimal or emergency diet in the US, then we can safely conclude that the Bank's IPL of $1.25 PPP 2005 is absurdly low in its base country and base year: in the US in 2005[112] – especially if we remember that the $1.25 per day would need to cover not merely nutrition, but also minimal requirements of clothing, shelter, medical care, water and other utilities.

What can be said to justify the Bank's chosen IPL level? It is obvious that the Bank cannot justify its decision by saying that the IPL must be set at such a low level in order to show the world to be on track toward achieving MDG-1. A lower IPL entails lower poverty headcounts and also, as we have seen, much prettier trend figures than would be derived from higher IPLs. But this cannot be a *justification* for choosing a low IPL.

One also cannot defend the Bank's chosen IPL level by pointing out that the blatant insufficiency of $1.25 per day in the US in 2005 proves nothing, because, in the locations where in 2005 very poor people actually lived, dollars bought much more than they did in the United States. This attempted defense involves a common misunderstanding of the Bank's procedure. Dollars converted at going currency exchange rates in 2005 did indeed buy more in poor countries than in the US. But the Bank is using for its conversions not exchange rates but PPPs, which supposedly preserve purchasing power. Thus the Bank counts someone who, in 2005 in India or Vietnam, was living on the exchange rate equivalent of $0.40 or $0.45 per day as non-poor because this amount, converted at 2005 PPPs, equals or exceeds $1.25.[113]

This raises the question whether the general household consumption PPPs employed by the Bank are an adequate guide to what poor people must actually pay for necessities. Can we conclude from the fact that $1.25 per day was not enough to meet the basic needs of a human being in the US in 2005 that the PPP equivalent of $1.25 per day in any other currency was similarly insufficient? As the following chapter shows, PPP conversions indeed fail to preserve command over basic necessities. But this does not help the Bank's case. For one thing, the prices of foodstuffs are, in every poor country, *higher* than PPPs suggest, and this by a whopping 50 percent on average (see endnote 127). Moreover, the Bank cannot defend the level of its IPL by disqualifying as inadequate the PPPs it is using because, by doing so, it would fatally undermine the very methodology it employs, which assumes that PPPs provide suitable conversion rates for comparing incomes and consumption expenditures of poor people worldwide and for fixing the level of the IPL.

Let me restate this point a little more elaborately. I have shown in this third reflection that consumption expenditure of $1.25 per person per day was much too low to access even the most basic subsistence minimum in the US in 2005. It follows that the use of 2005 PPPs to convert this amount into another currency cannot be relied upon to yield an amount sufficient to purchase in 2005 the most basic subsistence minimum in the territory of that other currency. This follows from considering two jointly exhaustive possibilities. Suppose PPPs reliably preserve purchasing power with respect to basic necessities. Then any 2005 foreign currency equivalent of $1.25 per person per day was as inadequate abroad as $1.25 per person per day was in the US. Alternatively, suppose PPPs do not reliably preserve purchasing power with respect to basic necessities. Then a person's position relative to the IPL – calculated through PPP conversion into 2005 international dollars – does not tell us whether this person has access to a minimally adequate set of basic necessities.

3.4 Reflection four – on relating the IPL to the global product

There is one more possible justification for the very low IPL chosen by the Bank and employed by the UN for tracking MDG-1. This justification invokes the IPL's normative significance. We are monitoring the evolution of extreme poverty not merely out of curiosity, but also with the aim of its reduction and eventual eradication. Given this aim, one might say, we ought to define the IPL in such a way that the magnitude of the world poverty problem implied by this definition is reasonably related to the world's resources: we should not define poverty so broadly that its eradication becomes wholly impractical. Doing so might even be counterproductive by discouraging efforts to reduce poverty to the extent that we can.

Table 3.4 provides the data we need to assess this worry.[114] Using the IPL favored by the Bank and the UN, we find that the aggregate shortfall of the 1,377 million people living below this IPL amounts to merely 0.17 percent of the global product – or about $76 billion per annum or one-ninth of US military spending.[115] It is *this* poverty problem that the world's privileged see themselves as reducing at the stately pace of 1.25 percent per annum, with the affluent states contributing some $12 billion annually in official development assistance for basic social services (see endnote 71).

Were we to double the Bank's IPL, both the number of poor and their average shortfall from the poverty line would greatly increase. A seven times larger 1.13 percent change in the distribution of the global product would then be required to eradicate poverty so defined. Yet, even this shift would hardly be discouragingly large – not when one considers that poverty causes some 18 million premature deaths annually,[116] thus killing at more than twice the rate of World War II during its worst period. Winning that war cost the lives of some 15 million Allied soldiers as well as half or more of the gross domestic products of the US, the UK, and the USSR during the war years.[117] Ending world poverty would not require sending any young people into battle. And it would not – even on a broader definition of $2.50 PPP 2005 per day – seriously affect the economies of the affluent countries. It would lower the growth path of these countries a bit so that they would reach any future standard of living a little later than would otherwise be the case – perhaps half a year, or a year later on the $2.50 PPP 2005 per day definition of poverty. It is for the sake of

Table 3.4: How the size of the global poverty gap varies with the level of the IPL

Poverty line expressed in 2005 international dollars (PPP 2005) per person per day	Poor people in 2005		Aggregate shortfall from the poverty line		
	Number in billions	Average shortfall from the poverty line	in percent of the global product		in $ billions p.a.
			at PPPs	at current (2005) exchange rates	
$1.25	1.38	30%	0.33%	0.17%	76
$2.00	2.56	40%	1.28%	0.66%	296
$2.50	3.08	45%	2.2%	1.13%	507

comparatively trivial gains, then, that we let poverty destroy billions of human lives.

3.5 Concluding thoughts

In 2015, the world's privileged will likely be able to celebrate the achievement of MDG-1: of the goal to halve world poverty by 2015. But this achievement will owe much more to the clever shifting of goalposts than to reductions in poverty. It crucially depends on two revisions that effected a triple dilution of the goal. These revisions have raised the number of those whose extreme poverty in 2015 will be deemed morally acceptable from 828 million to 1,324 million – and they have shrunk the reduction in the number of poor that is to occur during 1996–2015 from 50 percent to 20 percent. The foreseeable achievement of MDG-1 also crucially depends on choosing an absurdly low IPL. Were we to track poverty by reference to a broader poverty criterion, more commensurate to basic human needs and human rights, then we would find that world poverty has been either rising or else decreasing much more slowly than would be required for achieving MDG-1.

Recall the genocide in Rwanda, when the UN and nearly all the rest of the world stood idly by while some 800,000 people were hacked to death (see chapter 8 below). Suppose some Western politician had said, in April 1994, that the slaughter in Rwanda is morally unacceptable and that the world's governments ought to commit themselves to reducing the slaughter by 1.25 percent per annum. Or imagine Franklin Roosevelt in 1942 preparing a speech about the German atrocities in Europe: a speech promising that the US would lead a collective effort to achieve a 20 percent reduction of these atrocities by 1957. Add to this hypothetical scenario a shrewd White House advisor urging Roosevelt to express his promise more appealingly in terms of a larger percentage reduction in the *proportion* of the world's population, or of the world's non-Aryan population, being victimized by the Nazis.[118] And imagine Roosevelt making this reformulated promise to widespread celebration and self-congratulations in the media and among the general public.[119]

This imagined response to the Nazi menace may seem horrifying. But this just *is* our actual response to world poverty. Or are there morally relevant differences that render our actual response to world poverty less bad than the imagined US response to fascist atrocities?

There are such differences – but they actually weigh in the opposite direction: making our response to world poverty morally worse than the imagined US response to the fascist atrocities.

I have already stated two such differences: world poverty produces substantially more harm than the fascists ever did (more each year, and this over much longer periods than the fascists could have sustained), and the cost of ending world poverty is tiny in comparison to the cost of ending fascist rule. These two points combine to show a large discrepancy in the moral cost–benefit ratios associated with the two scenarios. In the 1942 scenario, the great moral urgency of fighting the axis powers is balanced by the huge losses in blood and treasure that such a fight would predictably involve. Yet, there are no morally significant costs that come anywhere near balancing the great moral urgency of ending world poverty. Instead, there is a morally grotesque incongruity between the human and the economic magnitude of world poverty. The problem is so large that it causes one third of all human deaths and blights well over half of all human lives with hunger, disease, oppression, exclusion, and abuse. Yet, global inequality has increased to such an extent that such poverty is now avoidable at a cost that would barely be felt in the affluent countries.

There is yet a third morally significant reason why our actual response to world poverty is worse than the imaginary Roosevelt response to fascism. The US was not a substantial contributor to the harms the fascist states were inflicting in Europe. By letting these harms continue, the US would have failed to live up to its positive duties to protect and to aid people in mortal distress. The governments and citizens of today's affluent countries like to conceive of their relation to world poverty analogously: most of us believe that we bear no significant responsibility for the persistence of this problem and that our only moral reason to help alleviate it is our positive duty to assist innocent persons caught in a life-threatening emergency. We have seen in the preceding chapter that this belief is highly questionable. The governments of the world's more powerful countries negotiate the design of the global institutional architecture with an eye to their own advantage and convenience, and they collaborate with one another and with the elites of the less powerful countries to impose this order on the world. They know that this regime maintains severe poverty on a massive scale and that such poverty is avoidable. But they are not willing to bear the small opportunity costs that a poverty-avoiding global institutional architecture would impose upon them.

Avoiding most of the severe poverty existing in the world today is not expensive. But making progress through gimmickry is much cheaper still. It is not especially difficult to see through these statistical gimmicks and, more generally, to appreciate the ways in which the picture of world poverty widely held in the affluent countries is false. But the prevailing picture is more attractive than the truth, and so it is reaffirmed by the media and uncritically absorbed by the public. Beholding the Millennium Development Goals, we are moved by the loftiness of our goals and the selfless nobility of our effort – and happily continue to take from Africans their natural resources while paying their oppressors, and happily continue to consume the rapidly diminishing fish stocks in African waters.[120] We celebrate ourselves for the thousands of lives we figure we are saving here and there through one or another generous initiative, without noticing that most of these lives need saving only because of the gravely unjust global institutional order our countries design and impose.

Perhaps the most fundamental obstacle to the eradication of poverty is such stunning thoughtlessness of the affluent in the face of a problem that destroys vastly more lives than many problems we do pay at least some attention to – such as the conflicts in the Middle East, the massacres in Rwanda and East Timor, or the 2004 tsunami. Our inattention to world poverty is all the more remarkable because we may bear a far greater responsibility for it than for those local eruptions of violence and also because we can actually do a great deal, even as individuals, toward reducing world poverty, while most of us can do very little toward protecting innocent people from violence in the world's trouble spots.

In a sense, such thoughtlessness in the affluent countries is not really surprising. Of course people do not like to think too hard about harms that they themselves may share responsibility for and can do something about. Many Germans in my parents' generation avoided moral reflection under the Nazis. But were they innocent merely because they did not think? Or wasn't their very lack of thought a great moral failing? The latter judgment is now widely held. Germans who could truthfully say that they had never thought about the fate of those whom state agents were taking from their neighborhoods and about the foreigners crushed by the Nazi war machine were not therefore innocent. Rather, they were guilty of violating their most fundamental moral responsibility: to work out for oneself what one's moral responsibilities are in the circumstances in which one finds oneself. In this respect, we are in the same boat with those Germans. They could not possibly have judged it obvious that Nazi conquests and mass arrests required no further thought from them. And we cannot possibly judge it obvious that we need give no further thought to world poverty. Apart from our involvement in the perpetuation of world poverty, we commit a separate crime of thoughtlessness. The global poor pose a morally inescapable question: what responsibilities do we have in regard to the social conditions that blight their lives? We owe them a reflective answer.

4

Developing Morally Plausible Indices of Poverty and Gender Equity: A Research Program

4.0 Introduction

The previous chapter has shown that the level at which the World Bank's International Poverty Line (IPL) is set greatly affects the appearance of the world poverty problem. The present chapter explores the use of indices more generally.

Why should indices – instruments for measuring and tracking phenomena in the world – attract the attention of philosophers? Beginning to answer this question, let me distinguish three types of index, or rather three distinct ways in which an index might be understood by its creators and users.

An index might be understood, first, as merely delivering convenient aggregates of information. Some baseball statistics are commonly so understood. For example, a batting average aggregates information about what happens during games. It is not understood to be the "right" way of aggregating such information, just one way that has become prominent through use. When so conceived, indices do not pose philosophically interesting problems.

An index might be understood, second, as serving an explanatory and/or predictive function. An index of risk factors for heart attack is an example. Here the index is designed and redesigned – by adding and deleting components perhaps, or by changing the formula used for aggregating information from the various components – toward maximizing its predictive power. This is an intellectually more ambitious enterprise, but an empirical, not a philosophical one: one needs to explore what the relevant risk factors are and how they interact with one another in order to fine-tune the index.

An index may also be understood, finally, as a standard of evaluation, typically used in a normative role. To be sure, the preceding case can also be described along these lines: a doctor evaluates a patient's lifestyle and exhorts him to avoid cigarettes or fatty foods. In that case, however, there is a clearly defined end – avoiding a heart attack – whose desirability is unproblematic. Matters are different with an index of gender equity, for instance, because here much conceptual and normative work is needed to specify a conception of gender equity that captures what is desirable about it and can serve as the basis for identifying and measuring it in real-life settings. This is philosophical work: furnishing a general basis for ranking as better or worse alternative states of a population as well as alternative changes in such states and for moral judgments and prescriptions based upon such rankings.

Insofar as morally significant indices have actually been constructed and applied, this work has differed from typical philosophical work in two respects. Generally ignored by professional moral philosophers, index construction has received uneven philosophical attention mostly from non-philosophers, including prominent ones like the economists Joan Robinson and Amartya Sen. And, unlike most philosophical works, some indices have become highly influential: followed and cited by the media, policy-makers, and the general public. This is an unfortunate combination – unfortunate for those who suffer the effects of deeply flawed indices and unfortunate also for academic philosophy, which is marginalizing itself and missing an opportunity to bring its wisdom to bear on something that really matters.

The present chapter marks the beginning of a major research effort – supported by the Australian Research Council, Oxfam, the International Women's Development Agency, and the Philippine Health Social Science Association – aimed at reflecting critically on how gender equity, development, and poverty have been, and on how they ought to be, measured and tracked across a plurality of diverse natural and social environments. This project is important insofar as such indices guide – and often misguide – the efforts of policy-makers in governments, NGOs, and international agencies. Taking such indices seriously, political actors will use them as proxies for the values they purport to measure: governments will aim to use the means at their disposal to effect the largest achievable reduction in the poverty index, for example, on the assumption that they will thereby have brought about – or be perceived to have brought about – the largest achievable reduction in what makes poverty objectionable. Insofar as this assumption is mistaken, money and human effort go to waste.

This danger is real. This is so, first, because index construction has thus far received too little systematic moral attention and reflection. A second reason is that indices tend to have great inertia: once an index has been introduced and has become widely known, people tend to go on using it, despite known flaws, because it allows comparisons with the past that would become impossible, or at least very difficult, if the index were to be replaced or substantially revised. A third and perhaps most important reason is especially relevant to prominent indices used for evaluation or prescription. Because the outputs such indices deliver can have serious political repercussions – for instance by serving as ammunition in debates about WTO globalization – the construction, refinement, and application of such indices can be subject to intense lobbying efforts. This is well known in domestic contexts but less widely recognized with respect to transnational indices. When governments and corporations have billions at stake in their efforts to shape and empower the emerging global trading regime, then they will take an interest in how the performance of this regime is being monitored. To be successful in their rule-shaping efforts, politicians and corporations need to attract political support and to disarm political opposition. Their ability to do this, in turn, depends in part on whether citizens and other politicians, at home and abroad, believe that WTO globalization "works," for instance by reducing poverty or by fostering development and gender equity. My discussion, in the preceding chapter, of the grand promise to halve world poverty by 2015 provides ample evidence of the length to which decision-makers will go to create the appearance of success. In examining existing indices of gender equity, development, and poverty, vigilance is needed.

The next two sections illustrate these points by discussing one of the most influential indices: the World Bank's poverty index. In section 4.3, I take up the indices of Human Development and Gender-Related Development maintained by the United Nations Development Program.[121] The final section outlines some ideas toward better indices of poverty, development, and gender equity.

4.1 How the World Bank is tracking poverty by counting people below some IPL

In chapter 3, I disputed the absurdly low consumption level above which the World Bank deems people not to be poor. Here I offer a more comprehensive critique of the Bank's methodology.

The first and most obvious problem is that tracking poverty by means of a headcount figure indefensibly prioritizes people living just below the IPL. Moving such people to just above the IPL is the cheapest and easiest way of reducing the poverty headcount. But why should only moves crossing the IPL count as progress? There is no good reason for ignoring changes in people's economic situation when these occur entirely below the IPL or slightly above it.

A second, related problem is that, when poverty is tracked as a headcount, our picture of the distribution and evolution of poverty may be excessively sensitive to the level at which the IPL is set. This problem was extensively discussed in section 3.2 above. We saw there that, for all available time periods, the poverty trend looks better the lower the poverty line is set. Regarding the 1990–2005 period, we found that, depending on the level of the IPL chosen, the achieved poverty reduction puts us 86 percent ahead of schedule or 40 percent ahead of schedule or 59 percent behind schedule or 103 percent behind schedule (see table 3.2). With an opportunity to affect so profoundly how the numbers look, those in charge of monitoring poverty are bound to come under pressure to adjust their IPL, and are bound to be suspected of having chosen their IPL with an eye to what the resulting trend figures would look like.

A third problem with the Bank's counting of the poor arises from the fact that the exclusive focus on monitoring income and consumption expenditure leaves out factors that are relevant to poverty as intuitively understood. Someone who survives by working in a cold climate, which requires additional expenses for staying warm, is poorer than another who can earn the same income without having to bear such extra costs. Likewise for someone who faces additional expenses due to local disease vectors or other challenges of the natural or social environment.

Another crucial factor is labor burden: someone who reaches the IPL by working 70 hours a week is poorer than another who can maintain the same level of consumption by working only 20 hours per week. Any plausible measure of poverty must take account of necessary labor time – including here not merely paid work, but also the work on family food production, housekeeping, and child-rearing, which is typically unpaid and still very predominantly performed by women and girls.

A fourth problem arises from the Bank's reliance on household surveys that seek to value, in local currency, the totality of a household's consumption or income. This amount is then simply divided by the number of household members to determine each member's economic position. This simple division ignores variations in course-of-life needs: as persons' needs vary with age, so do the requirements of poverty avoidance.[122] The Bank should not then ignore a household's age composition when assessing the adequacy of this household's consumption expenditure. The easy division also ignores how consumption and labor are distributed within each household, and thereby systematically overlooks, in particular, gender biases in the distribution of work, food, education, and health care. A closer look would often reveal what the Bank's method renders a priori impossible: that some – typically female – household members are poorer than others.[123]

4.2 The problematic reliance on CPIs and PPPs

A fifth problem for the Bank's method arises from how the results of household consumption surveys, expressed in the currencies of many countries and years, are compared against one common IPL. How does the Bank determine whether the consumption of an Indian household in 1987, say, valued at some amount of 1987 rupees per person per day, is above or below $1.25 PPP 2005? The Bank makes such determinations through two transformations. It uses purchasing power parities (PPPs) of the base year to convert its chosen IPL into base-year amounts of all other currencies (including 2005 rupees).[124] It then uses national consumer price indices (CPIs) to convert the results further into national currency amounts of other years (including 1987 rupees).

This conversion method is unreliable on account of the CPI and PPP conversions it involves. One difficulty here is that the accurate tracking of prices and consumption patterns is data-intensive and therefore subject to much debate and uncertainty. Recently published new PPPs (for 2005), for example, have resulted in huge revisions: increasing the estimate of Nigeria's GDP(PPP) by 58 percent and decreasing the GDP(PPP)s of Bangladesh, China, India, Indonesia, the Philippines, and Vietnam by 37, 39, 40, 17, 41, and 31 percent, respectively.[125] Such amazingly large revisions have an immense impact on any poverty counts that rely on PPPs: lowering previous poverty estimates for Nigeria and dramatically raising previous poverty estimates for Bangladesh, China, India, Indonesia, the Philippines, and Vietnam.

A further difficulty affecting CPI and PPP conversions is that prices often vary greatly within one country. In response to the new PPPs, the Bank has recently begun to take account of this fact by effectively creating, for several populous countries, a second PPP for the countryside, thereby attributing greater purchasing power to money earned or spent by rural households. In regard to China, for instance, the Bank now posits that rural yuan are worth 37 percent more than urban yuan. The Bank uses then two distinct conversions of its IPL into yuan: it uses the calculated 2005 PPP (4.09 yuan to the dollar) to compute the poverty threshold for urban households only ($1.25 \times 4.09 = 5.11$ yuan); and it then divides the result by 1.37 to obtain the poverty threshold for rural households ($5.11 \div 1.37 = 3.73$ yuan).[126] Thus, to count as non-poor in China in 2005, an urban household had to spend at least 5.11 yuan per person per day, while a rural household achieved this status by spending merely 3.73 yuan ($1.25 was worth 10.35 yuan at the 2005 exchange rate). This adjustment may well improve the Bank's sorting of Chinese households into those that are poor and those that are not. But it is obvious, nonetheless, that cost of living varies in China in rather more complex ways than this simple model suggests.

A third difficulty affecting CPI and PPP conversions is due to the fact that price comparisons across years (within the same country) and across countries (within the same year) yield different results for diverse commodities: the price of computers may be falling even while the price of rice is rising, and dollars in the US may buy more bread but less maid services than yuans do in China. CPIs and PPPs aggregate such diverse price data, weighting the prices of the various commodities according to their role in national (CPI) and international (PPP) consumption expenditure. This fact renders CPIs and PPPs unreliable within a poverty measurement exercise, because national and international consumption patterns do not come close to reflecting the consumption needs of the very poor. The prices of cars and services, for instance, play a much larger role in CPI and PPP calculations than in the lives of poor people. Conversely, prices of basic foodstuffs have importance in the lives of poor people that is vastly greater than their influence on CPI and PPP calculations reflects. The doubling of food prices during 2006–8, for example, made much less of a difference to national CPIs, and hence to the official poverty statistics, than to the poor who typically must spend well over half their incomes on basic foodstuffs.

In the case of PPPs, the resulting errors systematically exaggerate the consumption possibilities of poor people in regard to basic foodstuffs. This is so because international differentials in the price of any commodity will tend to be smaller the more "tradable" this commodity is. When a commodity can be easily conveyed across national borders, its price at prevailing exchange rates will tend to be about the same everywhere – if the price were much higher (or lower) somewhere, supply would promptly be moved to (away from) that location. If all commodities were easily tradable in this way, then PPPs would be close to prevailing exchange rates. The fact that the PPPs of poor-country currencies diverge from their exchange rates – often by a factor of three or more – is then due to differentials in the prices of commodities that, like land, cannot be conveyed across borders or, like (in our world) most services, can cross borders only in small quantities or at high cost.

Being sensitive to the prices of all commodities consumed by households, both tradable and non-tradable, the PPPs of poor countries can then be expected to imply overestimates of the prices of non-tradables balanced by underestimates of the prices of tradables such as foodstuffs. We can observe this effect when we compare poor countries' PPPs for "individual consumption expenditure by households" with those for "food and nonalcoholic beverages." Prices for food and nonalcoholic beverages are higher, in each and every poor country, than what PPPs for individual household consumption expenditure would suggest, and higher by about 50 percent on average.[127] This means that households that, in 2005, lived on what the Bank regarded as the equivalent on $1.25 per person per day could – concentrating their consumption on food alone – buy about as much food as could have been bought in the US for $0.84 per person per day.

We have seen that CPIs and PPPs do badly at tracking the prices of the commodities poor people need and that PPPs moreover systematically overstate poor people's consumption possibilities in regard to basic foodstuffs. Plausible poverty comparisons across space and time can therefore not be generated by using CPIs and PPPs for the purpose of mapping any amount, denominated in any currency of any year, onto the common currency of the IPL.

All this is not to suggest that the Bank should be working with CPIs and PPPs that are based on the prices of foodstuffs alone. Clearly, poor people need commodities other than food and water: such as clothing, shelter, and medical care. Nor would it be satisfactory to use indices based on the actual consumption spending of poor people (identified through some iteration procedure) – so-called PPPs for the poor, or PPPPs – because the observed spending pattern of the poor often fails to disclose what they need most. Unmet needs, ignorance, and advertising lead poor people to spend some of their income on alcohol, tobacco, or quackery. Yet, unlike a rise in food prices, a rise in cigarette prices does not make them poorer in an intuitive sense: it does not reduce their ability to meet their basic needs. Conversely, millions of poor people worldwide do not spend any money on buying patented medicines they urgently need. This fact does not show that the price of such medicines is for them irrelevant. In fact, this price is killing many of them. The observed spending pattern of the poor – itself heavily influenced by existing prices and other extraneous factors (such as advertising) – is not then a good indicator of what they require to meet their basic needs.

In the end, judgments of poverty must invoke, then, a notion of basic needs that is itself partly value-based. With such a notion on hand, one can identify the commodities capable of fulfilling these needs. It is the prices of these and only these commodities – "necessities" – that are relevant to poverty measurement.

This said, let me once more illustrate how the Bank's employment of CPIs and PPPs leads it astray. Imagine a simple world with three commodities: *necessities, discretionaries,* and *services* (always in this order). If their prices do not move in lockstep, the CPI will reflect a weighted average of their price movements, based on the national spending pattern. By relying on the CPI, the Bank thus loses track of the price of necessities. Falling prices of discretionaries (e.g., consumer electronics) may lead to a falling CPI even while rising biofuel demand is driving up food prices. Poor people on constant incomes become poorer relative to what they need to buy (necessities), yet by the Bank's calculations they become richer (relative to what their country's population is consuming).

Similar errors are introduced through the use of PPPs, as can be shown with a numerical example. Suppose the prices of our three commodities, in pesos, are 5, 6, and 1 in some poor country and $3, $4, and $9 in the US. What is the PPP? The answer depends on the spending patterns in *both* countries. Suppose this pattern is 30%, 50%, and 20% in the poor country and 10%, 50%, and 40% in the US. The way PPPs are computed, this yields a bilateral PPP of 1.55 – each peso is deemed to be equivalent to $1.55. (Here the hypothetical peso is valued so highly in dollars because it buys nine times more services and because services constitute so large a portion of US consumption expenditure.)

But this bilateral PPP is inadequate for assessing the incomes of the very poor, who do and must concentrate their consumption expenditure on necessities – relative to which each peso is worth only $0.60 (5 pesos buy as much necessities in the foreign country as $3 buy in the US.) Again, many who are extremely poor, relative to what they really need to buy, may not show up in the Bank's poverty statistics.

This distortion is compounded once additional countries enter the picture. Bilateral PPPs calculated without regard to other countries would not satisfy transitivity, that is, the condition:

for all countries A, B, C: $PPP(A,B) \times PPP(B,C) = PPP(A,C)$

Transitivity fails to hold because the left side of the equation is substantially influenced by the spending pattern in country B, while the right side is not so influenced at all. It is highly desirable, however, that PPPs be transitive because the Bank's poverty measurement exercise would otherwise not be robust with respect to the choice of base country (the relation between the domestic poverty lines of any two countries would change depending on which currency they are converted into and compared in). To ensure transitivity, the calculation of PPPs conventionally involves a final step that adjusts all preliminary bilateral PPPs to one another in a way that guarantees transitivity. As a result, the PPP assigned to any local currency is affected by the prices and spending patterns not only of its home country and the United States (base country), but also by those of every other country. In the Bank's method, then, the classification of any person as poor or nonpoor is influenced not merely by the money she has and the prices she faces, but also by the prices and spending patterns of all countries included in the PPP exercise.

The dependence of PPP calculations on the spending patterns of all other countries and on the prices of commodities that are irrelevant to poverty avoidance distorts the World Bank's poverty assessment exercise. This distortion could be reduced by leaving affluent countries out of account entirely. When counting the poor, the Bank is looking only at less developed countries – on the plausible assumption that virtually no one in the affluent countries lives in extreme poverty. But then the Bank includes the affluent countries in its calculation of PPPs, thereby allowing the prices of necessities to be drowned out by the prices of discretionaries and services, which play a much larger role in the consumption of affluent than in that of poor countries. The Bank would do better if it excluded affluent countries also from its PPP calculations, using the currency of some less developed country rather than the US dollar as the common measure – though this revision would only reduce, not eliminate, the error.[128]

The fifth problem then with the Bank's method is that it is hugely over-inclusive in its informational base. To determine whether a person is poor or not, the Bank rightly takes account of the local prices of necessities: nutrition, shelter, clothing, basic medical care, water, and other utilities. But it marginalizes this information by also incorporating much additional information that is irrelevant: the local prices of other commodities, the prices of all commodities in other countries, and national spending patterns in all countries. By making all this information relevant through its CPI and PPP conversions, the Bank distorts our picture of world poverty in ways that have not yet been fully analyzed.

Perhaps the best evidence one can have against any method is that its applications can deliver massively divergent results. The two notions of equivalence invoked in CPI and PPP calculations rely on very different (national and global) spending patterns. As a consequence, the comparison of two amounts in different years and countries varies with the base year chosen for PPP conversion. For example, one can use the CPIs of the two countries to convert into 1993 amounts and then compare via 1993 PPPs – or one can use these national CPIs to convert into any other year and then do the comparison in PPPs of that year. One can get as many different results as there are available PPP base years.

An intuitive way of displaying the problem involves taking a national currency amount – denominated in 1993 Chinese yuan, say – on a "round trip": using 1993 PPPs to convert it into Bangladeshi taka, then the Bangladeshi CPI to convert into 1985 taka, then 1985 PPPs to convert into 1985 yuan, and then finally the Chinese CPI to convert it back into 1993 yuan. The final amount resulting from such a round trip is typically quite different from the initial amount, in this case 31 percent higher.[129] This is so because the CPI and PPP conversions performed involve very different notions of purchasing power equivalence, based on different consumption patterns. And the comparison of a 1993 yuan amount and a 1985 taka amount will then vary depending on whether this comparison is made via 1993 PPPs and the Bangladeshi CPI or via 1985 PPPs and the Chinese CPI (or in some other way). Using 1993 rather than 1985 as the base year raises all Chinese amounts – prices, incomes, consumption expenditures – in all years by 31 percent relative to all Bangladeshi amounts in all years. And conversely, using 1985 rather than 1993 as the base year raises all

Bangladeshi amounts in all years by 31 percent relative to all Chinese amounts in all years.

The choice of PPP base year thus has a large impact on the relative position of national poverty lines – often much greater than 31 percent.[130] Bound to be arbitrary, the Bank's choice of base year affects the classification – as poor or non-poor – of hundreds of millions of people, though some of these effects do cancel out, of course, as poverty is shifted from one country or continent to another.[131]

Intuitively, whether people are poor and how poor they are depends on whether and to what extent they can, at reasonable cost in necessary labor, gain access to the goods and services they need to meet their basic human needs within their actual natural and social environment. To assess their ability to do this, one must know their age-specific human needs, the relevant environmental factors (such as climate and disease vectors) that co-determine what nutrients and other necessities persons require to satisfy their needs, the cost of the locally cheapest way of meeting these requirements in a culturally acceptable way, and the amount of labor necessary to gain access to these required goods and services.

The World Bank's poverty monitoring method bases its binary output (poor/non-poor) on the per capita cost of household consumption. It completely ignores household composition (age and gender), intra-household distribution, necessary labor, culture, and other environmental factors. And it marginalizes the local prices of necessities by swamping them with an enormous wealth of irrelevant data: about prices of commodities that are irrelevant to poverty avoidance, about the cost of all commodities in all other countries and other years, and about the proportions in which all national populations all over the world allocate their spending over commodities. There are strong reasons to doubt that this method can reliably identify the poor, assess how poor they are, or reveal whether world poverty is in decline and, if so, at what rate.[132]

Given the great political importance that tracking the evolution of poverty, and the possible feminization of poverty, have assumed in the wake of MDG-1 and in the heated debates about WTO globalization, it is high time to specify and try out an alternative approach that would draw on the right information base and would combine this information in a plausible way. The rich data produced by such an approach would not merely give us a more comprehensive picture of world poverty and its evolution, but would also enrich our empirical understanding of poverty, thus enabling more effective poverty avoidance.

4.3 Tracking development with the HDI and gender equity with the GDI

Designed principally by Amartya Sen,[133] the UNDP's Human Development Index (HDI) is meant to measure the degree of development a population enjoys. It is calculated as the average of three components, each normalized to a scale of 0–1. These components are the national population's life expectancy at birth (L), its education (E),[134] and its gross domestic product (GDP) per capita (P). Each country (C) receives a score in each of these components, and its overall HDI score is then the average of these three scores.[135] In a simple equation:

$$HDI_C = (L_C + E_C + P_C)/3$$

The Gender Development Index (GDI) uses the same three components. The only difference is that these three scores are now calculated in a more complicated way. First, the population is divided into its male and female subpopulations. Each subpopulation is then scored just like the entire population would be scored for HDI purposes. The GDI then uses, in each component, the weighted harmonic mean of the male and female scores.[136] When the male and female scores in some component are equal, then the harmonic mean is simply this equal score. The more unequal the two gendered scores are, the more the harmonic mean sinks below the average, reflecting a penalty for gender disparity.

To illustrate, suppose a country's education score is 0.6. The value of 0.6 would enter directly into the calculation of the HDI. In order to calculate the GDI, however, the two genders must be examined separately. Suppose that, with the population being half male and half female, the female education score is 0.3 and the male one 0.9. In this case, the GDI calculates the country's education score as the harmonic mean of the two scores, which is 0.45. In the education component, the country is thus assigned a GDI score that is 0.15 below the corresponding HDI score; this diminution constitutes a gender disparity penalty.[137]

The HDI/GDI method usefully complements income with other factors. But the choice of these factors as well as their aggregation (as implied by their normalizations and relative weights) remain rather arbitrary. By valuing the contributions that life expectancy, education, and income make to a society's development, these indices have implications about how valuable life years, educational gains, and money are relative to one another. These implications are neither further discussed nor is their plausibility examined. In addition, the HDI and GDI have grave defects to which we now turn.[138]

The first and most general problem is that both indices are focused on countries and also marketed as standards of achievement for countries. This is a step backward from the World Bank's poverty head-count measure which is focused mainly on the *global* poverty count (though headcounts disaggregated by country and region are also provided). This focus on the global poverty count strongly suggests that what matters is the impoverishment of *individual human beings* and that the responsibility of avoiding such poverty is shared world-wide. The HDI and GDI, by contrast, focus on the ranking of countries and thereby sustain the common view – well liked in affluent countries – that underdevelopment is the responsibility of the poor countries themselves.

The shift in focus away from individuals is most obvious in the first and last components which, together, constitute two-thirds of both indices. Life expectancy is simply averaged across a national population, or across its male and female subpopulations, and all information about its distribution within such (sub)populations is discarded as irrelevant. This is implausible, because inequalities in life expectancy – not merely between men and women, but generally – must be con-sidered relevant for any morally plausible conception of development. Thus an increase in a society's life expectancy cannot be celebrated as development when it derives from the fact that a gain in life years, above 80 years of age, for the affluent slightly outweighs a loss in life years, below 50 years of age, for the poor.[139]

Analogous thoughts apply also to the last component – and even more so, because the inequalities that are ignored by the HDI and GDI tend to be even greater in income than in life expectancy. The HDI uses GDP per capita, which averages over an entire country, while the GDI divides the GDP – in proportion to men's and women's shares of earned income – in order to calculate separately a male and a female GDP per capita. Inequalities within the population (HDI) and within the two gendered subpopulations (GDI) are entirely ignored. Thus, the HDI sees no difference in development between one society, in which income is heavily concentrated at the top so that the poor major-ity lives in dire poverty, and another society, with the same GDP per capita, in which income is widely dispersed so that no one must endure severe poverty. A given increase in per capita GDP is considered by the HDI to make the same contribution to development, regardless of whether the poorer majority of the population is gaining or losing ground.

Similarly, what matters for the GDI is the average earned income of females relative to the average earned income of males. It makes no difference to gender-related development, as the GDI conceives it, whether overall gender income parity exists because a few women at the top have enormous pay packages or because women in all strata of society enjoy employment opportunities and wages that roughly match those of their male counterparts.

This total neglect of distribution is obviously morally implausible. More important, it also provides perverse incentives. When policymakers are concerned to improve their country's HDI, they will seek to enhance its GDP without regard to whether the additional income goes to the rich or to the poor. They may well emulate the example of Angola, which achieved huge gains in per capita GDP between 2001 and 2007 thanks to rising crude oil production and crude oil prices, without worrying whether the extra income was earned by foreigners or embezzled by a small ruling clique. Likewise, insofar as policymakers are concerned to reduce their country's gender disparity penalty, they will seek to shift the income distribution in favor of females – but again without regard to whether the additional income goes to rich or to poor women. The GDI thus encourages such policymakers to boost their country's GDI score through policies that double to $200,000 the incomes of 10,000 women executives if this is even slightly more convenient to them than it would be to achieve the same female-income boost by doubling to $2,000 the incomes of 1 million female domestics. The GDI here values doubling an affluent woman's income *100 times* more highly than doubling a poor women's income – even though poor women typically have more at stake, in terms of both human needs and gender disadvantage.

The data in table 4.1 illustrate two hypothetical scenarios that attract identical gender disparity penalties from the GDI. Looking at the female-to-male earned-income ratios decile by decile, we see that the first scenario displays substantial disadvantages suffered by a large majority of women while the second displays much smaller disadvantages suffered by a minority of women at the top of the socioeconomic distribution. It is intuitively obvious that gender disparities are much worse in the first scenario than in the second. Nonetheless, the GDI ranks them as equals and thus guides policy-makers toward the first if achieving it is even slightly less costly for them than achieving the second. This evidently absurd conclusion arises from the GDI giving equal weight to each unit of income rather than to each woman. It

Table 4.1: How the GDI can fail to register great gender disparities affecting most women

	First Scenario				Second Scenario		
Female average	Male average	Female share of earned income		Female average	Male average	Female share of earned income
0	43	0.0000	Decile 1	44	43	0.5057
0	96	0.0000	Decile 2	99	96	0.5077
13	148	0.0807	Decile 3	147	148	0.4983
77	202	0.2760	Decile 4	204	202	0.5025
129	294	0.3050	Decile 5	292	294	0.4983
189	383	0.3304	Decile 6	385	383	0.5013
288	519	0.3569	Decile 7	520	519	0.5005
449	731	0.3805	Decile 8	711	731	0.4931
979	1,293	0.4309	Decile 9	1,192	1,293	0.4797
6,180	6,441	0.4897	Decile 10	4,710	6,441	0.4224
830	1,015	0.4500	AVERAGE	830	1,015	0.4500

thereby implicitly assigns much greater importance to disadvantages and percentage gains in the incomes of affluent women than to disadvantages and percentage gains in the incomes of poor women.

The shift in focus away from individuals manifests itself also in how the HDI and GDI aggregate information about a population into a single index number. They do so by first aggregating within each component indicator across the population, and then averaging the results across these components. They thereby ignore how different aspects of deprivation are correlated. This is not plausible because deprivations that persons suffer are morally more problematic when they – concentrated on the same individuals – aggravate rather than mitigate one another.[140]

The GDI inherits these problems. And it adds another one by discarding information about whether gender disparities aggravate or mitigate one another. The GDI calculates the gender disparity penalty separately in each component and simply adds up the penalties – regardless of whether women are disadvantaged in all three components, say, or one gender is disadvantaged in two and the other in one component.

In order to promote development, governments, international agencies, and NGOs should, other things equal, prioritize the neediest. Yet, in order to pinpoint those who are in greatest need overall, any multidimensional index must be constructed to aggregate in the opposite order: aggregating first intra-personally across the component indicators, and then aggregating the results across the population.

4.4 Toward new indices of development, poverty, and gender equity

Today's leading indices of development, poverty, and gender equity suffer from one or more of the following deficiencies:

1 Lack of a moral rationale, which results in some aspects of development or gender disparity being selected in preference to others without a sound justification of the former as being of greater constitutive or instrumental importance.
2 False universality – a focus on deprivations (e.g. income poverty) that anyone may suffer combined with relative neglect of deprivations that differentially affect persons according to gender, age, and environment.

3 Bias toward the better-off, which manifests itself in:
  (a) a focus on indicators that are relevant mostly to the more privileged, such as women in parliament[141] or women in higher education, which matter but are less important than gender disparities that constitute much greater burdens for much larger numbers of more disadvantaged women and girls; and
  (b) implausible aggregation that ignores correlations among different aspects of deprivation, for instance, or compares male and female income totals and thereby implicitly gives much greater weight to income inequalities at the top.
4 Lack of integration, as when several partial indices are presented side-by-side without any guidance for how to resolve conflicts among them about the ranking of programs and policies.

Because indices thus flawed provide faulty guidance and incentives to policy-makers, it is important to explore the possibility of constructing better indices. This is the point of the research project I am commencing with a group of scholars and international NGOs.

We have two broad, constructive ideas that serve as a starting point. First, handling distributional issues correctly requires a holistic measure of individual deprivation. An index is supposed to provide summary information about a group. To do so, it must track how group members are doing. This purpose is much better served when the interpersonal aggregation is performed last, after the relevant aspects of each person's situation have been holistically assessed. This is so because the significance of these situational aspects depends on the age and gender of the person and because these aspects are also interrelated in their significance. If individual lives are what ultimately matters, then we must attend to these interdependencies. For example, a credible index of development must be sensitive to whether an increase in literacy goes to landowners or the landless, an improvement in medical care goes to children or to the aged, an increase in enrolment to privileged university students or to children in slums, an increase in life expectancy to the elite or to the marginalized, enhanced physical security to males or to females.

The second idea is that a holistic measure of individual deprivation, grounded in a sound conception of basic human needs or requirements or capabilities, can serve within different aggregation exercises. Thus, the poverty of a population, or its level of development, can be defined as the mean level of individual deprivation. And gender disparity in a group can be defined as the mean difference across population fractiles (averaging over male/female ratios as calculated for each fractile).[142]

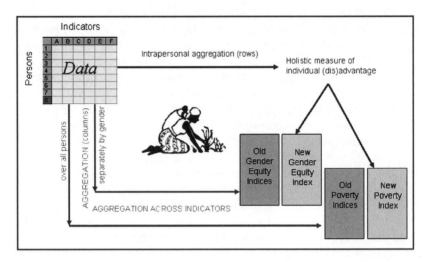

Figure 4.1: New indices based on a holistic measure of individual (dis)advantage

Obviously, these ideas – illustrated in figure 4.1 – are rough and preliminary. But they show in general terms at least how better indices might be specified – indices that would support plausible judgments about whether, for instance, WTO globalization has fostered development or fueled the feminization of poverty.

5

Growth and Inequality: Understanding Recent Trends and Political Choices

5.0 Introduction

In current debates about the world economy, "growth is good" often appears as a truism. Growth leads to affluence, it is said, and greater affluence is surely desirable, especially for the poorer developing countries. Closer inspection, however, leads to a far more nuanced assessment.

Legend has it that there was a time when economists celebrated economic growth, regardless of its distribution. Such economists would have judged alternative economic practices and policies exclusively by their relative impact on the inflation-adjusted (per capita) social product. I am not sure such economists were ever dominant. Economists have long seen the point of income and wealth in the satisfaction of human preferences and understood that, insofar as such satisfaction increases with rising income or wealth, it does so at a declining rate. In any case, the legend of the growth-only economists is useful by allowing real economists to stress that they are different, that they favor pro-poor growth, growth-with-equity, or some such thing. This is crucial to their theological role of appeasing the conscience of their wealthy constituents and of reconciling rich and poor alike to the great globalization push of the past 30 years. If economic experts committed to equity and poverty eradication celebrate this push and the growth it produces, how can we withhold our approval?

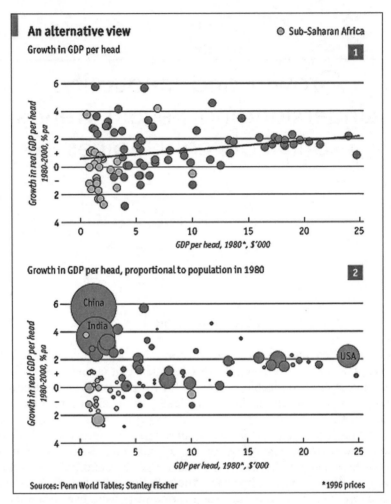

Figure 5.1: *The Economist's* growth distribution charts
Attentive readers of *The Economist* will remember seeing before [this] panel of charts. . . . We make no apologies for showing them to readers again: at a stroke, they cut through much of the statistical fog surrounding this subject. In both charts, the horizontal axis shows the average level of GDP per head in 1980, and the vertical axis shows the rate of growth in inflation-adjusted GDP per head between 1980 and 2000.[143]

Consider the example from *The Economist* shown in figure 5.1. The message conveyed with the two charts is that critics of WTO globalization are mendacious or confused when they complain of inequitable growth. Only when the population size of countries is ignored (as in the top chart) can it appear as though global economic growth is benefiting the rich disproportionately. Once population size is taken into account (as in the bottom chart) it becomes clear that the poor are benefiting mightily – the rise of China and India is living proof of this. A further message here conveyed is that the supporters of WTO globalization, such as *The Economist*, care about poverty and inequity and would not be such ardent supporters if the poor were not benefiting along with the rich.

5.1 Who benefits from recent growth?

Growth can benefit rich and poor alike, and thereby reduce poverty. But to what extent has WTO globalization actually done so? *The Economist* is right to suggest that the top chart in figure 5.1 cannot answer the question. And it rightly prefers the bottom chart: the added information about population size matters in that, other things equal, it is better for faster growth to occur in more populous poor countries than in less populous ones.

Nonetheless, the bottom chart cannot settle the matter either. One reason is that it reports growth in gross domestic product (GDP) rather than growth in gross national product or income (GNP/GNI). Both concepts allocate each unit of income uniquely to one country. But they do so differently. When residents of country A derive income from country B – returns on investments, for instance, or revenues from the sale of natural resources they own in B – then such income is counted toward the GDP of B yet toward the GNI of A. When our concern is with poverty of and equity among countries, we should assess national growth trajectories in terms of GNI which excludes the earnings accruing to foreigners and includes earnings that residents derive from abroad. If the oil price rises and a US company, owned by and paying dividends to US investors, therefore earns more from the oil it extracts in Nigeria, then this extra gain should count as enriching the US rather than Nigeria.[144]

For GNI per capita, Atlas method (current US$), the World Bank reports the trend shown in table 5.1.[145] Inequality increased considerably in *The Economist*'s chosen time period, though it has fallen again since 2000.

Table 5.1: Growth in GNI per capita 1980–2007

Year	GNI/cap of the high-income countries	GNI/cap of the rest of the world[146]	Ratio of high-income countries to rest of world
1980	$10,272	$655	15.7
1990	$19,098	$840	22.7
2000	$25,978	$1,157	22.5
2005	$34,622	$1,755	19.7
2007	$37,572	$2,370	15.9

Table 5.2: Growth in GNI per capita of the richest and poorest countries

Year	Richest countries	Poorest countries	Ratio
1980	$11,840	$196	60
2000	$31,522	$274	115
2005	$40,730	$334	122
2007	$43,503	$374	116

The increase in inequality is even more pronounced at the extremes. Define the poorest and the richest countries in any year as groups of countries that each contain 10 percent of the world's population; per capita GNI (in nominal dollars) in these two groups[147] has evolved as shown in table 5.2, with the corresponding inequality ratio nearly doubling over *The Economist*'s chosen time period.

Clearly, then, in terms of the more appropriate GNI per capita measure, the less developed countries, and the poorest of them especially, have not participated proportionately in global economic growth during the globalization period. In fact, the distance between the richest and the poorest countries has increased to a staggering 116:1 ratio.

An even more important problem with *The Economist*'s bottom chart is that the focus on international inequality, however measured, loses all information about how actual people in these countries are faring. Being told that China enjoyed 6 percent average annual growth in real per capita GDP, we learn nothing about how this growth was distributed within China. And this is what ultimately matters to those concerned with equity and poverty: how did the Chinese poor do in the globalization period? And how did the global poor do, relative to the rest of the human population? By looking only at country averages, one is focusing on the morally least significant inequality, *international* inequality or inequality among country averages, while ignoring the far more important *intra-national* and *global* inequalities among persons.

In criticizing the top diagram, *The Economist* is attacking a straw man that does not represent, let alone exhaust, the arguments that real critics of WTO globalization, appealing to the importance of equity and poverty avoidance, have actually set forth.[148] By endorsing the bottom diagram, *The Economist* sets aside what is morally most important: poverty and equity among human persons.

5.2 Intra-national inequality

Consider two large poor countries that, thanks to their resource endowments, have achieved enormous growth in the 2000–7 period. Nigeria's reported GNI per capita jumped from $270 to $920, and Angola's from $420 to $2,540.[149] Is this progress? Yes, if the additional money eased the plight of the poor. No, if it was spent to prop up oppressive and corrupt rulers: on military equipment and on perks and payments to officers to ensure their loyalty. Where the second scenario is closer to the truth, impressive growth in GNI per capita may be detrimental by strengthening a ruling elite's power over a population whose severe poverty was barely reduced.

There is considerable international diversity in the evolution of intra-national inequality over the past three decades. The WIDER database on the subject lists 5,313 surveys for 159 countries and areas. Available data for 111 of these jurisdictions are spotty or show no clear trend. In Brazil, France, Mauritania, and Sierra Leone, income inequality appears to be clearly lower this decade than in the 1980s – in the remaining 44 jurisdictions, clearly higher.[150] The United States is a case in point. In the 1980–2007 period, the income share of the bottom half declined from 17.68 to 12.26 percent.[151] In roughly the same period (1978–2007), the income share of the top 1 percent rose from 8.95 to 23.50 percent (2.6-fold); that of the top 10th percent from 2.65 to 12.28 percent (4.6-fold); and that of the top 100th percent from 0.86 to

Table 5.3: Economic performance of rich countries' bottom decile

Country	2007 GNI (PPP)/ cap[152]	Bottom decile relative share[153]	Bottom decile absolute share	Economic position of bottom decile
Norway	$53,690	38.6%	$20,724	89.4
Finland	$35,270	40.2%	$14,179	75.5
Germany	$33,820	32.2%	$10,890	59.2
Hungary	$17,430	35.3%	$6,153	46.6
USA	$45,850	18.8%	$8,620	40.3

6.04 percent (7-fold).[154] The top 100th percent – some 30,000 people (14,000 tax returns) – have nearly half as much income as the bottom 150 million.

That growth has been accompanied by rising inequality matters for the poor in two ways. It reduces or even negates gains in their absolute share that would otherwise result from economic growth. And it also diminishes their relative share. Many things money can buy are positional or competitive: political influence, for instance, and access to education and even health care depend not merely on how much money one has to spend but also on how much others are willing and able to spend on those same goods. To model this crudely, we can take as a proxy for the overall economic position of an affluent country's poor the geometric mean of their absolute and relative shares – defining their absolute share as their per capita income and their relative share as the ratio of their per capita income to their society's. Table 5.3 presents a static cross-country comparison that takes the poor to be each country's bottom income decile. The table shows that, even though the US does very well in terms of per capita GNI (PPP), its poor have only about two-fifths as much income as the poor of Norway and little more than the Hungarian poor. Taking relative share into account as well, the US poor do much worse than the poor in the other countries. From their standpoint, less economic growth more evenly distributed would have been much better.

My crude index for the economic position of the poor – giving equal weight to their absolute and relative shares – is implausible when we extend the assessment to poorer countries. Even if we here give three times more weight to the absolute share of the poor than to their rela-

Table 5.4: Economic performance of poor countries' bottom decile

Country	2007 GNI (PPP)/ cap[155]	Bottom decile relative share[156]	Bottom decile absolute share[157]	Economic position of bottom decile[158]
Turkey	$12,090	19.1%	$2,309	22.0
India	$2,740	36.4%	$997	13.8
South Africa	$9,560	12.8%	$1,224	12.4
Vietnam	$2,550	30.8%	$785	11.1
Brazil	$9,370	10.6%	$993	10.1
Ethiopia	$780	40.7%	$317	6.0
Colombia	$6,640	7.6%	$505	5.6
Nigeria	$1,770	19.9%	$352	5.4
Bolivia	$4,140	4.7%	$195	2.4

tive share, we still find astonishing discrepancies to the usual economic ranking of countries in terms of per capita GNI (PPP), as table 5.4 shows. Bolivia, Colombia, and Brazil drop precipitously in the rankings, while Ethiopia, Vietnam, and India rise substantially. Discrepancies are so dramatic because variations in intra-national inequality are even larger among poor countries, where the share of the bottom decile ranges from 5 to 61 percent of the national average (as against a range from 19 to 48 percent among the affluent countries).[159]

Consider what difference such a pro-poor assessment of economic growth would make to an economic planner – in a high-inequality country, say, such as Bolivia. If such a planner focuses on (per capita) GNI, she will ignore the people in the poorest decile who, though they comprise 10 percent of the national population, constitute less than 0.5 percent of the national economy. One percent more income growth for the poorest decile adds 0.0047 percent to national growth – one percent more income growth for the richest decile adds 100 times as much: 0.441 percent. But if such a planner assesses her performance in terms of the economic position of the poor, she will realize that substantial improvements in the position of the poor are possible at tiny opportunity cost to the rich. Those in Bolivia's richest decile live on nearly $18,300 PPP per capita as compared to $195 in its poorest decile. A shift of $200, barely noticeable to the former, would raise the latter from 4.7 percent to 9.5 percent of the average income and their economic position from 2.4 to 4.9.

5.3 Growth and poverty in China

Let me illustrate this point by examining dynamically the recent economic evolution of China, poster child of globalization. China has achieved dramatic economic growth over the recent globalization period. This growth was accompanied by a rapid increase in intra-national inequality. But surely, many believe, lamenting this trend would be silly, even callous, in light of the unprecedented gains China's growth has brought to its poor. Despite continued population growth, the number of Chinese living below $1.25 PPP 2005 per day has reportedly declined from 585.7 million in 1987 to 207.7 million in 2005, and the number living below $2.50 PPP 2005 per day from 1,001.7 to 645.6 million in the same period.[160] Given such huge poverty reductions, must we not approve of China's economic policies and the global institutional changes that made them possible?

Before we approve, we should consider four cautions. That severe poverty in China has declined substantially is beyond reasonable doubt. But the magnitude of this decline since the early 1990s is uncertain. As we saw in the preceding chapter, there are serious flaws in the poverty measurement method employed by the World Bank, and there are doubts also about the accuracy of the official estimates of the Chinese consumer price index and the 2005 PPP of the Chinese currency (see section 4.2 above).

Second, it is unknown whether the sharp rise in intra-national economic inequality was necessary for China's amazing economic growth and poverty reduction. In fact, it is likely that more equitable growth would have been much better for the Chinese poor. Thus consider (see table 5.5) China's recent economic evolution from the standpoint of its poorest decile, using my crude mode of assessment for developing countries.[161] We see that, while per capita GNI increased a spectacular 236 percent over the period, the income of the poorest decile – set back by a severe erosion of their relative share – increased by only 75 percent and their economic position by a mere 29 percent. The same is true, to a lesser extent, when we define the poor more broadly: the second and third deciles gained 114 and 132 percent in absolute terms and 58 percent and 71 percent in economic position. These are very

Table 5.5: Economic performance of China's bottom decile

Year	GNI/cap (PPP) in constant 2005 $	Bottom decile relative share	Bottom decile absolute share	Economic position of bottom decile[162]
1990	$930	30.8%	$286	5.2
1992	$1,128	25.7%	$290	5.0
1995	$1,533	22.2%	$340	5.4
1998	$1,927	23.9%	$461	7.0
2001	$2,381	18.0%	$429	6.1
2004	$3,127	16.0%	$500	6.7

respectable gains for a 14-year period. Yet, due to erosion of their relative share, the poorest quintile (fifth) realized not even half the country's economic gain.

Now it is often said that more equitable growth is slower growth: that the increase in inequality was necessary for China to grow as fast as it did. I do not think this view is empirically well supported; but let us, for the sake of the argument, suppose that preserving relative shares would have cost China fully 2.3 percentage points in annual per capita GNI growth, so that for the whole 14-year period its aggregate per capita GNI growth would have been 150 percent instead of 236 percent. The poorest decile would have done *much* better under this scenario, ending the period at an average income of $715 rather than $500, thus with a gain of 150 rather than 75 percent. In fact, the bottom four deciles would each have done better with such a uniform 150 percent gain – better in *absolute* terms, that is, without even considering that more equitable growth would have spared the poorer half much of the marginalization, social exclusion, and vulnerability to domination they are now experiencing.

Another great beneficiary of the alternate scenario would have been the global environment which China is now burdening with a huge upsurge in pollution and resource depletion. One may object that we should not expect China to moderate its ecological footprint so long as the affluent countries continue to pollute and deplete at even higher per capita rates. I do not contest this objection. The example of China is meant to illustrate quite general points about intra-national inequality. *All* countries should conceive growth much more from the stand-point of their poorer population segments. Doing so, they would do much better in terms of avoiding poverty and (if equity slows aggregate growth) environmental degradation.

The increasing vulnerability to domination and marginalization of China's poor are aggravated by the dramatic rise in the share of the richest decile from 25 to 35 percent of the average income. (This mirrors the development in the combined share of the bottom six deciles, which went from 36 to 26 percent.) This expansion gives the rich much greater opportunities to influence political decisions, to give unfair advantages to their children, and to dominate the poor directly. In 1990, people in the top decile had about 8 times as much income as people in the bottom decile. By 2004, this ratio had risen to 21.6, as China has moved from an income distribution comparable to that of Central Europe to one between Nigeria (17.8) and Mexico (24.6). If its decile inequality ratio were to treble again, China might find itself near the top of the chart in 2020, close to where Colombia (63.8) and Paraguay (65.4) are now.[163]

This brings me to my third caution. Intra-national inequality is not a simple economic parameter that clever economic planners can, in light of prevailing conditions, move up or down like the overnight interest rate. The most affluent know well that their future wealth is affected by the social rules. So they generally use their influence on the design of the social rules toward defending and expanding their advantages. The richer those at the top are relative to the rest of the population, the more their interests will differ from the interests of the rest and the greater their influence will be on the design of the social rules. For these reasons, large economic inequalities are far easier to create than to eliminate through ordinary political processes.

Some optimists may contend that China's rich or its political leaders will be so imperturbably committed to the common good, including poverty avoidance, that the economic interests of the rich will not affect the design of China's economic order. Such optimism is risky, even naive. Wealth affects one's perceptions and sentiments, makes one less sensitive to the indignities of poverty and more likely to misperceive one's affluence as richly deserved and in the national inter-est. Also, wealth and the prestige that comes with it influence public officials and divert them from serving the interests of ordinary people toward serving those of the wealthy (while perhaps sincerely identify-ing the latter with the interest of the nation).

These points are supported by our international historical experi-ence. High-inequality countries like those of Latin America have been highly resistant to inequality-lowering reforms, because any government must cooperate with those whose economic power enables them severely to damage the country's economy. By contrast, low-inequality countries like those of Scandinavia find it easy to keep inequality low. Some citizens are richer than others even there, but they lack sufficient power and incentives to manipulate the political process to expand their advantage. The historical evidence suggests that China's rising economic inequality will eventually level off, but that any reduction in economic inequality below the level then reached will be slow and politically difficult to achieve.

5.4 Global inequality

My fourth and final caution before celebrating China's spectacular growth provides a good transition to the third and last economic inequality: *global inequality* among human beings worldwide. Much of China's export-driven success has come at the expense of other poor populations. We must therefore not conclude from China's example that all poor countries could have done, or could still do, similarly well. To be sure, the world economy is not a constant-sum game, where growth is fixed so that some can gain more only if others gain less. But export opportunities into the affluent countries' markets are tightly limited by protectionist barriers (tariffs, anti-dumping duties, quotas, export credits, and subsidies) that the richer countries have insisted on being allowed to retain. These barriers contribute to making export results for the poor countries strongly interdependent. China's exporters could succeed only by out-competing exporters from other poor countries, thereby lowering export prices, along with wages and labor standards, for all poor exporting countries. More recently, China's huge imports have raised prices of crucial resources (petroleum and food, most notably), thus slowing the development of other poor countries dependent on imports of the same resources. These interdependencies surely go some way toward explaining why, outside China, the reported number of people in poverty has actually been stagnant, even rising.[164] We must consider the full picture, not merely China in isolation, when we assess, with equity and poverty concerns in mind, the growth WTO globalization has engendered.

Looking at humanity at large, we find once more a relentless rise in inequality. The World Bank reports that in the high-income countries, household final consumption expenditure per capita (constant 2005

Table 5.6: Economic gains of the poorer half of humanity

Relative position	Real consumption gain 1984–2004 (1993 PPPs)	Real consumption gain 1984–2005 (2005 PPPs)
Median, or 50th percentile	48.6%	60.1%
40th percentile	47.2%	55.8%
30th percentile	42.2%	50.9%
15th percentile	33.7%	45.1%
7th percentile	31.9%	44.3%
2nd percentile	22.9%	42.0%
1st percentile	9.6%	30.5%

international dollars) rose 59 percent over the 1984–2005 globalization period.[165] World Bank interactive software can be used to calculate how the poorer half of humankind have fared, in terms of their real (inflation/PPP adjusted) consumption expenditure, during this same period. Table 5.6 shows the gains at various percentiles of world population labeled from the bottom up. I present data produced with the Bank's old (1993) PPP alongside the latest data calculated with the new (2005) PPPs because – unless 2005 was a outstandingly good year for the global poor – the Bank's new accounting for intra-national cost-of-living variations (see endnotes 124, 161) seems to have affected the results.[166] Consumption expenditure is growing faster at the top, more slowly lower down, and most slowly at the very bottom.[167]

To get a sense of the rise of global inequality and the avoidability of poverty, it is also worth looking at the global income distribution assessed at current market exchange rates. Here we see that, while inequality among persons is rising more slowly worldwide than in China, it is also much further along. In China, the poorest quintile still accounted for 4.3 percent of household income in 2004, and the bottom two quintiles for 12.8 percent.[168] Globally, in 2002, the bottom quintile of humanity accounted for about 0.67 percent of household income, and the bottom two quintiles for 1.96 percent. Table 5.7 gives the full picture.[169] The table shows a pattern already familiar from the cases of the US and China: massive gains for the top decile while the majority of the population is losing ground. The morally most important losses occurred at the bottom, where the relative income share of the

Table 5.7: Evolution of global income inequality (current exchange rates)

Ventile	1988	1993	1998	2002	1988–2002 change	1988–2002 % change
Bottom ventile	0.139%	0.091%	0.076%	0.109%	−0.030%	−21.4%
Second ventile	0.198%	0.136%	0.142%	0.150%	−0.048%	−24.4%
Third ventile	0.239%	0.167%	0.180%	0.187%	−0.052%	−21.8%
Fourth ventile	0.275%	0.196%	0.215%	0.222%	−0.053%	−19.2%
Fifth ventile	0.304%	0.230%	0.253%	0.254%	−0.050%	−16.3%
Sixth ventile	0.364%	0.266%	0.301%	0.297%	−0.067%	−18.4%
Seventh ventile	0.389%	0.304%	0.349%	0.342%	−0.047%	−12.0%
Eighth ventile	0.462%	0.360%	0.424%	0.398%	−0.064%	−13.8%
Ninth ventile	0.523%	0.432%	0.506%	0.467%	−0.056%	−10.7%
Tenth ventile	0.632%	0.508%	0.584%	0.552%	−0.079%	−12.6%
Eleventh venile	0.736%	0.604%	0.701%	0.663%	−0.073%	−9.9%
Twelfth ventile	0.953%	0.773%	0.888%	0.810%	−0.142%	−14.9%
Thirteenth ventile	1.210%	0.995%	1.112%	0.994%	−0.216%	−17.9%
Fourteenth ventile	1.692%	1.285%	1.467%	1.306%	−0.386%	−22.8%
Fifteenth ventile	2.383%	1.845%	1.982%	1.666%	−0.717%	−30.1%
Sixteenth ventile	3.673%	3.076%	3.227%	2.481%	−1.192%	−32.4%
Seventeenth ventile	7.317%	6.566%	6.504%	5.344%	−1.973%	−27.0%
Eighteenth ventile	13.844%	13.696%	13.223%	12.678%	−1.166%	−8.4%
Nineteenth ventile	21.797%	22.610%	22.335%	22.280%	+0.483%	+2.2%
Top ventile	42.872%	45.860%	45.532%	48.799%	+5.926%	+13.8%

poorest 30 percent of humanity was reduced by about one fifth during the 1988–2002 period: from 1.52 to 1.22 percent of global household income. Had this bottom 30 percent merely maintained its measly 1.52 percent share of global household income over the 14 years, then (other things equal) it would have ended the period with 25 percent more income, and world poverty would have been substantially less.

Even the huge inequalities in income worldwide are dwarfed by global inequalities in wealth. In 2000, the bottom quintile held just 0.12 percent of all personal wealth, and the bottom two quintiles 0.62 percent. The top 1 percent, by contrast, held 39.9 percent of all personal wealth, and the top ventile held 70.6 percent.[170] Doubling the wealth of all in the bottom two quintiles would take only 1.55 percent of the wealth of the top 1 percent of the human population. Doubling the wealth of all in the bottom four quintiles would still take just 15.3 percent of the wealth of the top 1 percent, or 8.7 percent of the wealth of the top ventile.

To put these staggering inequalities in perspective, we must recall that the poor around the world lack not merely pocket money, denying them the toys of the rich, but access to the most basic necessities of human life. I described the astonishing extent of global poverty in section 1.1. Let us pause to recall some of the numbers we encountered there (see endnotes 5–10): some 18 million human deaths each year are due to poverty-related causes; 1,020 million human beings are chronically undernourished, 884 million lack access to safe water, and 2,500 million lack access to basic sanitation; 2,000 million lack access to essential drugs; 924 million lack adequate shelter and 1,600 million lack electricity; 774 million adults are illiterate; 218 million children are child laborers.

We must recall also that global economic inequalities influence and are influenced by the rules of the world economy. As an important component of globalization, the world has come to be dominated by an increasingly dense and consequential global system of rules that govern all kinds of transnational, and increasingly also purely national interactions. Because these rules have a profound impact on the distribution of global economic growth and the global product, their design is heavily contested. We discussed the ways that the affluent and privileged have shaped the institutional order in their favor in section 2.4.3. In the struggle over the rules of the world economy, those already more affluent enjoy enormous advantages in expertise and bargaining power. They have much greater means to influence the design of the rules and also much better opportunities to research how to use their influence to maximum advantage. The global poor, by contrast, have no influence on the design of global rules, and those who do have such influence have no incentives to take account of the impact their decisions will have on the global poor. The ruling elites of developing countries have far more reason to accommodate the interests of powerful foreign governments and corporations, who can offer substantial rewards for such accommodation, than to protect the interests of their poorer compatriots. In this way, the thorough marginalization of a majority of humankind is self-reinforcing and self-perpetuating. With only 8.4 percent of global household income and 4 percent of global private wealth, the poorer three-quarters of humankind predictably find their interests ignored in international negotiations. With 49 percent of global household income and 71 percent of global private wealth, the top ventile is calling the shots and still gaining further ground.

5.5 What next?

Having persisted through chapters 3–5, the reader deserves a nod of recognition. The discussion has been tedious and unpleasant. But without engaging with the measurement and evaluation of globalization and economic growth at this level of detail, it is difficult to reach an independent judgment that can withstand the daily onslaught of our Panglossian media and experts.

The analysis shows that the problem of world poverty is both amazingly small and amazingly large. It is amazingly small in economic terms: the aggregate annual income shortfall from the World Bank's $2 PPP 2005 per day poverty line of all those 40 percent of human beings who in 2005 lived below this line is merely $296 billion annually – 0.66 percent of the global product or 0.83 percent of the combined GNIs of the high-income countries, well under half of what the US spends on its military. On the other hand, the problem of world poverty is amazingly large in human terms, accounting for a third of all human deaths and the majority of human deprivation, morbidity, and suffering worldwide.

Most of the massive severe poverty persisting in the world today is avoidable through more equitable institutions that would entail minuscule opportunity costs for the affluent. It is for the sake of trivial economic gains that national and global elites are keeping billions of human beings in life-threatening poverty with all its attendant evils such as hunger and communicable diseases, child labor and prostitution, trafficking, and premature death. Considering this situation from a moral standpoint, we must now assess growth – both globally and within most countries – in terms of its effect on the economic position of the poor.

Let me restate, more fully, my response to the predictable objection that prioritizing the poor will sacrifice economic growth. Existing global institutional arrangements are designed to promote growth not in the global product so much as growth in the affluence of the wealthy elites who dominate international negotiations. The hypothesis that the world economy would be growing more slowly if its rules were less unfavorable to the poor is not well supported. But let us just accept this claim for the sake of the argument. Let us suppose (as we did earlier in regard to the Chinese economy) that institutional reforms that accelerate growth for the bottom deciles would retard overall growth of the world economy.

We might then have to choose, for instance, between Growth Path One, which would increase global household income to $6,000 per capita by 2020, with the share of the bottom three-quarters of humanity gradually rising from 8.4 back to 10.5 percent, and Growth Path Two, which would raise global household income to $6,600 per capita by 2020, with the share of the bottom three-quarters of humanity being further eroded down to 7.5 percent. If we focus narrowly on total human affluence, then it seems obvious that Path Two is preferable: the level of global average income it achieves by 2020 is 10 percent higher. But let us disaggregate. Path Two is better for the top quarter, offering them an average annual income of $24,420 in 2020, 14 percent more than the $21,480 the top quarter would have on Path One. Path One is better for the bottom three-quarters, offering them an average annual income of $840 in 2020, 27 percent more than the $660 the bottom three-quarters would have under Path Two.[171] Which difference matters more: a 14 percent difference for one-quarter of humanity who would live comfortably either way, or a 27 percent difference for three-quarters of humanity who would continue to suffer greatly on Path Two and to die in larger numbers? Clearly the latter matters more. Economic growth is not an end in itself; its whole point is to satisfy human needs and desires.

A further point here is that the world would realize considerable ecological gains if global economic growth were slowed through the choice of a more poverty-avoiding growth path. These gains derive from three factors. First, slower overall growth would mitigate the harm from pollution and resource scarcity that is threatening future generations. Second, avoidance of severe poverty would also have beneficial ecological effects because poor people – though they do far less environmental damage *per person* than is typical among the more affluent – tend to do more environmental damage *per unit of income or consumption* because they typically cannot afford to take proper account of the long-term environmental impact of their conduct. Poor people cannot afford fuel-efficient and low-pollution cooking, and must use what combustible materials they can find regardless of cost to the environment. Third, very poor people also cannot afford to limit the number of their offspring because they face serious uncertainty about whether any given child will survive and about whether, without surviving children, they themselves could survive beyond their prime. As is now very well confirmed empirically through evidence from all regions and cultures, severe poverty fuels rapid population growth,[172] which in turn is one main driver of environmental degradation. Eradicating severe poverty is thus a plausible and effective strategy of working toward an early leveling-off of the human population, hopefully below the 10 billion mark.

Compelling as these supporting considerations are, they pale beside the main point: we must not continue to impose upon the world institutional arrangements that avoidably keep billions in life-threatening poverty.

6

Dworkin, the Abortion Battle, and Global Poverty

6.0 Introduction

There is, in many countries today, an intense and sometimes acrimonious public and academic struggle over abortion. The main intellectual dispute – henceforth the abortion debate or controversy – concerns the question of what position the state, and specifically the law, *ought* to take: should they tolerate abortions on demand, at least in the early stages of pregnancy? Or should such abortions be legally prohibited, and those having and performing them be punished? This debate is part of a larger, political struggle – henceforth the abortion battle – which is about what position the state and the law do and will *in fact* take on abortion.

Ronald Dworkin has made a serious and sensitive contribution to the abortion debate.[173] His central claim is that this controversy is best understood not as a debate over whether unborn human beings are persons with interests and a right to life, but rather as a debate over how best to interpret a profound belief in the intrinsic value of human life that is shared on all sides. The main motive behind Dworkin's attempt to understand the abortion controversy in this new way is political: he shares the goal of various authors of finding common ground between the disputants or helping Americans live together even while they disagree about abortion (and much else).[174] But he firmly asserts that achieving this goal is unrealistic so long as one side believes that women have a fundamental right to choose an abortion, while the other side holds that abortion violates an unborn person's right to life.[175]

But aren't these precisely the beliefs on the two sides? According to Dworkin: yes and no. Those on the pro-choice side do indeed believe that women have a fundamental right to choose an abortion, and Dworkin fully agrees with them that women have this right, and ought to have it legally, during the first two trimesters of pregnancy. Ostensibly, Dworkin then addresses those on the pro-life side. His argument is supposed to show that they – the great majority of them, anyway – do not really believe that a human fetus has a right to life, however firmly they may *think* that they believe this. It is supposed to show that these pro-lifers really hold two other beliefs. They believe, *first*, that human life in all its forms has intrinsic value, a certain sanctity, which is violated when a human fetus is aborted. Dworkin says that this belief is shared by most on the pro-choice side, including himself. Most pro-lifers believe, *second*, that, even in the early stages of pregnancy, the violation of the sanctity of human life through an abortion morally outweighs the ordinary frustrations a pregnant woman may have to endure by carrying her fetus to term, and that it is therefore morally wrong to have or perform an *ordinary* abortion, i.e., one not involving special circumstances (as when the mother is extremely young or her pregnancy is threatening her own health or due to rape or incest). This second belief is, of course, rejected by Dworkin and his allies on the pro-choice side.

If Dworkin's restructuring of the pro-life position succeeds, then the abortion debate is about how much weight to give to something we all agree is a disvalue: to the violation of the sanctity of human life through an abortion. This would be nice for both sides in that the disagreement would turn out to be based upon a deeper agreement and also in that the disagreement would turn out to be about the weighing of competing values – just the sort of issue about which reasonable persons can disagree without losing respect for one another. It would, moreover, be *very* nice for Dworkin's own pro-choice side. How much weight should be given to the violation of the sanctity of human life through an abortion? This seems to be just the kind of question we do not want the state to settle for everyone. This is so, because this question is intensely personal,[176] extremely controversial in our culture,[177] and also, most importantly, "*essentially* religious."[178] By frequently expressing the belief that we supposedly all share in terms of the *sanctity* (and only rarely in terms of the intrinsic value) of human life, Dworkin prepares the ground for the refrain of his text, which appears throughout with minor variations: "The crucial question is whether a state can impose the majority's conception of the sacred on everyone."[179] Not surprisingly, Dworkin maintains that the only reasonable answer to this question is "No." And he warmly invites his pro-life opponents to come around to the view that the disagreement about whether ordinary abortions are wrong, like other spiritual and religious disagreements, calls for mutual tolerance rather than criminal law coercion by the state. Since we all have come firmly to accept that the state should not be mobilized to prevent citizens from making what some of us regard as religious errors, reformed pro-lifers will be glad to accept that the state should not be mobilized to prevent what they regard as a serious underestimate of how gravely an abortion offends the sanctity of human life.[180] They can still hold that the state may encourage reflective, responsible, and conscientious decisions about abortions by requiring women to absorb relevant information and by imposing a waiting period upon them.[181] But reformed pro-lifers will agree that the state must not force a particular decision upon women.

It takes some chutzpah to announce – in the third decade of an intensive public debate over whether abortion on demand should be legal – that one side to this debate has severely misunderstood its own most basic beliefs, that those who often refer to themselves as the right-to-life movement do not really believe that every human fetus has a right to life. Should it turn out that many pro-lifers will indeed – convinced by Dworkin's explanation of the true nature of their own beliefs – accept his restructuring of their position, then I will surely not want to stand in their way. But this does not seem to be happening, and I doubt that Dworkin himself seriously believed this would happen. I suspect rather that, while Dworkin ostensibly addresses the pro-life side, his real target audience is his own pro-choice camp. His message is that good liberals owe no accommodation to pro-lifers who seek to outlaw abortion on demand, because such pro-lifers are really only trying to impose their religious convictions upon their fellow citizens.

In the remainder of this chapter, I will first give reasons for doubting that Dworkin's argument will make any headway with those on the pro-life side. I will do this by criticizing his argument – showing why I do not find his restructuring of the pro-life position compelling (6.1) and why the usual pro-life position does not seem to me to be infected by the deep inconsistencies Dworkin claims to find in it (6.2). I will then try to show that what Dworkin declares impossible is possible after all: that significant common ground can be developed between the pro-choice and the pro-life sides, even if the latter do reaffirm their harshest claim: that abortion, at least in ordinary circumstances, is murder (6.3–6.6).

6.1 Dworkin's problematic reconstruction of the pro-life perspective

While the new self-understanding Dworkin offers to the foes of abortion has considerable intellectual appeal – much more, certainly, than my brief sketch could reveal – his argument nonetheless has three important weak spots. The next section (6.2) will discuss two of these, which are weaknesses in how Dworkin supports his claim that those now committed to the standard pro-life position have compelling reason to embrace the dramatic revisions he offers.

The present section discusses the third, which is the weakness of the link between Dworkin's new construal of the pro-life position and the political attitude he believes follows from it. I find it doubtful, that is, whether Dworkin's construal of the pro-life position leads as easily to toleration as he suggests. In fact, his argument becomes rather sketchy at this point. He simply says that construing the pro-life position as giving greater weight to the sanctity of human life "ties it to an important tradition of religious toleration with substantial roots in all genuine modern democracies."[182] But surely someone might accept Dworkin's construal of the pro-life position and nevertheless hold that, quite apart from any religious beliefs, the violation of the sanctity of human life through an abortion *so plainly* morally outweighs the ordinary frustrations a pregnant woman may have to endure by carrying her fetus to term that the state *must*, or at least (through democratic legislative procedures) *may*, ban the abortion of any healthy fetus, when the pregnancy is not due to rape or incest and does not seriously endanger the mother's vital interests. Analogous settlements prevail throughout the developed countries on such issues as animal sacrifices, polygamy, and pedophilia. In the first issue, two disvalues must be balanced against each other: a violation of the value of animal life and of our human stewardship for all life on Earth against the frustrations endured by those prevented from worshipping as their religion requires. The second issue involves balancing the concern to discourage morally offensive relations between men and women against the frustrations endured by those prevented from shaping their private lives as they prefer. In these cases, Dworkin as well as most citizens of the developed West – with strong support from the dominant religious denominations – do not believe that the state must allow each adult to balance the two disvalues as he or she deems fit. Rather, we hold that our states must (or at least may) prohibit the practices in question, which is precisely what in fact they do.[183] It remains an open question, then, why those accepting Dworkin's new construal of the pro-life position should end up supporting the political settlement Dworkin himself favors: the legality of any abortion on demand during the first two trimesters.

Dworkin is not the only one who has sought to support this political settlement by appeal to some ideal of religious toleration. During the past 15 years or so, many arguments of this sort have been produced in the United States. The two put forward by Mario Cuomo, then Governor of the State of New York, and John Rawls are the best known.[184] Their general strategy, pervasive in Dworkin's book as well,[185] is to argue for restrictions on the reasons that may legitimately be adduced in public political debates and in justification of state coercion. Any exercise of state power ought to be justifiable with reasons that are available in the shared public culture and thus generally accessible to all those subject to this power. Even if one is convinced, for instance, that requiring citizens to attend religious services would save countless souls from eternal damnation, one is not to support, to vote for, or to help enforce such a measure if all one can adduce in its support is one's own religious faith, however firm and sincere. The same constraint – by Rawls referred to as the "duty of civility" – is then invoked to settle the abortion controversy, along these lines: "You propose that abortions be legally prohibited and punished by the state. Implementation of this proposal would constitute an exercise of state power against your fellow citizens. Such an exercise of state power must be justifiable with public reasons. The notion that an early human fetus has a right to life on a par with that of a human being already born is, however, grounded in certain religious convictions – concerning ensoulment, perhaps, or the sanctity of human life – that are not part of our public culture and so not generally accessible. Hence the proposed use of state power is illegitimate."

Though I cannot here discuss this view thoroughly, let me mention three objections to it that have not so far, I believe, been satisfactorily answered. First, significant doubts have been raised about whether a reasonably clear and uncontroversial distinction can be drawn between justifications that are and those that are not "generally accessible" or "available within the public culture." Second, is it really reasonable to demand that citizens put aside their most deeply held moral convictions, that they ignore what they firmly believe to be wrongs and injustices of the greatest gravity, merely because the reasons for their convictions are not part of the public culture?[186]

Third, it can plausibly be argued that the constraint cuts not only one way. In the argument we have just considered, the constraint works only in conjunction with a certain assumption about the burden of proof. It is assumed that what stands in need of justification is the exercise of state power against women and their doctors. Dworkin, though he relies on this assumption throughout, does not argue for it or even formulate it clearly. An exemplary formulation of it is offered by Judith Thomson:

> One side says that the fetus has a right to life from the moment of conception, the other side denies this. Neither side is able to prove its case. . . . Why break the symmetry by letting the deniers win instead of the supporters? The answer is that the situation is not symmetrical. . . . What the supporters want is a licence to impose force; what the deniers want is a licence to be free of it. It is the former that needs the justification.[187]

But one might assign the burden of proof to the other party on the ground that it is really the *pro-lifers* who want a license to be free of force: a license for unborn human beings not to be forced out from where alone they can continue to live; and that it is really the *pro-choicers* who want a license to impose force: a license for pregnant women to force their unviable offspring out of their bodies to certain death. To be sure, those forcibly prevented from having an abortion have the capacity to demand a justification, while those forcibly removed from a womb do not. In this respect, the situation is indeed asymmetrical. But why should this be a morally relevant asymmetry? And, if it were, if the exercise of force against a human being needed a justification only if that human being can demand one, then should we not legalize the killing of late fetuses, and babies, as well?

In the absence of a response to this challenge, one could then turn the tables and argue *for* the legal prohibition of ordinary abortions, as follows: "You demand that the exercise of state power for the sake of protecting the physical integrity of human beings be confined to those who have been born (or to those beyond the second trimester). But such discrimination must be justifiable with reasons that are available in our public culture. The view that the moral status of an early fetus is far below the equal moral status of human beings already born is, however, grounded in convictions – concerning the falsehood of certain religions perhaps – that are not part of our public culture and so not generally accessible. Hence the proposed discriminatory use of state power is illegitimate."[188] The availability of such a parallel argument makes clear that the constraint by itself cannot settle anything so long as we lack an authoritative assignment of the burden of proof.

6.2 Review of the alleged inconsistencies of the pro-life perspective

Let us proceed to what I consider the other two important weak spots in Dworkin's argument. First, it is doubtful whether Dworkin has really shown the standard pro-life position to be in the kind of deep trouble that would, he believes, push its adherents to look for a plausible alternative. Without such a push, they may not take enough of an interest in his alternative construal to experience the pull of its intellectual appeal. Second, it is doubtful whether pro-lifers would really find Dworkin's construal of their position to be the next most attractive alternative. Indeed, Dworkin does not assert this and does not even consider the question. Should the standard pro-life position really come to be seen as untenable, then other plausible new construals, perhaps much less conciliatory ones, will also emerge; and pro-lifers might well find one of these other restructurings more attractive than the one Dworkin proposes. These two weaknesses run into each other; their identities depend on how precisely or vaguely the standard pro-life position is understood. Either way, the key question is whether pro-lifers really have compelling reason to accept as dramatic a restructuring of their position as Dworkin is urging upon them.

The position Dworkin thinks pro-lifers should abandon, on pains of inconsistency, can be sketched through the following four claims:

(0) Even an early human fetus has interests.
(1) Even an early human fetus is a person.
(2) Even an early human fetus has a right to life.
(3) Abortion is murder.

Pro-lifers generally believe (3) on the basis of (2) and, in some cases at least, (2) on the basis of (1). Dworkin holds that both (1) and (2) presuppose (0), though he correctly concedes that pro-lifers typically take no position on (0).

Clearly, the crucial claims here are (2) and (3). Claims (0) and (1) are abstract, philosophical claims that do not seem to have a clear and shared meaning within the public abortion controversy – and the extensive poll data Dworkin provides do not elucidate how these claims are understood or how widely they are endorsed. If (2) and (3) fall, the pro-life position will have been dramatically transformed and, if they survive, the standard pro-life position will also have survived in its essentials. Once someone has firmly endorsed or denied (2) and (3), his or her views on (1) and (0) are of precious little political, practical, or personal relevance. Dworkin denies this on the ground that claims (2) and (3) presuppose (1) and (0) – that, in particular, it makes no sense to attribute a right to a being that has no interests. But he offers no defense for this assertion. Judith Thomson, a leading philosophical theorist on rights and a staunch defender of abortion rights, allows that "we lack a compelling rationale" for asserting the dependence of rights on interests and that she therefore "know[s] of no conclusive reason for denying that fertilized eggs have a right to life."[189] This should suffice to show that it is not, *pace* Dworkin, unreasonable to affirm (2) while denying (0).

The inconsistencies that put pressure on standard pro-life position derive from the fact, says Dworkin, that the great majority of pro-lifers are also committed to

(4) Abortion should be legal in some circumstances.

Dworkin adduces various polls in support of this attribution.[190] Among the findings he cites are the following. A 1991 Gallup poll found that 48.3 percent of Americans hold that abortion is murder.[191] A 1990 Wirthlin poll found that 60 percent of Americans consider the statement that "all human life, including that of the unborn, should be protected" either extremely convincing or very convincing and that roughly the same was true for the statement that "every unborn child has a basic right to life." The same poll found, on the other hand, "that only 7 percent said that abortion should be illegal in all circumstances, and only 14 percent said that it should be legal only when necessary to save the life of the mother."[192] This is confirmed by a 1992 Time/CNN poll, finding only 10 percent maintaining that abortion should be illegal in all circumstances. The polls do indeed show, then, that large majorities of pro-lifers – namely somewhere between 79 percent and 89 percent of those who profess to believe that abortion is murder or that every unborn child has a basic right to life[193] – are willing to permit abortions in cases of rape, incest, fetal deformity, or a threat to the mother's vital interests.

Before proceeding to examine whether (4) really is inconsistent with (2) and (3), I should point out that, even if it were, the inconsistencies could still be resolved either way. Dworkin reasons that, since (4) is inconsistent with (2) and (3), those who are committed to (4) cannot *really* believe that a human fetus has a right to life and that abortion is murder. But one might just as well reason the other way around: since (4) is inconsistent with (2) and (3), those who believe in (2) and (3) cannot *really* believe that abortion should be legal in some circumstances. Politically, it is a wide open question how those 38–50 percent of Americans who now believe (2), (3), and (4) would react if they were to accept the inconsistencies Dworkin alleges. It is entirely possible that many of them would join the ranks of what is now a minority (of 11–21 percent) among pro-lifers: those who hold that abortion should be illegal in all circumstances.[194] Such a backfiring of Dworkin's effort is all the more likely, because he offers no argument at all against this most radical pro-life view – his entire effort is concentrated on those moderate pro-lifers who accept (4), i.e. favor some exceptions.

It is then perhaps fortunate on the whole for Dworkin's cause that the inconsistencies he purports to find are rather dubious. Let us consider first the alleged inconsistency of (2) and (4). Much intellectual energy has been spent on showing how these two beliefs are consistent, and Dworkin does nothing to show that these attempts have failed. I can here only discuss one well-known and formidable attempt, exemplified by Judith Thomson,[195] who justifies limits on the right to life by appeal to basic liberty rights. Two other classic efforts, which would justify fewer exceptions than Thomson, involve the doctrines of self-defense and double effect.[196]

Thomson takes as widely accepted the view that I do not violate your right to life by failing to rescue you from mortal danger when this rescue would impose upon me considerable cost. Appealing to this view, she argues that a woman does not violate the right to life of her fetus if – through a drug, hot bath, or physical procedure – she separates the fetus from herself. A right to life includes no right to be nurtured and sustained at considerable cost. One is not required to offer the hospitality of one's body to others for months at a time, even when their lives depend on it. Thomson's essay vividly stresses the great cost involved in undergoing an unwanted pregnancy. Even the right to life of a grown person does not, she maintains, require others to preserve this life at such high cost. Her defense of the permissibility of abortion is then compatible with assigning to human beings the same stringent right to life before and after birth.[197]

It may be thought that a view like Thomson's justifies all abortions and is thus incompatible with anything recognizable as a pro-life position. But this is not so. One can plausibly hold that I do have a duty to rescue you even at very considerable cost, if your being in mortal danger is a foreseeable consequence of something I have voluntarily done. And one can then insist, analogously, that a woman has a duty to complete a normal pregnancy if her pregnancy is the foreseeable consequence of her own prior voluntary conduct. Conceived along these lines, the right to life of the fetus could rule out the legalization of abortion on demand and still be consistent with the usual indications of rape, fetal deformity, and serious danger to the mother's vital interests.

Let us now consider the alleged inconsistency of (3) and (4). It is unlikely that many Americans would affirm that murder should be legal in some circumstances. It is therefore also unlikely that many respondents understood (3) in the sense of "*every* abortion is murder." For, so understood, (3) and (4) together do entail – in a very straightforward way that makes this implication hard to miss – that some murders should be legal. Instead of assuming that 38–50 percent of the respondents were either extremely stupid or in favor of legalizing some forms of murder, we should therefore rather assume that they understood the word "abortion" in (3) as referring only to those abortions that they believed should be illegal. This conjecture is not implausible: the class of ordinary abortions on demand vastly outnumbers all other abortions (some or all of which these respondents claimed should be legal), and this class is also, after all, what the great public abortion debate is almost exclusively about. People holding that abortion should be legally available only in exceptional circumstances (rape, incest, fetal deformity, and/or danger to the mother) often refer to themselves as anti-abortion. And this shows that they use "abortion" to refer to the largest, central class of unexceptional cases.

Whether my conjecture is correct or not is, of course, an empirical matter which only additional poll data could settle conclusively. One needs to ask those who endorse (3) and (4) what the special circumstances are under which they believe an abortion should be legally permissible, and then whether abortions under these special circumstances are also murder. Now suppose that my conjecture turns out to be mistaken. Suppose, that is, that significant numbers of Americans really do believe that certain kinds of abortion, though murder, should be legal nonetheless. Even then, they still would not hold inconsistent beliefs. There would be an inconsistency in their beliefs, and hence a compelling reason for them to restructure their position, only if they also affirmed

(5) Murder should be illegal in all circumstances.

But to attribute this inconsistency to large numbers of Americans strains credulity. It is simply incredible that many happily believe that all abortions are murder and all murders should be illegal and some abortions should be legal. In any case, if Dworkin is targeting those who hold this happy belief triplet and hopes to convince them of the complex pro-life view he suggests, then he surely has his work cut out for him.

In this section, I have shown that Dworkin has failed to prove his assertion that the standard pro-life position is inconsistent. In fact, he has not even seriously tried. I have also sketched, with the help of Thomson's work, how exceptions can fit into this position. I have not shown that this sketch can be specified in a philosophically satisfactory way. But this is irrelevant. The decisive point is that, at the current state of public and philosophical debate, it is entirely reasonable to believe that claim (4) is consistent with both (2) and (3).

Of course, the fact that Dworkin has shown no good reasons for taking (2) and (3) to be inconsistent with (4) does not mean that his political appeal will fail. Just as people often cling to their beliefs even when they have good reasons to revise them, so they often revise their beliefs even when they lack good reasons to do so.

6.3 The search for common ground

I have criticized a man and a book that I admire. It is time, then, to make myself a target as well by offering a constructive argument of my own. My argument parallels Dworkin's insofar as it also seeks to mobilize elements within the conventional pro-life position toward a certain modification of it. It differs from his by asserting no inconsistency in this position. My conclusion asserts something Dworkin explicitly denies: that significant common ground can be developed between the pro-choice and pro-life sides even if the latter adhere to their harshest claim: that ordinary abortions are murder.

The common ground I will try to develop is on a third level, which is generally ignored (and not only by the protagonists in the abortion debate). Let me recapitulate the two familiar levels. On the first level, we have the substantive issue how abortion ought to be treated by the law: whether, to what extent, and how severely abortions should be proscribed and punished. In this debate, a central role is played, quite properly, by the question whether having or performing an abortion is morally wrong and, if so, how grave a wrong it is. As we have seen, those who hold that abortion should be outlawed generally claim that any unborn human being has a moral right to life, a right to be brought to term, which has the same weight as the right to life of those already born. They could also, however, defend their opposition to permissive abortion laws by taking a somewhat weaker position: that there is a moral duty not to terminate a human life and that this duty overrides all other ordinarily available moral considerations, such as a woman's moral right to exercise control over her body and a couple's right to pursue their own happiness.[198] Those who hold that ordinary abortions on demand should be legal often claim that there is no such duty (and hence no moral right to life) at least early in a pregnancy. But it would be sufficient for them to claim that the duty (and the right), if it exists, is not strong enough to override a woman's moral right to exercise control over her body and a couple's right to pursue their own happiness.

On the second level, we have the meta-issue concerning what arguments may properly be advanced on the first level and how the burden of proof should be assigned. Here those favoring legal abortions argue that it would be wrong to impose severe restrictions on the liberty of women on grounds that are "*essentially* religious" or at least are dependent on a conception of the meaning of human life which is not shared by all and which it is not unreasonable to reject. Those opposed to legal abortions on demand can give a similar argument: that it would be wrong to withhold from some human beings the most basic legal protections extended to all others and to do so on grounds that depend on a conception of the meaning of human life that is not shared by all and can reasonably be rejected.

Claims and counter-claims on these two levels have been put forward, defended, and disputed many times. Yet, they have had little impact on the abortion battle. However much we might wish to see this battle decided by arguments rather than by sheer political clout, there seems to be little evidence at present that the vast energies expended on attempts to develop common ground on these two levels will lead to progress by convincing significant numbers on either side to change their minds.

The importance of the third level depends on the fact that, in our world, wrongdoing, injustice, and suffering are so pervasive that those working to mitigate these evils must make painful choices about the allocation of their scarce time, money, and energy. There is not merely the problem that we must, often under conditions of great uncertainty, choose how to combat some particular morally significant evil.[199] There is the further problem that we must choose which particular morally significant evil(s) we should try to combat in the first place. This latter problem, unlike the problem of choosing means, is a genuinely moral problem. It has not, however, been much examined. There is a good bit of discussion of moral conflicts and dilemmas, where an agent must violate one of several determinate rights or duties (hurt someone or break a promise, kill one innocent or let two innocents die, etc.). Much less attention has been paid to what one might call *moral competition*, where scarce resources must be allocated among several morally important projects or causes. This lack of discussion may indicate a preference for leaving such questions to private reflection. In a world in which so many people do little to combat the evils around them, one is not eager to criticize those who care and are doing something for having the wrong priorities. Even at the risk of doing just that, I will here conduct a somewhat more public reflection.

What I want to examine is whether, in the world as it is, one can sustain this appeal: "Let us, for the time being, quit the abortion battle and let us instead concentrate on another task with respect to which we can agree that it has at least equal moral urgency." Politically, this appeal favors one side – the status quo, whatever it may be in a given jurisdiction at a given time – by steering both sides away from the abortion battle. But intellectually the appeal differs from arguments on the other two levels in that it does not bear on the abortion controversy. It does not touch the merits of the case and thus, substantively, does not favor one side or the other. Relatedly, my appeal can be addressed to both sides at once – not with exactly the same justification perhaps, because, in order to convince someone that another cause is of at least equal moral urgency, we may have to appeal to particular moral beliefs of hers connected to her stand on abortion; but perhaps with similar justifications. It would be highly desirable if both sides could be shown to have reason to work together for the alternative moral cause instead of working against each other in the political battle over abortion.

To save space, I will here present my appeal only to one side: to those who believe that abortion ought to be illegal. One reason for addressing them first is that it is they who are currently more heavily involved in the attempt to change the legal status quo. Another reason is that my appeal must initially seem especially hopeless when addressed to the proponents of outlawing abortion. They are being asked to put up with (what they see as) the legally authorized killing of millions of innocent and defenseless human beings. What existing or impending evil could be of comparable moral importance? The proponents of permissive abortion laws, in the opposite scenario, are being asked to put up with (what they see as) massive legally mandated infringements of women's rights to exercise control over their own bodies and of couples' rights to pursue their own happiness. This is surely, for them, a very grave evil. But it does not entirely outclass other moral evils, such as the horrifying evils of rape and domestic violence and the evils of sexual harassment and discrimination, which are still all too pervasive in our culture. So I am rather confident that, if my appeal can be made plausible to those who believe that abortion must be outlawed, then it will also be possible to make this appeal plausible to those who believe it should be legal to have and perform early abortions on demand. Here I attempt only the first, more difficult task.

6.4 Global poverty as a competing moral priority from the pro-life perspective

My appeal must point to some cause that can compete for moral priority with the cause of outlawing abortion. I choose for this role the cause of mitigating and eradicating global poverty. Simplifying to some extent, we can then entertain the following straightforward binary choice. Consider someone who is sincerely convinced that every abortion constitutes the deliberate destruction of an innocent human life and that this is a grave moral evil. Such a person has moral reason to join the battle against abortion: to participate in demonstrations and blockades of abortion clinics, to engage in political work aiming for laws or constitutional amendments that outlaw abortion, and so forth. But then this same person also lives in a world in which some 18 million persons, many of them children, die every year from poverty-related causes such as starvation, diarrhea, and other cheaply curable diseases.[200] Since the needless deaths of unborn human beings constitute a grave moral evil, so, too, must the needless deaths of innocent children. Our sample person, accordingly, has moral reason to join the fight against global poverty: to donate time and money to food aid organizations, to engage in political work designed to stimulate concerted government initiatives, and so forth.

Given scarcity, it is clear that the two causes compete: any bit of effort (time, money, energy) devoted to either one of them could be devoted to the other instead. Hence the question: does it matter, morally, which of these two causes one supports? And, if so, which cause ought to be given precedence?[201] Let me sketch three moral considerations that favor giving precedence to the struggle against global poverty.

First, *the argument from doubt*. The proper legal status of abortion is highly controversial. Honest, intelligent, knowledgeable, and well-intentioned persons have come to opposite conclusions – there are many such persons on either side. This fact gives me some reason to doubt the soundness of my own conviction in this matter. This doubt is of little relevance in situations where I must act on my conviction or its opposite, where I am, for example, asked for advice by a woman who is considering an abortion. But the doubt may be of great relevance when I face competing moral claims. There is virtually no serious dispute over the question whether the starvation of children constitutes a significant moral evil. Almost everyone agrees that it is morally important to mitigate and, if possible, to eradicate such unnecessary suffering. Therefore, I have (other things being equal) less reason to doubt my belief in the moral importance of joining the struggle against global poverty than I have to doubt my belief in the moral importance of joining the abortion battle. Hence I have a reason to devote my efforts to the former cause in preference to the latter – guided by the thought that, other things being equal, I should direct my efforts toward causes in whose moral importance I have more confidence at the expense of other causes whose moral importance is more doubtful.

This argument is quite different from the second-level argument we have considered in section 6.1 above. There, the key idea was that I have a duty of civility to abstract from certain of my most deeply held convictions when I find that they cannot be based on ideas available in the shared public culture. I am not to act on such convictions in the public arena – at least when this would result in significant state coercion of persons who reasonably reject these convictions. Here, by contrast, what is invoked is not a moral duty, but an epistemic principle: when a conviction finds less support among those whom I consider competent to judge matters of the relevant sort, then I should be less certain of it and act accordingly. This principle is of broad application. Suppose you are a meteorologist and your calculations show that a major storm will hit some island, destroying both of its main cities. Other meteorologists, whom you respect, believe that only the southern city is in danger. You are not convinced. You will insist that both cities be put on alert. But you should nevertheless recommend, I believe, that (other things being equal) scarce evacuation efforts be concentrated on the southern city.[202]

Second, *the argument from moral waste*. Most efforts devoted to the abortion battle simply cancel each other out. This waste is not merely temporary, because it is likely that neither side will be able to achieve a permanent victory, i.e. a victory that would not need to be defended through continued political mobilization.[203] So the battle will go on, and much moral effort will continue to be wasted on shifting the legal situation back and forth over the same terrain. In the struggle against global poverty, by contrast, there is no moral waste. Here we have virtually no opponents who feel morally called upon to ensure that starvation continue despite our efforts to eradicate it. Hence I have another reason for devoting myself to the struggle against global poverty – guided by the thought that, other things being equal, I should give precedence to causes where people's moral efforts will support and complement one another rather than cancel each other out.

Third, *the argument from civil harmony*. When we face each other across the seemingly unbridgeable abyss of a deep moral controversy – with each side convinced that what the other advocates is morally intolerable – then it is all too easy to forget how much, morally, we have in common. A protracted battle over abortion tends to weaken the moral cohesion of our society by undermining the sense that we are jointly committed to a scheme of shared principles, values and ideals. A protracted struggle for the eradication of global poverty would heighten this sense: it would unite us against a common "enemy" rather than pit us against each other as in a civil war. Hence I have a third reason to devote my efforts to the struggle against global poverty – guided by the thought that, other things being equal, I should give precedence to moral causes that unite me with others over causes that put me at odds with them.

One might object to the last two arguments that no one should be asked to switch causes, as it were, without assurances that those on the other side are willing to do likewise. I disagree. For one thing, such assurances are impractical. It is simply impossible to negotiate a phased withdrawal from the abortion battle on the model of the phased with-drawal of intermediate-range nuclear missiles from Europe. Moreover, the above arguments are meant to demonstrate (for now only to the pro-life side) that even the worst-case scenario of unilateral withdrawal is preferable to continuing the battle over abortion. Suppose that only those on one side of the abortion controversy were to heed my appeal. They would then be doing something that, from their own point of view, is of at least equal moral importance as continuing to hold up their side of the abortion battle. Yes, the other side might then win. But this, too, could have its good side. For the other side would then have no more work to do on the abortion front, and at least some of the moral effort they would have devoted to that cause is therefore likely to flow into other moral causes, such as the eradication of global poverty, which are supported by both sides.[204]

6.5 Comparing the responsibilities for abortion and global poverty

Turning now to possible objections against giving precedence to the anti-poverty struggle, let us first consider the *distinction between doing and letting happen*. Deliberately bringing about some given harm is generally considered to be much more wrong than merely failing to prevent a like harm. So while the evil of a child dying of hunger is indeed at least equal to the evil produced by an abortion, it is still far more wrong to have or perform an abortion than to fail to save a child from death by hunger. It is therefore more important to support the battle against abortion than to work against global poverty.

As it stands, this counterargument is unsuccessful, because its conclusion does not follow from its premise. The premise entails only that it is more important not to have or perform an abortion than to save a child from starvation. But the conclusion (and our initial question) concerned a different comparison: the importance of preventing abortions had or performed *by others* versus the importance of preventing poverty deaths. Such failures to prevent are, in both cases, instances of letting happen. And nothing in the argument shows that it is more important not to let abortions happen than not to let (the same number of) children die of hunger. Of course, it might be said that to prevent killings is always morally more important than to prevent other deaths. But this is a different distinction whose moral significance (so far) enjoys little recognition in ordinary or academic discourse. It is generally not thought less important to rescue one innocent child from drowning than another from being deliberately killed.

The objection can be renewed by invoking the further *distinction between the responsibilities of participants and those of non-participants*. The children who are starving to death in the poor countries are foreigners. Insofar as we fail to help them, we let their deaths happen; we surely do not participate in their deaths in any way. The human beings whose abortion we might be trying to prevent by changes in the law are, however, our compatriots. In their deaths we do play a role and we thus do, in a sense, help bring these deaths about. For, as citizens of a democratic society, we co-determine, and thus share a special responsibility for, its laws and social institutions. Permissive abortion laws are unjust in that they engender a larger number of abortion deaths than would occur if abortion were more stringently prohibited and strictly punished. By upholding such laws, we citizens are responsible not merely for letting these additional deaths happen. We are responsible for helping to bring these deaths about by participating in maintaining and enforcing a legal system that, by permitting abortions, foreseeably results in these extra deaths.

To illustrate the force of this revised counterargument, consider the case of slavery as it existed in the US before 1860. Slavery was not a popular crime committed by individuals, like the robbing of mail coaches, but it was an injustice deeply embedded in the practices and institutions of the United States: in its voting laws, fugitive slave laws, and so forth. The creation, continuation, and enforcement of these laws were authorized by the electorate. And the members of this electorate, unlike their foreign contemporaries, were therefore, morally, participants in this slavery. A wealthy Swede might have been as well positioned, causally, as most US citizens were to protect slaves or to lobby for legislative reform. But he was not a participant in the injustice, and for him the suffering of these slaves was thus morally on a par with much other suffering the world over. US citizens, by contrast, even those who owned no slaves themselves, did bear a special responsibility, because it was their legislation that authorized, and thereby engendered, widespread slavery.

I fully accept the significance of distinguishing between the responsibilities of participants and non-participants. I agree that the more advantaged participants in an institutional scheme bear an especially weighty responsibility for the justice of this scheme and the harms it produces. If the scheme is unjust and these persons do nothing about it, then they are violating not merely a positive duty to help victims of injustice anywhere, but a more weighty negative duty not to participate in the imposition of unjust institutions.

I challenge, however, a key supposition of the revised counterargument: that our role with respect to global poverty is that of non-participants. I dispute that, insofar as we do not protect the global poor, we merely let their deaths happen, that we do not participate in their deaths in any way. I argued in chapter 2 that the following hypothesis is plausible: the present global scheme of political and economic institutions profoundly affects the living conditions of the global poor. So long as the present global institutional order remains intact, we can expect, for example, that vast income differentials will persist and that the daily number of deaths from poverty-related causes will remain in the tens of thousands. By foreseeably producing these effects, the present global order is unjust insofar as there are feasible (i.e., practicable and reachable) institutional alternatives that would not produce such catastrophic human suffering.

If our global institutional scheme is indeed unjust on account of its foreseeable distributional effects, then the developed countries and their more affluent citizens – being the most advantaged participants of this scheme – bear a special responsibility for this injustice: it is through our participation and support that those institutions are upheld; and we are also in the best position to alleviate their worst effects and to work for institutional reforms. We are then not like uninvolved bystanders, who merely let massive starvation happen. Rather, our position is analogous to that of non-slaveholding US citizens before the Civil War, who were participants in the enslavement of blacks. By collectively imposing the existing global institutional arrangements, we are bringing about a stable and predictable incidence of deprivation, thereby effectively excluding large segments of humankind, those who cannot translate their basic needs into effective market demand, from all but the most minimal benefits from planetary resources. By supporting this regime, we participate in the starvation of millions.

The objection can be renewed one last time by invoking the further *distinction between established and engendered harms*.[205] What makes abortion deaths especially outrageous from a moral point of view is that they are officially and explicitly permitted by the law, for whose content we citizens share responsibility. Hunger deaths, by contrast, however regularly and foreseeably the current global "rules of the game" may produce them, are not officially permitted by these rules. That this distinction makes a moral difference is shown, for instance, by reflection upon penal systems: we find it morally intolerable officially to authorize certain harms – rough interrogation methods by the police, low standards of evidence in criminal trials, disproportional punishments (such as the death penalty for drunk driving) – even if harm overall is thereby reduced.[206] This shows that, in assessing the justice of an institutional scheme, we assign more weight to harms it officially authorizes than to harms it merely foresee-ably produces.

What this argument shows, convincingly in my view, is that it would be unjust for a society officially to authorize the killing of some human beings even if a much larger number of deaths from poverty could thereby be avoided. But I have not been trying to convince pro-lifers that permissive abortion laws are to be accepted as just – e.g., on the ground that there will be fewer premature human deaths with them than without them. To the contrary, I have accepted all along, if only for the sake of the argument, that permissive abortion laws are a very grave injustice, and I am willing to concede on this basis that, if we had to choose between institutions that authorize abortions and others that produce extreme poverty (both roughly at current levels), the latter should be morally preferred. But our situation is not this, not one in which we must settle on a *design* priority among *conflicting* values. Institutions that do not permit abortions and also do not produce extreme poverty are easily feasible in this world. Current institutions are then unjust in both respects. As participants in such doubly unjust institutions, we thus face a situation in which we must settle on an *implementation* priority among *competing* values: which of these two injustices is it more urgent to overcome?[207]

My claim is that in this case the priority is reversed: in implementa-tion, the larger injustice, which kills more human beings, must take precedence over the smaller that kills fewer (assuming equal prospects for eradicating either). This is so because the key reason for the oppo-site priority in matters of design does not apply here: by giving priority to the eradication of global poverty, one is not morally accepting the legal authorization of abortions on demand. The priority becomes even more compelling in the present case where, as we have seen in the previous section, considerations concerning doubt, moral waste, and civil harmony all favor the greater urgency of combating the global poverty problem.

6.6 Objections to the comparative moral priority of poverty

This claim can surely be attacked in various ways. I will here focus on the three objections that strike me as the most important.

First, it may be said that, though the problem of global poverty is of greater magnitude than the problem of abortion, moral responsibil-ity for this problem is much more widely diffused. Every one of us thus bears a smaller share of responsibility for the former problem than for the latter. We should, therefore, other things being equal, concentrate our moral efforts on the abortion problem at home, for which our individual responsibility is greater.[208]

Let us accept the moral mathematics this objection invokes[209] and concede that each well-placed US citizen, sharing responsibility for both injustices, bears a smaller share of responsibility for the global poverty problem than for the US abortion problem. If roughly three times as many persons bear significant responsibility for the injustice of our global institutional scheme (on account of the poverty it produces) as bear responsibility for the injustice of the domestic institutional scheme of the US (on account of the abortions it produces), then each advantaged US citizen bears a roughly three times larger share of responsibility for US abortion deaths than for global poverty deaths.[210]

This factor of three is handily overcome, however, by the much larger number of poverty deaths. The number of persons dying from starvation and treatable diseases each year is estimated to be somewhere around 18 million, while the number of annual abortion deaths in the US is only 1/22 of that.[211] While three times more persons share responsibility for the injustice (on account of global poverty) of our global institutional scheme, this is more than made up for by the 22 times greater magnitude of this problem. I assume here that the weight of (the responsibility for) an injustice increases with the number of deaths it engenders. This is in the spirit of the moral mathematics stipulated by the objection under discussion. For, surely, if the responsibility for an injustice gets diluted as more persons participate in it, then it must increase as more people get victimized by it. Otherwise, those imposing unjust institutions could reduce their responsibility simply by pooling their operations. Our moral responsibility for poverty deaths outweighs then our moral responsibility for abortion deaths: each of us, those who help uphold the current world order and also the current permissive abortion regime in the US, is responsible for about seven times as many poverty deaths as abortion deaths.[212]

Second, it may be said that, even so, responsibility for domestic injustice (producing deaths of compatriots) should count for more than responsibility for global injustice (producing deaths of foreigners). If this view were put forward as a piece of national chauvinism to the effect that American lives, say, are intrinsically more valuable than those of non-Americans, it would not be worth discussing. But the view may be perfectly universalizable: each person has more moral reason to care about her or his compatriots than about foreigners.

This is indeed something many believe firmly. One role national borders play in our world is that of defining spheres of responsibility. The pre-eminent responsibility for any person's security and welfare is assigned to his or her compatriots.[213] And so we may indeed be tempted to think that, when children are starving in Ethiopia, Brazil, and Bangladesh, this is primarily the responsibility of other Ethiopians, Brazilians, and Bangladeshis, and only very tangentially ours.

However convenient, this thought cannot support a plausible objection. After all, the assignment of pre-eminent responsibility to compatriots is itself part of our present institutional scheme, whose justice was put into question by the above explanatory hypothesis about global poverty. The fact that our global economic institutions produce such high rates of deprivation is in good part a consequence of the current assignment of responsibilities, in which the poor are told to look for relief from others little better off than themselves, while the affluent take care of one another. We have a deeper, ultimate responsibility for imposing the current global order, together with this assignment of responsibilities. And we cannot disconnect ourselves from this ultimate responsibility, no matter how many borders we institute and no matter how firmly we declare that our preeminent moral task is to look after one another rather than to eradicate global poverty.[214]

There is another flaw in the objection. The widely accepted moral priority for compatriots is understood to cover only positive, not negative, duties: not rescuing a compatriot is considered worse than not rescuing a foreigner, but killing a compatriot is not normally considered worse than killing a foreigner. My argument has been that, by helping to uphold unjust global institutions, we share a negative responsibility for the deaths these institutions produce just as we share a negative responsibility for the deaths produced by unjustly permissive national abortion laws. Since negative duties are at stake, the suggested priority for compatriots does not apply in any case.

Third, someone with consequentialist leanings, convinced that we should make those moral efforts that offer the best probability-weighted cost/benefit ratio, may claim that we can be more effective if we devote our efforts to the abortion battle rather than to the struggle against global poverty. Assessing such a claim is anything but straightforward. We might begin by splitting the comparison into two central cases: extrapolitical efforts aimed at mitigating the effects of unjust institutions, and political efforts aimed at reforming such unjust institutions themselves. In both cases, we might initially do the comparison in terms of lives saved.

Consider two organizations supported by volunteers and donors. One works to convince US women that they should not have abortions. It prints information, organizes demonstrations at abortion clinics, counsels women considering an abortion, helps arrange adoptions, and so forth. What difference does such an organization make to the US abortion rate? The honest answer is, I suspect, that no one really knows. But it is entirely credible that such an organization may every year convince thousands of women who would otherwise have had an abortion.

The other organization combats global poverty. It provides food, water, and shelter to persons in acute distress. We can get a sense of how cost-effective such measures are from the fact that much of today's misery occurs in regions with annual per capita incomes below $300. In such regions, where a family of five can get by on $1,000 a year, it is extremely cheap, by Western standards, to improve people's living conditions enough to increase their chances of survival dramatically. As is well known from UNICEF advertisements, one pack of oral rehydration therapy (ORT) can cure life-threatening diarrhea for just 20 cents. Such an organization can be even more cost-effective when it is not responding to acute emergencies: it may provide capital and expertise for investments that very poor people, compelled to live hand to mouth, cannot make on their own: grants or microloans for seeds, wells and irrigation, tools and simple machinery, livestock, literacy and numeracy, medical knowledge and supplies, and start-up capital to open a business or cooperative. Support for such investments helps save lives not just in the current year, but for years to come. Funding the construction of a well that supplies safe and convenient drinking water, for example, can have a lasting impact on the infant mortality rate in some area. This is one reason why it is difficult to calculate anything like a precise ratio of dollars donated to lives saved: the larger a time horizon we choose for evaluating the difference made by some program or initiative, the more uncertainty we face about how things would have developed in its absence. It is entirely possible that a $300 investment will save thousands of lives over the next 50 years. But it is virtually impossible to be certain of something like this, even *ex post*.

The first comparison does not support a clear-cut conclusion. But there are two factors that favor the cause of global poverty. Even with somewhat higher start-up and monitoring costs, it is much cheaper to operate in a developing-country environment than in the United States. Moreover, it is easier to make lasting contributions to the struggle against poverty: contributions that, without requiring additional efforts, will continue to save lives in years to come. These considerations are surely not conclusive. But they may suffice to cast doubt upon the claim that extrapolitical efforts to prevent abortions are more cost-effective than extrapolitical efforts to reduce global poverty.

The second comparison concerns organized political efforts aimed at institutional reform. As regards abortion, the aim is to have laws against abortion (providing for severe punishments) adopted and enforced in one's state. Even if this project succeeds, the abortion rate would not be reduced to anywhere near zero. Many women would travel elsewhere to have abortions. Others would obtain abortifacient drugs from abroad or on the domestic black market, or would use other means of inducing an abortion themselves. Others again would find doctors or quacks willing to perform illegal abortions. Still, the number of abortions would probably decline significantly, as more care would be taken to avoid unwanted pregnancies and a larger share of such pregnancies would be brought to term.

As regards global poverty, the aim is to induce the US government to take an active role, in concert with other Western governments, in enabling the global poor to meet their basic needs. To some extent this will involve increasing development aid to truly needy areas (which are often of little political or strategic interest). It may involve reforms in our global market system designed to insulate developing-country populations from precipitous declines in their exchange entitlements due to fluctuations in the price of some essential export or import commodity.[215] It may also involve reforms in our global political system designed to reduce the incentives toward undemocratic forms of government. Finally, it may involve some institutional mechanisms through which the benefits of the world's resources, as well as the burdens of various externalities, would be more fairly shared around the globe.[216] It seems entirely realistic that popular pressure on G-7 governments could lead to significant reforms of this kind. In fact, it is possible to eradicate global poverty in a decade – and at a cost below 1 percent of GNIs of the affluent countries.

The second comparison, again, does not support a clear-cut conclusion. Significant political efforts would be required to induce the US government, and state legislatures, to take effective action against abortion. The same is true for initiatives against global poverty. But there are two factors that favor the latter cause. If we concentrate on the abortion battle, much effort will be lost to moral waste. Moreover, even a small stab at the global poverty problem – say one tenth of the reform needed to eradicate it – would save at least two million persons annually from starvation.[217] No realistically achievable victories on national abortion fronts could save that many lives.

I conclude that arguments from cost-effectiveness are unlikely to undermine my thesis that we should give precedence to the struggle against global poverty over the battle against abortion. I have based this conclusion solely on considerations concerning lives saved.[218] If we take a broader view, my conclusion becomes even more compelling. First, efforts to combat poverty-related misery cannot be neatly targeted at those 18 million persons who will needlessly die next year (as if we could know in advance who they will be). Such efforts must be directed, more broadly, at the global poor now at risk. Reducing needless deaths among them by two million would involve helping some tens of millions of persons to become more self-sufficient. Second, if tough laws against abortion were passed and enforced, many women and doctors would end up with lengthy prison terms. This may be just what they deserve. But as these people are jailed, they leave behind family members and relations: spouses, children, parents, and friends. These other persons suffer as well, though they can hardly be said to deserve it. Third, joining the battle against abortion rather than the struggle against global poverty also has significant costs in terms of civil harmony – a topic to which I will now return in the concluding section.

6.7 Conclusions

You may think that the appeal I have presented may itself undermine civil harmony. So far, those who were primarily concerned to combat global poverty had no quarrel with those fighting on either side of the abortion battle. My appeal is liable to open up a new front by initiating a battle over which of the two causes is morally more important.

In response, let me say that my appeal can at most initiate a new controversy, not a new battle. What is at stake in the abortion dispute is a question that must and will be answered, one way or another. There is only one position the law can take on abortion in each jurisdiction. What is at stake in my appeal, however, is of an entirely different character. I am certainly not trying to have morality legislated, so that it will be illegal to devote time, money, or energy to the abortion battle in preference to the struggle against global poverty. The choice between moral causes is one that each of us makes privately, guided by our own conscience; and this is certainly the way it should be. Still, we normally do not make such choices in isolation. We discuss moral topics and priorities with one another. My appeal is meant as a contribution to such a discussion. If it is controversial, and will lead some readers to consider new ideas or arguments, so much the better. This poses no threat to civil harmony.[219]

By contrast, one great cost of the abortion battle is the breakdown of trust and good faith among citizens. One side suspects its opponents of considering abortion a convenient method of birth control; the other suspects its opponents of a self-righteous attempt to enslave everyone else to their religious convictions. My hope is that we can begin to overcome such deep suspicion and animosity by working together on a common moral cause. A concerted effort to eradicate global poverty could do wonders for the moral cohesion of our societies.[220]

It might even help us resolve the abortion controversy sometime in the future. Having worked together against global poverty, each side will be able to appreciate the moral sincerity of its opponents, and we will then be in a much better position to find a solution that both sides can live with. Here we can begin with mutually acceptable measures designed to reduce the number of abortions: improved availability of, and information about, birth control, day care, and adoption, as well as improved social support for single mothers. We will also be able to draw upon rapidly expanding medical expertise: It will be possible to abort many pregnancies in ways that do not result in a death. To be sure, political and medical progress cannot completely resolve the controversy. There may still be more born and unborn infants than adults are willing to raise (or bring to term). And there will still be the tragic cases of rape, incest, grave fetal deformities, and serious danger to the pregnant woman. It is not clear what sort of regulation or deference to conscience the law should impose in these matters. My point is that citizens with faith in one another's moral sincerity will be in a much better position to fashion a solution that is morally tolerable for most of them.

This brings me to a final thought. Whatever our moral convictions, we must be disheartened and alarmed by the low esteem in which morality is held in our culture. Two factors play major roles in explaining this fact. First, those who put forward moral claims and arguments are routinely, and often accurately, suspected of self-righteous bigotry or of being concerned to promote their own interests. Where such selfish or self-righteous motives are not readily apparent, they are gladly constructed and imputed by opponents. Second, and relatedly, serious moral disputes are almost always interminable, so that it must seem as though morality is just so much background noise, so many rhetorical effusions that never make a difference to what happens, because they never convince anybody anyway.

In this respect, a concerted effort to eradicate global poverty could have a tremendous positive impact. It would focus our attention on a moral topic on which we can share a deep conviction: it is morally intolerable that we have arranged a world of plenty so that many human beings, through no fault of their own, must live on the brink of starvation. It rings hollow to say of this conviction that it is merely an opinion that can be just as easily denied as affirmed. And it also rings hollow to suspect those who are working to eradicate global poverty of self-serving motives or of self-righteous bigotry. So the struggle against global poverty has the potential of deepening our understanding of what morality is, and of what role it could play in a healthier public culture. Though materially costly, this struggle may greatly enrich our lives and our culture. This is not to deny the obvious: the most important reason for making a concerted effort to eradicate global poverty is, of course, the prospect of reducing global poverty.

7

Making War on Terrorists: Reflections on Harming the Innocent

7.0 Introduction

The countries of the developed West are fighting a war on terror. More accurately: the governments of some of these countries are conducting a war against terrorists. This war effort was stepped up dramatically after the terrorist attack of September 11, 2001, which killed about 3,000 people in New York, Virginia, and Pennsylvania. The most notable terrorist attack before then was the car bomb attack on the US embassies in Dar es Salaam and Nairobi of August 7, 1998, which killed about 257 people, including 12 US citizens. After the September 11 attack, 202 people, including 88 Australians, were killed in Kuta on the Indonesian island of Bali on October 12, 2002; some 191 people were killed in the Madrid bombing of March 11, 2004; and the terrorist attack in London on July 7, 2005 killed 52 people.[221]

Why wage war against these terrorists? Offhand, one might think that such a grand response to terrorism is undeserved. This thought is supported by comparisons with other threats to our life and well-being – cardiovascular disease and cancer, for instance, annually kill some 1.2 million and 700,000 people, respectively, in the US and UK alone, while traffic accidents kill about 46,000 each year in these two countries. In the UK, only about one per 10,000 deaths in 2005 was due to terrorism. And even in the US in 2001, the corresponding ratio was about one in 750 deaths, that is, 0.13 percent. It would seem that even a small increase in the effort to combat cardiovascular disease, cancer, road accidents, or any of several other, similar threats would do much more to protect our survival and well-being, at lower cost, than revving up the war on terror.

This point has been made repeatedly with dramatic facts and figures.[222] Since 2001, the Global Fund to Fight AIDS, Tuberculosis, and Malaria, funded by all willing governments and devoted to combating diseases that kill about 4.4 million people each year, has committed about $12.6 billion and spent about $8.6 billion.[223] This expenditure comes to roughly $220 per fatality. Between 2001 and 2009, the US government alone has spent $944 billion on the war on terror.[224] This amount comes to roughly $314 million per US fatality – over a million times more per fatality. Millions of deaths from extreme poverty and curable diseases could be avoided each year if the world's governments were willing to devote even one quarter as much to the fight against world poverty as they are now spending on their war on terror. Such a war on poverty and disease would also avoid the substantial human costs of the war on terror. Some 6,000 coalition soldiers have been killed and several tens of thousands wounded in Iraq and Afghanistan. Fatalities among Iraqi and Afghan civilians have been vastly higher.

So why is terrorism being taken so seriously? This question requires nuances. We need to distinguish reasons and causes. And we need to differentiate the various groups involved in this war.

7.1 The uses of terrorism for politicians and the media

I see two main explanations (sections 7.1 and 7.2). One explanation is that public attention to terrorism serves important domestic constituencies. It serves most obviously the news media. Their economic success depends on their ability to attract the public's attention; and it is vastly easier to attract the public to stories about terrorists and their plans and victims than to stories about cancer and cancer victims or to stories about traffic accidents.[225]

Public attention to terrorism also serves the interests of politicians, especially incumbents. They can gain greatly increased attention, authority, and deference from a frightened public as well as acquiescence when they withhold information, increase surveillance, disrespect civil liberties, and curb political opposition. Many Western government policies – from the invasion of Iraq to the secret monitoring of citizens and the detention of political opponents at home and abroad – have been marketed as anti-terror measures.[226] Many non-Western governments have eagerly followed our example, often defending severe violations of basic human rights as necessary responses to terrorist threats.

The politicians of some countries derive a further benefit from a major war on terror also in the international arena, namely the benefit that this war strengthens the political power of their country. Assume simplistically that a country's political power depends on three components: military might (capacity for violence), economic might, and international moral standing. Countries differ in regard to the composition of their political power: Russia and the US are strong militarily relative to their moral and economic strength. Japan is strong economically relative to its military and moral strength. And Iceland's moral standing in the world is strong relative to its military and economic strength. Now, how much each of the three components contributes to political power depends on the regional or global environment. Military strength will be a much larger contributor to political power in the midst of a world war than in a time of universal peace; and a country's moral reputation will matter much more in peaceful times than in a period of war or conflict. Therefore, governments of countries whose military strength is relatively larger than their economic and moral strengths will tend to benefit from heightened insecurity and tension by enjoying greater freedom of action due to greater acquiescence on the part of their own citizens and other countries. The political leaders of such countries with comparatively greater military strength therefore have a further incentive to foster an international climate of conflict and hostility. Such a climate stands to enhance not only their domestic standing, but also the power they wield on their country's behalf internationally.

These points are worth further thought because, by playing up terrorism in pursuit of their own ends, our media and politicians are helping the terrorists achieve exactly what they want: attention and public fear. By helping to ensure that terrorist attacks are successful in the way their perpetrators want them to be successful, the media and politicians are multiplying the damage our societies suffer from terrorism and also encouraging further terrorist attacks.

7.2 Public support for anti-terror policies

Those ordinary citizens in the UK and US who have been supporting
the war effort, at least tacitly, are a different matter. Why have they
been so supportive of the new war? One reason is, of course, that such
citizens have been persuaded that this war enhances the security of
themselves and their friends and relatives from terrorist attacks. But
this more prudential reason does not explain the enormous public
attention paid to terrorism, nor the great cost, in terms of money and
basic freedoms, that many citizens seem willing to bear to combat terrorism, because the war on terror is not a cost-effective way of protecting our health and survival. Of course, citizens are not fully informed
and perfectly rational. They may not realize how small terrorism's
damage has been, and how costly the counter-measures. But I think
an important part of the explanation is our moral judgment that these
terrorist attacks are exceptionally heinous. This judgment lends special
urgency to fighting this terrorism as the effort promises not merely a
reduction in the risk of harm each of us is exposed to, but also the
suppression of a dreadful moral evil. Because we perceive these terrorist attacks as so exceptionally heinous, we attach to their suppression
an importance that is greatly disproportional to the immediate harm
they inflict.

Is it correct to consider these terrorist attacks especially heinous
and thus to attach such disproportional importance to suppressing
them?

Before examining this question (section 7.3), let us address a prior
concern. Some find such an examination offensive. They find it obvious
that these terrorist attacks are very wrong. And they feel that the self-
evidence of this proposition is denied when we examine its meaning
and grounds. They feel that the question "What is wrong with these
terrorist attacks?" suggests that these attacks are among the things
about which people can reasonably disagree. And they firmly reject
this suggestion.

Let me be clear then that, by asking what is wrong with these terrorist attacks, I am not suggesting that people can reasonably disagree
about their wrongness, but merely that it is important to understand
why these attacks are wrong. Even if we are perfectly certain they are
wrong, understanding why is still important for two reasons. I will
state one reason now, the other in sections 7.6–7.

The first reason has to do with moral theorizing. We are often faced
with moral questions or decisions that are difficult to resolve. When

this happens, we engage in moral reflection. Such reflection looks at relevant empirical evidence and also at other, less difficult moral questions or decisions that may be analogous or related in some way to the problem at hand. John Rawls has analyzed this ordinary method in some detail and has compared it to how we make difficult judgments in linguistics: when we are doubtful whether some particular phrase is proper English, we can hypothetically formulate grammatical rules that would forbid or allow it and then test these general hypotheses against other phrases whose status is certain. In this way, some of the rules we try out will be confirmed and others refuted. Confirmed rules can then be brought to bear on the questionable phrase to resolve our doubt.[227]

With this method, which Rawls calls reflective equilibrium, our most firmly held convictions, collectively, are the standard by which we judge difficult questions. But the method can work only if we can bring some of our most firmly held convictions to bear on the difficult question or decision we confront. This requires that we generalize from these most firmly held convictions. We can do this by hypothetically formulating more general moral principles that may then be confirmed or refuted by our firmest moral convictions, such as the conviction that these terrorist attacks are wrong. A confirmed moral principle helps us understand why these attacks are wrong, or what makes them wrong. And such a principle can then also be used to help resolve other, more difficult moral questions or decisions.

7.3 One failure in the moral justification for terrorism

So what is wrong with terrorist attacks such as the five I described at the outset? In first approximation, we might say that what makes these attacks presumptively wrong is that, foreseen by the agent, they harm and even kill innocent people. I assume it is clear enough for present purposes what it means to harm or kill people. By calling a person innocent, I mean that this person poses no threat and has done nothing that would justify attacking her with lethal force. To be sure, the terrorists may have believed that some of those they attacked were not innocent in this somewhat technical sense and were thus justifiably subject to lethal attack. But they could not have reasonably believed this of the great majority of the people they attacked. They clearly foresaw that their conduct would harm and kill many innocent people. In fact, the time of day they chose for their attacks, and the lack of any prior warnings such as were often issued by the IRA and the ETA, strongly suggest that they not merely foresaw it but even intended to harm and kill many innocent people.

We need not claim that it is always wrong to do what one foresees will harm or kill innocent people. It is enough that there is a firm presumption against it, which may be overcome by showing that so acting is necessary to achieve some greater good (which may consist in the prevention of some greater harm).

Justifications of this kind come in two types. Justifications of the first type assert that those who will be harmed stood to gain from the action *ex ante*. We can give this type of justification for a doctor who administers a live vaccine to 10,000 children while knowing statistically that roughly one or two of them will die from the resulting infection. This doctor's conduct is nonetheless permissible if each child's prospects of survival are expected to increase relative to no treatment and also relative to other feasible treatment options. With justifications of this type, it is enough that the expected good should outweigh the expected harm so that there is a net expected gain for each person affected. Since it is plainly false that each of the persons attacked by the terrorists stood to gain from this attack *ex ante*, we can set aside this type of justification in what follows.

Justifications of the second type assert that the harm done to innocent people is outweighed – not by some good for these same people, but – by a greater good of some other kind. Some philosophers reject justifications of this second type altogether. But I find such absolutism implausible. If the brutal reign of a tyrant who is killing many thousands can be ended with a violent strike that unavoidably also kills an innocent child, then this strike seems morally acceptable, perhaps mandatory, if indeed it can save thousands from being murdered and millions from being oppressed and brutalized. Similarly, the aerial bombardment of cities may be justifiable when this is the only means of defense against a horrible aggressor state. At the opposite end of the spectrum, some philosophers hold that justifications of the second type can succeed even when the greater good just barely outweighs the harm foreseen. Such philosophers might approve of killing 19 children when this is the only way of saving 20 others. Like most, I find such an act-consequentialist standard too permissive. When the greater good an agent intends to achieve with her action will not be a good for the innocent persons whom this action will harm, then that good can justify the action only if it *greatly* outweighs the harm this action foreseeably inflicts. (This requirement is often thought to be especially significant when the harm to be inflicted is a means to attaining the purported good, rather than a foreseeable side effect.) In addition, a successful such justification also requires, of course, that the harm be *necessary* for achieving the greater good in question, so that the same good could not have been achieved using any other less harmful means.

Can such a justification be provided for the terrorist attacks at issue? I believe not. To show this conclusively, one would need to run through indefinitely many candidate "greater goods" that might be offered. This we cannot do. Instead, let us focus on three such candidate greater goods that have actually been appealed to by the terrorists or their supporters. This exercise may give us a clearer sense of how we might respond to other such justifications yet to be advanced.

One justification refers to various regimes in the Middle East – that of Saudi Arabia prominently included – which are regarded as dictatorial or un-Islamic or pro-Western. The terrorist attacks were meant to discourage the US and other Western countries from supporting these regimes, especially through the stationing of troops in their territories, and to boost the morale of those who are seeking to overthrow these regimes. A second justification appeals to the alleged good of weakening Israel by discouraging other governments from supporting it and by boosting the morale of Palestinians resisting the occupation of their lands. A third justification appeals to the alleged good of punishing Western countries for their past and present support of Israel and/or of dictatorial and un-Islamic Middle Eastern regimes.

To succeed, any such justification must discharge four burdens of proof. It must show that the alleged good really is a good. It must show that the terrorist attacks in question contribute to this good, at least probabilistically. It must show that the value of this contribution greatly outweighs the foreseen harms to innocent people. And, finally, any such justification must also show that all these harms were really necessary for the intended contribution to the greater good, that the same good could not have been achieved using any other less harmful means.

The quickest and clearest way of seeing that these justifications fail focuses on the fourth burden of proof. Equivalent contributions to all three candidate greater goods could have been achieved with far less harm to clearly innocent people. In fact, the manner and timing of the attacks suggest that such harm was intended. In any case, the terrorists at minimum displayed great disregard for what is often euphemistically called collateral damage. The terrorists could have attacked their US targets early on a Sunday morning, for instance, when the World Trade Center area would have been nearly deserted. Such a palpable effort to spare innocent people would not have reduced attention to the terrorists' cause. On the contrary: by signaling clearly their intent to spare innocent people as far as reasonably possible, the terrorists would have made local and Western citizens less unreceptive to their ends and grievances, and would still have demonstrated their terrifying capabilities and willingness to die for their cause. Most of the harm the terrorists inflicted on innocent people was not necessary for promoting the alleged good they sought, and was quite possibly even counterproductive.

We might remember in this context that the disregard for the lives of innocent persons is not a defining feature of terrorism and is in fact absent from much historical terrorism. The IRA and ETA frequently issued bomb warnings beforehand in order to minimize harm to persons. And some of the 1905–6 Russian terrorists – sometimes called moral-imperative terrorists and immortalized by Albert Camus in his play *The Just* as well as in his essay *The Rebel* – were absolutely determined not to harm innocents. Thus Kaliaev abandoned his first attempt to kill Sergei Aleksandrovich when he saw that the Grand Duke had his niece and nephew, two children, in his carriage.[228]

Moral justifications of the terrorist attacks fail, then, because the fourth burden of proof cannot be discharged: the attacks inflicted great harms on far more innocent people than was, given the goal, reasonably unavoidable.

To this it may be objected that the terrorists and their supporters may feel that no justification is needed for their killing of innocent people. They see themselves as involved in a war in which their opponents have inflicted even greater harms upon the innocent. When one's enemy in war employs immoral methods, then it is morally permissible to employ the same methods in return.

In earlier work, I have discussed this objection under the label "sucker exemption."[229] The basic idea is that an agent in a competitive context is not required to observe constraints that other, competing agents fail to observe. I believe that this idea can indeed be plausible, but only when the victims of an agent's constraint violations are themselves previous violators of the constraint. If you have various agreements with another person, for instance, and he turns out routinely to violate these agreements whenever it suits him, then you are not morally required to honor your agreements with him when it does not suit you.

The sucker exemption is distinctly implausible, however, when those whom the agent's conduct would victimize are distinct from those who have victimized her. You are not morally permitted to violate your agreements with one person because some other person has violated his agreements with you. Similarly, an agent is not morally permitted to harm the friends or relatives of someone who has harmed her friends and relatives. A man is not permitted, for example, to rape the daughter of his own daughter's rapist. And likewise for the terrorists and their supporters: they are not morally permitted fortuitously to harm and kill innocent compatriots of people who have harmed innocent compatriots or associates of theirs. A person can forfeit ordinary moral protections against being harmed only through something she herself has done, not through the actions of another. Therefore, whatever wrongful harms the terrorists or their associates or compatriots may have suffered do not alter their moral relations to third parties who are not culpable for those wrongful harms.

Interestingly, Osama bin Laden has professed to share these sentiments in his early denials of any involvement in 9/11. Thus he is reported as saying, in his *Daily Ummat* interview dated September 28, 2001:

> I have already said that I am not involved in the 11 September attacks in the United States. As a Muslim, I try my best to avoid telling a lie. I had no knowledge of these attacks, nor do I consider the killing of innocent women, children and other humans as an appreciable act. Islam strictly forbids causing harm to innocent women, children and other people. Such a practice is forbidden even in the course of a battle.[230]

That bin Laden's interpretation of Islam is at least a plausible one is confirmed by various passages in the Quran, such as this one: "whosoever kills a human being for other than manslaughter or corruption upon earth, it shall be as if he had killed all mankind."[231]

7.4 Other problems for the moral justification of terrorism

To show that the terrorist attacks were morally unjustifiable, I have focused on the weakest link in the purported justifications for them: any plausible purpose of the attacks could have been achieved with much less harm to innocent civilians. This focus on the fourth burden of proof should not be taken to suggest that the other three burdens can be met. I do not believe that they can be. In particular, it is unclear what genuine greater good these attacks might conceivably have contributed to. Perhaps there were some people among the victims who, in the eyes of the terrorists, were sufficiently guilty to deserve death. But this is not enough for these attacks to count as successful punishment operations serving an aim of focused deterrence. The attacks were far too indiscriminate for that – both by making no effort to include specific persons perceived as guilty and also by making no effort to exclude persons who were clearly innocent. "It is better that ten guilty persons escape, than that one innocent suffer," the proverb says.[232] To justify the attacks as punishment of guilty individuals, the terrorists would have to deny a much weaker principle. They would have to assert something like this: "It is better that ten innocent persons be killed than that one guilty person should continue to live." And even then they would have to identify 337 among their victims – one in 11 for each attack – who deserved the death penalty and whose deaths would then justify the deaths of 3,365 innocent people as well as all the other collateral damage.

The attacks might be understood as collective punishments of a group, presumably a country, serving the aim of deterring this country, and others, from continuing their foreign policies relating to the Middle East. In fact, I don't know how else to make sense of the Bali bombing. But are such reprisal killings a good? Is it appropriate to punish Australia and Spain for their – let us assume: wrongful – foreign policies by killing a random selection of their citizens? Such lop-sidedly distributed punishment of groups is known from history – from the Roman practice of decimating a military unit, for example, typically for cowardice or insubordination. But the moral implausibility of such punishments is no longer seriously contested. Moreover, even if such a randomly biased group punishment were a good thing, one would still need to show that this good is large enough greatly to outweigh the harm done to innocents. These innocents include most or all of the group members randomly selected, who may be children or youths or active opponents of their government's foreign policy. And they also include those outside the targeted group. In the Bali attack, about one fifth of the victims were locals and another fifth were tourists from non-target countries. In the US embassy bombings, nearly 95 percent of victims were not from the target country.

Did these attacks, or could they reasonably have been expected to, weaken Israel or the rulers of Saudi Arabia or other disliked rulers in the Middle East, for instance by deterring Western support? The terrorist attacks have predictably increased, certainly in the US, sympathy and support for Israel: for Israel's security wall, settlement expansion, and check points in the West Bank, as well as for Israel's policies of targeted assassinations and deadly reprisals against civilians in the occupied territories and abroad (Lebanon, most recently). The attacks have greatly increased diplomatic, financial, and security support for the Middle Eastern regimes the terrorists despise and have also increased Western tolerance for, and collaboration with, these regimes' long-standing practices of severe repression of dissent and of Islamic dissent in particular. To be sure, the terrorists of September 11 would have welcomed the demise of Saddam Hussein's regime in Iraq, which their attacks facilitated; but they would not have welcomed the way he fell, the occupation of Iraq by Western troops, or the emerging successor regime. Their attacks predictably endangered the Taliban regime in Afghanistan, leading to its replacement with a regime they would have found much less congenial. The terrorist attacks did accelerate Western acceptance of the first acquisition of nuclear weapons by a Muslim country.[233] But this acceptance was predicated on Pakistan's military dictator agreeing to a range of domestic and foreign policies that the terrorists reject as anti-Islamic and pro-Western, including active participation in the war on terror. None of these Western reactions is surprising. And it is hard to see then what great good did, or could have been expected to, come out of the terrorist attacks – sufficient greatly to outweigh all the harm to innocents.

7.5 Taking morality seriously

I have briefly presented my reasons for believing that the five terrorist attacks in focus were morally unjustifiable acts of mass homicide. This conclusion could be further disputed. Other candidate greater goods might be adduced, or modifications of my account of what a successful justification would need to show might be proposed. A clever philosopher might be able to keep this game going a good while longer, and I cannot anticipate, let alone respond in advance to, all the moves such a philosopher might make.

But this is no reason for us to suspend moral judgment. These attackers and their supporters have made clear that they take themselves to be engaged in justifiable political violence. Their pronouncements are laden with moral and religious language that presents their conduct as justifiable, even noble, and urges others to follow their example. Such statements imply a responsibility to justify their attacks. They may not owe such a justification to just anyone. But they do owe a justification to their innocent victims and to the innocent friends and families of such victims. And they owe a justification also to the sincere adherents of their religion, in whose name they have attacked their targets.

Put yourself in the position of someone who is involved in planning an attack that he foresees will kill many innocent civilians. And imagine this person to be someone who takes morality seriously – understanding morality broadly here as including any religion that provides moral guidance and constraints. Such a moral person would think very hard indeed before killing large numbers of innocent people. He would not do this without having assured himself, up to a very high level of confidence, that his planned action is really justifiable – in one of the ways I have sketched or in some other way he finds compelling on reflection. For a religious person, especially when he is about to act in the name of his religion, there is the further need to make quite certain that he has really used his God-given capacities to the fullest so as to reassure himself that his planned action really accords with God's will. For a seriously religious person, what could be more terrifying than the possibility that one might not be careful enough and therefore make a mistake by killing, against God's will but in God's name, hundreds of innocent human beings?

With the cases before us, this is not a far-fetched possibility. As bin Laden has said, these attacks killed innocent human beings and Islam strictly forbids harming innocent human beings even in war. So it is – to put it mildly – not obvious that these attacks are permitted, let alone that they are God's will. Some serious thought is certainly required for a genuinely religious person conscientiously to reach the conclusion that these attacks accord with God's will.

Now suppose a genuinely religious person has conscientiously reached this conclusion. He would want to give his reasons, at least after the fact (and thus perhaps after his own death). He would feel a responsibility to explain to his innocent victims and their innocent friends and relatives why he felt compelled to harm them. He would want other Muslims not merely to follow his example, but to do so with a full appreciation of why this really is the will of God. And, perhaps most important, he would want any mistake in his understanding of Islam to be identified and corrected. A genuinely religious person seeks to live in accordance with God's will, in accordance with what his religion requires. This is distinct from seeking to live in accordance with what one *believes* to be God's will and *believes* to be required by one's religion. These two goals are distinct because of the possibility of error. To deny this possibility is to claim infallibility for oneself. This would be hubris in regard to morality, and blasphemy in any theistic religion.[234] It is true, of course, that all we have are our beliefs. We have no belief-independent access to the truth. Still, beliefs can be more or less well founded. To the person who seeks to live in accordance with what she *believes* to be God's will, it does not matter whether her beliefs are well founded or not. To the person who seeks to live in accordance with God's will, by contrast, nothing matters more. The more pains she takes to examine and correct her understanding and beliefs, the more likely she is to get it right. And even when she gets it wrong nonetheless, she will at least have done her best to get it right by making full use of the faculties and other resources God had endowed her with.

It is then of great importance to a genuinely moral or religious person to have a full justification for an action that he knows will kill many innocent civilians, and also to present this justification, at least after the fact. Such a full justification will then be examined and discussed by others whom it will help either to follow the agent's example conscientiously, with full appreciation of the reasons why it may or should be followed, or else to avoid the error he had committed in good faith.

It is stunning how far the terrorists and their supporters fall short of the conduct of persons with genuine moral or religious commitments and scruples. They traffic heavily in the language of morality and holiness, but there is no evidence that they have seriously thought about what their religion requires of them. What they give us are simple moral colorations of the world along with fervent professions of sincerity and commitment. They do indeed seem strongly committed – after all, many of them are willing to die for the success of their attacks. But for this commitment to be a sincere commitment *to Islam*, there would need to be a serious effort substantively to connect their activities and colorations to Islamic teachings. There would need to be reflective answers to questions such as "Why is this a holy war?" "Who counts as an enemy in this holy war, and why?" "What is one allowed to do in a holy war to enemies and to the uninvolved?" There is, and has been for centuries, sophisticated treatment of such questions among Islamic scholars.[235] But the terrorists and their supporters are conspicuously absent from this discourse, even though their pronouncements and actions are highly controversial within it. They seem to be quite unconcerned to rule out what I have called the most terrifying possibility for a genuine believer: the possibility that one might be mistakenly killing, in God's name but against God's will, hundreds of innocent human beings who, no less than oneself, are God's creation.

7.6 Acting under color of morality

I have discussed two moral failings of those involved in the five terrorist attacks. It was wrong of them to harm large numbers of innocent civilians for no compelling purpose. And they did wrong to perpetrate these attacks in the name of a religion without taking great care to work out whether their religion really justifies such attacks. Placing these two wrongs side by side, one may think that the latter pales to insignificance. But I will try to show that the latter wrong, too, is of great importance. This discussion will also bring out the second reason why it is so very important for us not merely to be certain *that* these terrorist attacks are wrong, but also to understand *why* they are wrong. We are in the same boat with the terrorists in the sense that we use moral language just as they do. Our moral judgments are fallible just as theirs are. And we have a moral responsibility, just as they do, to take great care to ensure that the important decisions we make are not merely ones that we, however sincerely, believe to be morally justifiable, but also ones that we can actually justify.

Moral language is all around us – praising and condemning as good or evil, right or wrong, just or unjust, virtuous or vicious. In all too many cases, however, such language is used only to advance personal or group interests. The speaker expresses the narrowest judgment that allows her to score her point while avoiding any further normative commitments that might encumber her now or in the future. This is quite common in politics. Politician *A* criticizes politician *B* as unethical for accepting a free trip to a conference in Brighton courtesy of Shell Oil. Without any further explanation of what makes *B*'s behavior unethical, this is rather too easy a way of scoring political points. *B* gets tarred with the label *unethical*, while *A* can look good for her ethical concern without imposing any ethical constraints on her own conduct. *A* remains at liberty, should she be found to have accepted some free trip herself, to say that her conduct was not unethical because of its different purpose, different destination, different sponsor, or whatever.

A's conduct is not atypical in our culture. Many seek to take advantage of morality to influence the sentiments and conduct of others while avoiding any interference by morality in the pursuit of their own ends. This is a moral failing, of course, but one that may seem rather mild in comparison to horrendous crimes of violence such as those we have discussed. And yet, this common abuse of morality is of great importance, as we recognize when we consider it, as I will now do, from three perspectives: from the perspective of morality itself, from the perspective of agents, and from the perspective of our society and culture.

The imperative to take morality seriously is not a command merely of this or that morality, but one that any plausible morality – and again I include religions – must make central. Though substantive in content, this central imperative flows from understanding what it means to have – not some particular moral commitments, but – any moral commitments at all.

In rough outline, we might say that the central imperative to take morality seriously involves at least these three injunctions. One must try to integrate one's moral judgments, one's religious beliefs and commitments, through more general moral principles into a coherent account of morally acceptable conduct. One must work out what this unified system of beliefs and commitments implies for one's own life. And one must make a serious effort to honor these implications in one's own conduct and judgments.

Some agents who disregard the central imperative are ones who simply set aside moral considerations and moral language altogether, and typically behave badly as a result. Let us set them aside, for they are fringe groups in the contemporary world. Much more important and much more numerous are those who take no interest in morality as such – in working out its content and living in conformity with it – but nonetheless employ moral language to influence the sentiments and conduct of others. They appeal to morality in bad faith, without a sincere willingness to work out what morality requires and thus in defiance of its central imperative. In order to advance their own ends, they falsely present themselves as friends of morality, as speaking on morality's behalf. Abusing morality in this way, they are not merely bad people, behaving badly, but unjust people, behaving unjustly.[236] Such people are the analogue to judges or police officers who use the law to advance their own ends: a judge who decides in the name of the people, but on the basis of what enriches himself or what advances his sectarian ideology; a police officer who falsely arrests a young woman for his own entertainment or to prevent her from expressing political views he dislikes. Such actions are not the worst violations of the law. And yet, committed under color of law, they are in one sense the most pernicious. Similarly, acting *under color of morality* – misrepresenting oneself as motivated by a sincere commitment to morality in order to advance one's own ends – is not the worst violation of morality, but one that strikes at its very heart. Acting under color of Islam or under color of Christianity are instances of this – acts of supreme defiance where the agent puts himself in the place of God. The content of religion becomes whatever the agent declares it to be. The agent is not seeking the guidance of his religion but merely uses its moral language to color the world as suits his distinct purposes.

Imagine a society whose public culture is dominated by people of this sort – trafficking heavily in moral language without any respect for morality's central imperative. In such a culture we get endless repetitions of specific moral assertions ("The United States is the great Satan" or "To withdraw our troops now would be a cowardly capitulation to terrorism"), and endless repetitions of unexamined generalities ("We must fight the infidels wherever they dishonor what is sacred" or "We must defend freedom against the enemies of freedom"). Such moral appeals are made on all sides. But since they remain unexplicated and unjustified, there is no substantive moral debate. The political effect of all the moral language thrown around depends then on media access and acting skills. To have an impact, one must manage to intone, on prime-time TV, the relevant sentences with an honest face and a good show of profound conviction, conveying to the audience that one cares deeply about moral considerations and is sincerely convinced that the policy one is defending is the moral policy. And to remain unencumbered with regard to other policies one might want to defend simultaneously or in the future, one must do all this without assuming any further, possibly inconvenient substantive moral commitments.

This imagined society is not so far from what we find in the real world today. We find it in much of the Arab world. And we find it in the UK and in the US as well. The model also resembles current international society pretty closely. To be sure, there is a great deal of serious moral discourse going on, not merely in universities, but also within other (for instance, religious) associations and in political forums such as in some committees of the United Nations and of various national legislatures. But the public visibility and impact of such serious moral discourse is small and diminishing, and the political forums in which it takes place are therefore increasingly shunned and marginalized. This may not seem like a calamity comparable to terrorism. And yet, such moral corruption is, in one sense, a more profound danger.

When moral language degenerates into just one more tool in the competitive struggle for advantage, then this struggle becomes ultimately unconstrained. To be sure, the power of political leaders and factions is limited by the power of other leaders and factions, and is restricted also by procedural checks and balances. But all these constraints are soft and flexible, themselves subject to indefinite modification through the use of political power. Insofar as political players understand that their competitive struggle for power is always also a struggle over the rules governing this competition, they tend to be ruthless in this competition because there is no other long-term protection of their interests and values. This problem is well explicated in Rawls's discussion of a *modus vivendi*. Rawls's preferred alternative model is that of an overlapping consensus focused on firm, widely recognized social rules to which all major groups, perhaps for diverse reasons, have a principled moral commitment.[237] But even without such an overlapping consensus, there can at least be that trust among adversaries which comes from recognizing one another as genuinely moral agents who are at least committed to *their own* morality. The moral importance of avoiding a world without trust and without shared social rules gives us further moral reasons to honor morality's central imperative in our applications of moral language to both domestic and international issues.

7.7 The measures taken in our name

We can now appreciate the promised second reason for considering it important – even if we have not the slightest doubt – to articulate the grounds of our firm belief that these five terrorist attacks were heinous acts: to articulate our understanding of why these attacks are wrong, or what makes them wrong, as I have tried to do earlier. We must do this to honor morality's central imperative, which requires us to elaborate and extend our moral commitments to the point where they impose clear constraints on our own conduct. This is crucial for being moral persons, rather than persons acting under color of morality. And it is crucial also for being recognized as moral persons, as persons with genuine moral commitments that we are willing to discuss and are determined to live up to.

There is considerable skepticism outside the affluent West about the moral fervor with which we have condemned the terrorists and prosecuted our war against them. Occasionally, such skepticism comes with sympathy for and even celebration of the terrorists. Far more frequently, however, the skeptics share our conviction that those terrorist attacks were very wrong. Their skepticism involves the judgment or suspicion that we are moralizing in bad faith, that we are interested in morality when this serves to win us support or sympathy or at least acquiescence, but that we have no interest in the moral assessment or adjustment of our own conduct and policies.

In my view, these skeptics are essentially correct. But before presenting some evidence to support their case, I should state clearly two points that I am not making and in fact strongly reject. I reject the view that wrongful conduct by our governments renders the terrorist attacks any less unjustifiable. My moral condemnation of such attacks is based on the harms they inflict on innocent civilians, who do not become permissible targets for lethal attack by wrongful policies of their governments. I also do not claim that it is impermissible for those who are doing wrong to fight the wrongs done by others. My main point in discussing our governments' conduct and policies is to show that our politicians take momentous action, in our name, without any effort to apply the morality they profess in our name to decisions that cry out for moral justification. That they can get by, comfortably, without any such effort is our fault as citizens.

Let me illustrate the point by recalling some well-known highlights of the "global war on terror" (GWOT) as orchestrated by the US and UK governments. Central to the GWOT as they conceive it is the doctrine that the terrorist danger justifies pervasive secrecy and disinformation toward the media and the general public, and even toward the legislature. The suggestion was, and still is, that the success of the war effort requires that most of this effort be exempt from public scrutiny and that even the scope of this exemption should not be disclosed.[238] A well-known and typical example is UK Attorney General Lord Peter Goldsmith threatening British media with criminal prosecution for reporting that President Bush had proposed to bomb the Al Jazeera television station in peaceful Qatar.[239]

An early episode in the GWOT was the overthrow of the Taliban regime in Afghanistan. In this initiative, our governments chose to rely heavily on the United Islamic Front for the Salvation of Afghanistan. This "Northern Alliance" had been losing the civil war against the Taliban, but massive Western air support, funding, and US teams of special forces turned the situation around in its favor. Thousands of Taliban fighters, who had laid down their arms in exchange for a promise of safe passage to their home villages in an orderly surrender negotiated with the participation of US military personnel, were instead crammed into metal shipping containers without air or water for several days. Between 960 and 3,000 of them died in agony from heat, thirst, and lack of oxygen. Some of the survivors were shot dead and all bodies buried in a huge mass grave.[240] The commander of Northern Alliance forces, Abdul Rashid Dostum, later used murder and torture to intimidate witnesses to the atrocity, and had the mass grave bulldozed, exhuming bodies and removing evidence.[241] While insisting on a full investigation of the mass graves at Srebrenica, Western governments blocked any official inquiry into the mass grave at Dasht-e Leili; and the mass murder of surrendering Taliban has now been largely forgotten in most parts of the world.[242] Implicated also in systematic and horrific crimes against women and girls,[243] Dostum currently serves as Chief of Staff to the Commander-in-Chief of the Afghan Armed Forces, reporting directly to President Hamid Karzai.[244]

The US and UK governments defended their 2003 invasion of Iraq, once again, as a necessary component of the GWOT. But the evidence for their claims that Saddam Hussein had weapons of mass destruction and ties to Al Qaeda was flimsy, and these claims are now known to have been false and preparations for the invasion are known to have been made well before 9/11. Hussein's regime had been responsible for horrendous human-rights violations, including massive chemical weapons attacks against Iraqi and Iranian civilians. But these were most severe in the 1980s, when Iraq, with Western encouragement and chemicals delivered by Western states, fought a nine-year war against Iran. At that time, our governments were on friendly terms with Saddam Hussein – though the US, eager to prolong the war, sold weapons and intelligence to Iran as well (the "Iran-Contra Affair").

The US and UK quickly took over the prisons of the regimes they had defeated and filled them with thousands of people they had taken captive in their war on terror. Labeled "unprivileged combatants," "unlawful enemy combatants," or "security detainees," these people have been routinely humiliated and degraded at will by coalition personnel: stripped naked, forced to masturbate and to simulate sex acts, abused with dogs, shackled in excruciating positions, kicked and burned, beaten with electric cables, hooded and deprived of human contact for months, and tortured with electric shocks, drugs, sleep deprivation, induced hypothermia, and "water-boarding" (simulated drowning).[245]

Such abuse is partly explained by the large and increasing number of "moral waivers" that allow people with serious criminal records to join the US armed forces.[246] A second contributing factor is that civilian contractors, who have played a major role in the abuse of civilians, can act with near total impunity.[247] A third important factor is that officers are virtually never prosecuted and punished, presumably to maintain the fiction that the abuse is coincidental and not related to any policies.[248] Accounts from former prison personnel make clear that, on the contrary, much of the abuse was systematic and deliberate, encouraged and condoned up the chain of command,[249] with the objective of breaking resistance to the occupation trumping any concern for protecting the innocent. This is confirmed by former US Army interrogator Tony Lagouranis who, in his *Hardball* interview with Chris Matthews, estimated that 90 percent of the people he interrogated were wholly innocent – not merely in the technical sense of innocent until proven guilty, but really innocent of any armed resistance to the occupation of Iraq or any serious crime that might conceivably justify their horrendous treatment.[250] Many were arrested for having once visited Afghanistan, for having had some association to an Islamic charity with suspected links to terrorists or their sympathizers, or even to help extract information from an incarcerated relative; others were simply turned over in exchange for cash.[251]

There are many facilities outside Afghanistan and Iraq where perceived enemies of the West are held indefinitely. Best known among these is the US-operated compound at Guantánamo Bay, Cuba. United Nations officials have been trying to inspect this prison since it opened in 2002, but declined the option to visit without full access and the opportunity to conduct private interviews with detainees.[252] The US Defense Department has been compelled by the judiciary to issue a list of the people it has been holding at Guantánamo Bay, and several people released from there have provided graphic accounts of how prisoners are treated.[253]

The US government asserts that the prisoners it holds at Guantánamo Bay are not entitled to *Geneva Convention* protections[254] and sought to try them by military commissions. But the US Supreme Court overruled the government on both counts, emphasizing the severe flaws of the constituted military commissions:

> The accused and his civilian counsel may be excluded from, and precluded from ever learning what evidence was presented during, any part of the proceeding that either the Appointing Authority or the presiding officer decides to "close." . . . not only is testimonial hearsay and evidence obtained through coercion fully admissible, but neither live testimony nor witnesses' written statements need be sworn.[255]

The Court concluded that trial by military commission, as envisioned, violates both the *Geneva Conventions* and the US *Uniform Code of Military Justice*, whose Article 36(b) requires that all pre-trial, trial, and post-trial procedures must be uniform with those applied to crimes allegedly committed by US military personnel.[256] The Court also found that trial by military commission as contemplated violates Article 3, common to all four *Geneva Conventions*, which requires that any punishments inflicted must be pursuant to a "judgment pronounced by a regularly constituted court affording all the judicial guarantees which are recognized as indispensable by civilized peoples."[257] In response to the Court's decision, the US Congress has since passed the *Military Commissions Act* attempting to reinstate trial by military commission in modified form.[258] Although this law was overturned by the Supreme Court as an unconstitutional violation of habeas corpus rights in 2008, the military commissions have continued.[259]

Coalition forces have also maintained secret detention facilities around the world, reportedly in Jordan, Pakistan, Qatar, Thailand, Uzbekistan, various locations in Eastern Europe, and on the British island of Diego Garcia.[260] At these "black sites" our governments are imprisoning so-called ghost detainees – unknown numbers of unknown persons for unknown reasons under unknown conditions. Our governments are telling us that nothing untoward is going on at such sites. But it would be irrational and irresponsible to trust that basic human rights are being respected in locations that no one else has access to when such rights are not being respected in locations from which a fair amount of information is leaking out. Common sense suggests that, once persons have been caught in the secret prison system, their captors are reluctant to release them even when they become convinced of their innocence. Wholly unaccountable for their actions, these captors much prefer innocent persons to remain missing indefinitely over their resurfacing with information about conditions in the secret facilities and possibly with knowledge that might be used to identify particular torturers, interrogators, or collaborating doctors.

The UK is the main "partner country" in this system of secret detention and torturous interrogation whose victims have no rights of any sort. UK officials sit with their US counterparts on the Joint Detention Review Board in Iraq, UK officials have participated in coercive interrogations, and UK officials have asserted that human-rights law does not bind UK forces in Iraq.[261] The US government relied, in the first few years of the GWOT, on a 50-page memorandum signed by

Assistant Attorney General Jay S. Bybee. This memorandum comments at length on the legal obligations of US military personnel under the *International Covenant on Civil and Political Rights* and the *Convention Against Torture and Other Cruel, Inhuman, or Degrading Treatment or Punishment* – both ratified by the US – and under implementing national legislation. Appealing to a Reagan Administration precedent, Bybee reiterates eight times that the word torture covers only the "most extreme" forms of physical and mental harm which result in "excruciating and agonizing" pain, such as "the needle under the fingernail, the application of electric shock to the genital area, the piercing of eyeballs":[262]

> [T]orture . . . covers only extreme acts. . . . Where the pain is physical, it must be of an intensity akin to that which accompanies serious physical injury such as death or organ failure. Severe mental pain requires suffering not just at the moment of infliction but it also requires lasting psychological harm, such as seen in mental disorders like posttraumatic stress disorder. . . . Because the acts inflicting torture are extreme, there is significant range of acts that though they might constitute cruel, inhuman, or degrading treatment or punishment fail to rise to the level of torture.

The Bybee memo also asserts that, even when torture in this narrow sense is used, "necessity or self-defense could provide justifications that would eliminate any criminal liability" and that judicial review of "interrogations undertaken pursuant to the President's Commander-in-Chief powers may be unconstitutional."[263] In plain language: most extreme forms of punishment are not extreme enough to count as torture. Even the infliction of clear-cut torture is justifiable by appeal to necessity or self-defense. And even if clear-cut torture is not so justifiable, the courts have no power to stop it when it is ordered by the President.

The Bybee memo was superseded by a memo signed by Acting US Assistant Attorney General Daniel Levin on December 30, 2004, stating that "we have reviewed this Office's prior opinions addressing issues involving treatment of detainees and do not believe that any of their conclusions would be different under the standards set forth in this memorandum."[264] The main change from the Bybee memo is that the second and third lines of defense are now declared superfluous. Because the President has directed US personnel not to engage in torture, it is unnecessary to consider whether torture is justifiable and whether the courts have the authority to stop torture ordered by the

President. The memo reiterates at great length that only the most extreme forms of inhuman and degrading treatment should count as torture. It thereby follows the Bybee memo in ignoring that what the US has signed and ratified is a convention against torture *and other cruel, inhuman, or degrading treatment or punishment,* and in ignoring as well that the US has signed and ratified the *Geneva Conventions* whose common Article 3 prohibits not only torture but also "cruel treatment" and "outrages upon personal dignity, in particular humiliating and degrading treatment."[265] This Article is common to all four *Geneva Conventions,* and its application can therefore not be refuted by claiming that detainees fail to qualify as prisoners of war.[266]

Among the treatments coalition partners use and officially classify as acceptable are:

Long Time Standing: This technique is described as among the most effective. Prisoners are forced to stand, handcuffed and with their feet shackled to an eye bolt in the floor for more than 40 hours. Exhaustion and sleep deprivation are effective in yielding confessions.

The Cold Cell: The prisoner is left to stand naked in a cell kept near 50 degrees F. Throughout the time in the cell the prisoner is doused with cold water.

Water Boarding: The prisoner is bound to an inclined board, feet raised and head slightly below the feet. Cellophane is wrapped over the prisoner's face and water is poured over him. Unavoidably, the gag reflex kicks in and a terrifying fear of drowning leads to almost instant pleas to bring the treatment to a halt.[267]

Another instrument in our war on terror is "extraordinary rendition" in which persons are transferred, without any legal process, to regimes known to practice even more severe forms of torture. According to former CIA officer Robert Baer, the CIA captures individuals it suspects of ties to terrorism and puts them on a plane. "The ultimate destination of these flights are places that, you know, are involved in torture. . . . If you send a prisoner to Jordan you get a better interrogation. If you send a prisoner, for instance, to Egypt you will probably never see him again, the same way with Syria."[268] Maher Arar, software engineer and Canadian citizen, was fortunate enough to be seen again. Coming from Tunis and headed for Montreal, he was detained during a stop-over at John F. Kennedy Airport and delivered to Syria where he was held in solitary confinement and brutally tortured on a regular basis. He was released more than a year after his arrest, completely cleared of any terrorism charges by a Canadian commission of inquiry.[269] The US ambassador to Canada, Paul Cellucci, commented that "the US government will continue to deport Canadian citizens to third countries if they pose a risk to American national security."[270] Khaled el-Masri, a German citizen abducted by the CIA while vacationing in Macedonia, also resurfaced after five months of detention in Afghanistan where he was shackled, beaten, and injected with drugs. He was released somewhere in Albania when his captors realized that his abduction was a case of mistaken identity.[271]

With regard to ghost detainees and extraordinary renditions, no information is typically provided to family members of missing persons, to the general public, or even to US or UK legislators about who is being detained, where, for how long, and under what conditions. People are being disappeared in the way people used to be disappeared in Latin America under the military dictatorships of the 1970s and 1980s. And even when the detention of specific persons by US or UK personnel is known to their relatives and friends, the latter are often unable to obtain further information. They do not know whether their loved ones are alive or dead and, if alive, where they are being held, by whom, and how they are being treated. The pictures from coalition-run prisons that such friends and relatives can see in the mass media – much more frequently abroad than in our own countries – cannot contribute to their peace of mind. And these pictures cast a terrible light on our words, such as these spoken on the occasion of the UN International Day in Support of the Victims of Torture: "The victims often feel forgotten, but we will not forget them. America supports accountability and treatment centers for torture victims. . . . We stand with the victims to seek their healing and recovery, and urge all nations to join us in these efforts to restore the dignity of every person affected by torture."[272]

As with regard to the terrorist attacks, we should ask whether all this barbarity, much of it inflicted on innocents, is really necessary to protect our societies from terrorist attacks. Would we be worse protected and, if so, by how much, if we did not transfer suspects to notorious torture countries? Would we be worse protected and, if so, by how much, if we allowed judicial oversight involving at the very least a public record of who has been detained as well as an opportunity for prisoners to communicate with independent doctors and lawyers? Reflection on these questions suggests that the barbarity of our response to the terrorist attacks may well be counterproductive by inciting more terrorism than it deters.[273]

7.8 How do we justify our policies?

What is remarkable is that our governments show so little interest in justifying, in moral terms, the great harms they are clearly inflicting on innocent persons. Of course, they traffic heavily in moral and specifically religious rhetoric, on both sides of the Atlantic. But is there any evidence that those who design and implement coalition methods in the global war on terror have thought carefully about their moral justifiability? Such serious reflection is what they would engage in if they were genuinely concerned that their conduct – or let me say, *our* conduct, for they are acting as our elected representatives in our names – be morally justifiable. And had they engaged in such serious moral reflection and convinced themselves that these methods are indeed morally justifiable under existing conditions, would they not want this justification to be publicly known so that we all can appreciate that what is being done in our names is, appearances notwithstanding, really morally justifiable?

The conduct of our politicians is better explained by their desire to act under color of morality. This requires no more than the bald assertion that we are doing the right thing, presented in appealing tones of sincerity and commitment. What is most astonishing here again is that our politicians get away with this so easily. This is astonishing not merely in the GWOT case here under discussion, but in US and UK foreign policy more generally.

In the 1990s, the United Nations maintained a stringent regime of economic sanctions against Iraq. These sanctions greatly reduced access to foodstuffs and medicines for poor Iraqis and further degraded Iraq's heavily damaged infrastructure, preventing the provision of electricity, water, and sanitation with devastating effects on the incidence of contagious diseases. Madeline Albright, then US Ambassador to the UN, defended the sanctions regime on *60 Minutes*:

Lesley Stahl: We have heard that a half a million children have died. I mean, that's more children than died in Hiroshima. . . . Is the price worth it?

Albright: I think this is a very hard choice, but the price – we think the price is worth it. . . . It is a moral question, but the moral question is even a larger one. Don't we owe to the American people and to the American military and to the other countries in the region that this man [Saddam Hussein] not be a threat?

Stahl: Even with the starvation?

Albright: I think, Lesley, it is hard for me to say this because I am a humane person, but my first responsibility is to make sure that United States forces do not have to go and re-fight the Gulf War.[274]

The interviewer left it at that, and the remarks drew scant media attention in the US and Europe and were not noted in Albright's Senate confirmation hearings for Secretary of State that same year. The remarks were much reported and discussed in the Arab world, however, and apparently motivated at least one of the terrorists involved in the attacks described above.[275] In her autobiography, Albright expresses deep regret about her remarks: "Nothing matters more than the lives of innocent people. I had fallen into a trap and said something that I simply did not mean."[276]

But if nothing matters more than the lives of innocent people, then why were these very severe sanctions continued without regard to their effects on Iraqi civilians? Despite considerable variation in the estimates, it was clear from the start that the sanctions' health impact on Iraqi civilians would be devastating.[277] The most careful studies I have found are Richard Garfield's, who estimates that mortality among children under 5 rose from about 40–45 per 1,000 in 1990 to about 125 per 1,000 during 1994–9, and stresses that many of the surviving children sustained lasting damage to their health.[278] Garfield estimates that there were between 343,900 and 525,400 excess deaths among children under 5 in the 1991–2002 period, which comes to about 3,000 per month.[279]

In 1998, Denis Halliday, coordinator of humanitarian relief to Iraq and Assistant Secretary-General of the United Nations, resigned after 34 years with the UN. Explaining his resignation, he wrote: "I am resigning, because the policy of economic sanctions is totally bankrupt. We are in the process of destroying an entire society. It is as simple and terrifying as that . . . Five thousand children are dying every month . . . I don't want to administer a programme that results in figures like these."[280] He added in an interview:

I had been instructed to implement a policy that satisfies the definition of genocide: a deliberate policy that has effectively killed well over a million individuals, children and adults. We all know that the regime, Saddam Hussein, is not paying the price for economic sanctions; on the contrary, he has been strengthened by them. It is the little people who are losing their children or their parents for lack of untreated water [*sic*].

What is clear is that the Security Council is now out of control, for its actions here undermine its own Charter, and the Declaration of Human Rights and the Geneva Convention. History will slaughter those responsible.[281]

In 2000, Halliday's successor, Hans von Sponeck, also resigned, after 32 years of UN service, while harshly criticizing the sanctions regime as well as the dishonesty of the relevant officials in the Blair and Clinton governments.[282] Jutta Burghardt, director of the UN World Food program in Iraq, also resigned for the same reasons.[283]

Nothing matters more than the lives of innocent people. Most of us would agree with Albright on this point. Most of us would also agree that her, and our, first responsibility is to our own country. And most of us endorse these two commitments in such a shallow way that, like Albright, we do not even notice the tension. Then, when a choice must be made between promoting the interests of our country – our government, citizens, or corporations – and those of innocent people abroad, we routinely prioritize the former without so much as examining the cost that our choices will impose on the lives of the innocent.

In this spirit, the US and UK governments have stated that they do not track civilian deaths in the aftermath of their invasions and occupations of Afghanistan and Iraq.[284] And in the same spirit our governments press their favored economic rules and policies upon the rest of the world: structural adjustment programs required by the IMF have deprived millions of African children of elementary schooling.[285] Protectionist trade barriers are unfairly depriving poor populations of a decent livelihood (see endnote 25). Loans and arms sales are keeping brutal and corrupt rulers in power in poor countries, and lax banking laws facilitate massive embezzlement by these countries' public officials (see endnote 45). Intellectual property rights mandated by the WTO cut off hundreds of millions of poor patients worldwide from cheap generic medicines.[286] In these cases and many more, our politicians take momentous action, in our name, without any effort to apply the morality they profess in our name to decisions that cry out for moral justification. Their bald assurances that their conduct is alright, morally, are accepted by the vast majority of citizens who are similarly inclined to avoid further thought about how our "first responsibility" to benefit our own might be constrained by the interests of innocent people abroad. It appears that, outside a few insulated forums, the distinction between what is morally right and what is believed and proclaimed to be so has all but collapsed. This is a disastrous flaw in our public culture – one that, quite apart from its horrific effects, fundamentally undermines our ambition to be a civilization that strives for moral decency.

* * *

Since this essay was written, a new American president has been elected and inaugurated. Barack Obama has taken important steps toward eliminating some of the more abhorrent policies described above: he has disavowed all legal advice on interrogation policies issued during the Bush administration, ended the use by the CIA and US military of water-boarding and other torture techniques, and has ordered an immediate shuttering of secret prisons. Other policy steps have been more tentative: he has ordered Guantánamo to be closed by early 2010 – suspending the trials by military commission – but has not decided on what to do with its prisoners; similarly, he has placed the extraordinary renditions policy under review but not halted it.[287] These initial moves led one commentator to exclaim, of the new president, that "with the stroke of his pen, he effectively declared an end to the 'war on terror,' as President George W. Bush had defined it."[288] As of January 2010, this exclamation seems premature.

Although I am hopeful that the Obama administration will continue along this promising course, only time will tell how committed it really is to human rights and the rule of law. In any case, this chapter is not so much about our politicians as about us citizens as the ultimate bearers of responsibility for our government's policies. Did the change in US policy signal a new reflective commitment on the part of the public to fundamental human rights as constraints on government policies? Did we recognize our responsibility for the massive harms that the Bush and Blair governments caused to innocent people in our names, so that similar abuses will be politically impossible for decades to come? My fear is that the answer to both these questions is "no" – that the American public has simply moved on, leaving our terrifying culpability for the horrors of the Bush administration behind to be benignly forgotten.

8

Moralizing Humanitarian Intervention: Why Jurying Fails and How Law Can Work

8.0 Introduction

Thomas Franck believes that the strict constraints imposed by the UN Charter on military intervention have become too constraining and that, so long as the Charter remains unrevised, we should condone violations of these rules as legitimated by a jurying process. The relevant UN Charter constraints he seeks to subvert are two. First, the Charter directs that "All Members shall refrain in their international relations from the threat or use of force against the territorial integrity or political independence of any state, or in any other manner inconsistent with the Purposes of the United Nations" (Article 2(4)). Without specific authorization by the Security Council, states may use military force across national borders only in "individual or collective self-defense if an armed attack occurs against a Member of the United Nations, until the Security Council has taken measures necessary to maintain international peace and security" (Article 51). Second, regarding the use of force by the UN itself, the Charter proclaims that:

> Nothing contained in the present Charter shall authorize the United Nations to intervene in matters which are essentially within the domestic jurisdiction of any state or shall require the Members to submit such

matters to settlement under the present Charter; but this principle shall not prejudice the application of enforcement measures under Chapter VII. (Article 2(7))[289]

Why does Franck want to see these constraints undermined through selective non-compliance? One reason he gives is "the immensity of changes in the state system's configuration, together with the intractability of the Charter to change through formal amendment."[290] The changes he lists are "the development of the hydrogen bomb, the end of colonialism and communism, and the emergence of terrorism as weapon of choice for the disempowered [,] . . . the consequences of responsible regionalism in Europe, Africa and the Americas, [and] the proliferation of states from fewer than sixty to almost two hundred."[291] Franck does not explain how these changes make strict adherence to the UN Charter constraints implausible. But in some cases it is not difficult to guess what he has in mind: to protect ourselves from terrorist attacks, we should be allowed to intervene militarily in states that seem either unwilling or unable to root out on their soil terrorist organizations capable of attacking our citizens. And, with modern weapons of mass destruction, such as hydrogen bombs delivered by intercontinental ballistic missiles, we should not be required to wait until an armed attack on us or our allies is actually in progress, but may instead, under appropriate circumstances, take preemptive action by striking first, as the US takes itself to be entitled to do.[292]

8.1 The amazing appeal to the Rwandan genocide

But instead of producing arguments that appeal in this way to our security interests, Franck invokes a quite different line of thought, one that appeals not to our entitlements but to our moral duties and has nothing to do with how the world has changed over the past 60 years. He invokes the Rwandan genocide – or rather, he draws on how UN Secretary-General Kofi Annan has invoked this case. Here is what Annan wrote:

> To those for whom the greatest threat to the future of international order is the use of force in the absence of a Security Council mandate, one might say: leave Kosovo aside for a moment, and think about Rwanda. Imagine for one moment that, in those dark days and hours leading up to the genocide, there had been a coalition of states ready

and willing to act in defense of the Tutsi population, but the council had refused or delayed giving the green light. Should such a coalition then have stood idly by while the horror unfolded?[293]

With Annan, Franck concludes from this case that there is a genuine predicament here, giving rise to serious conflict between the letter of international law, on the one hand, and "good sense and morality,"[294] on the other. Going beyond Annan, Franck stresses that committing or condoning violations of the law can be justified in such cases by reference to the rule of law itself:

[T]he power of law to secure compliance is undermined if the gap between it and the prevalent sense of justice, morality, and common sense is allowed to become too wide. The capacity of the law to pull towards compliance those to whom it is addressed is diminished whenever it is seen no longer to comport with shared notions of what is right. The law's self-interest, therefore, demands that a way be found to bridge any gap between its own institutional commitment to the consistent application of formal rules and the public sense that order should not be achieved at too high a cost to widely shared moral values.

If law permits – or even *requires* – behavior that is widely believed to be unfair, unjust, or immoral, it is not only persons but also the law that suffers. So, too, if law *prohibits* that which is widely believed to be just and moral.[295]

It is curious that the Rwandan genocide should be invoked in illustration of these points. This is curious, first, because this case is quite disconnected from the changes in the state system that Franck supposes to have been immense and unforeseeable by the drafters of the UN Charter. Indeed, the founding of the UN was in good part motivated by the German Holocaust of the same decade, so the possibility of another genocide was certainly not inconceivable to the drafters.

Appeal to this case is curious, second, because, as described by Annan, it is purely hypothetical. Perhaps it is good that, high up in remote ivory towers, there should be philosophers searching for moral guidelines for all possible agents in all possible worlds. But, surely, the UN Charter should answer to a narrower ambition: it should be formulated to work as well as possible in this actual world of human (and often inhuman) politicians. In order to judge whether certain articles of this Charter should be revised or subverted, we should then examine realistic cases in which strict application of international law actually did or actually would lead to morally intolerable results.

To be sure, the genocide in Rwanda was real enough, and it was certainly morally intolerable. What is entirely fantastic about Kofi Annan's case is his reference to states willing and able to stop the slaughter but held back by an unreasonable vote or veto in the UN Security Council. In the real world, there was only the coalition of the *un*willing: of those who did all they could *not* to get involved in Rwanda while suppressing any use of the word "genocide" (in favor of "chaos" and "civil war" and finally "acts of genocide") as long as possible. There were no saviors, willing and able, held back merely by the Charter text.

The choice of Annan's hypothetical example is curious for yet a third reason. Its author, Kofi Annan, played an absolutely essential role – with President Clinton, his UN ambassador Madeleine Albright, and Secretary of State Warren Christopher – in the grand coalition of the unwilling that enabled the genocide. His contributions as head of the UN Department of Peacekeeping Operations are well known from many sources, including the official reports by the UN itself and by the Organization of African Unity (OAU, since renamed African Union).[296]

On January 11, 1994, General Romeo Dallaire, commander of UNAMIR (United Nations Peacekeeping Mission for Rwanda, already legally stationed in the country), had sent his so-called Genocide Fax to UN headquarters. The fax recounts how Dallaire was put in contact with a high-level informant who told him of plans to distribute weapons to Hutu militias (Interahamwe, cooperating closely with the Rwandan army), to kill Belgian members of UNAMIR in order to "guarantee Belgian withdrawal from Rwanda," and then to kill large numbers of moderate Hutus and Tutsis. ("[The informant] has been ordered to register all Tutsis in Kigali. He suspects it is for their extermination. Example he gave was that in 20 minutes his personnel could kill up to 1,000 Tutsis.")[297] In the fax, Dallaire indicates that he trusts the informant and is planning to take action, within 36 hours, to seize a major weapons cache whose location the informant is prepared to divulge. Dallaire requested authorization to grant the informant, his wife, and their four children UN protection and safe exit from Rwanda in return for his information. Dallaire did not ask for authorization to seize the weapons cache, an action he apparently viewed as falling squarely within his mandate "to contribute to the security of the city of Kigali inter alia within a weapons-secure area established by the parties in and around the city."[298]

Without informing the then UN Secretary-General, Boutros Boutros-Ghali, of this fax, Kofi Annan, in a sequence of messages (January 10–13, 1994), repeatedly and categorically forbade the operation: "No reconnaissance or other action, including response to request for protection, should be taken by UNAMIR until clear guidance is received from headquarters." "The overriding consideration is the need to avoid entering into a course of action that might lead to the use of force and unanticipated repercussions."[299] Annan similarly refused various subsequent proposals and reinforcement requests sent to UN headquarters by Dallaire – on January 22, February 3, February 15, February 27, March 13, mid-March, and March 26.[300] Even on April 9, with the massacres in full swing, Annan still instructed Dallaire to:

> cooperate with both the French and Belgian commanders to facilitate the evacuation of their nationals, and other foreign nationals requesting evacuation. You may exchange liaison officers for this purpose. You should make every effort not to compromise your impartiality or to act beyond your mandate but may exercise your discretion to do [so] should this be essential for the evacuation of foreign nationals. This should not, repeat not, extend to participating in possible combat, except in self-defense.[301]

We can safely infer from the historical evidence (see endnote 304) that General Dallaire with his 2,500 troops could have done a great deal more toward preventing, and later toward reducing, the slaughter had he not been continuously obstructed by Annan – and that Annan would never have become UN Secretary-General, and thus would not have won the Nobel Peace Prize, had he not acted in accordance with US wishes.[302] In light of these facts about what actually happened, Annan's hypothetical is truly astounding.

Annan's words and deeds diverged unfavorably from the less-than-admirable conduct of his boss. On April 20, Boutros-Ghali at last sought "immediate and massive reinforcement of UNAMIR to stop the fighting and the massacres, requiring several thousand additional troops and enforcement powers under Chapter VII"[303] – in vain, as the Security Council voted unanimously the next day to *reduce* UNAMIR from 2,539 soldiers to 270.[304] Boutros-Ghali was also among the first key official to use the word "genocide,"[305] a word the Clinton Administration strictly forbade its staffers to use.[306] He thereby embarrassed Clinton who, just the day before, had signed Presidential Decision

Directive 25, imposing strict conditions on US support for any future UN peacekeeping operations.[307]

8.2 Would an intervention to stop the Rwandan genocide really have been illegal?

Now one may be tempted to think that – although there were no states willing and able to stop the genocide – Kofi Annan's hypothetical is realistic at least in this regard: the actions General Dallaire was proposing to take would have violated the UN Charter. As head of the UN Department of Peacekeeping Operations in 1994, Annan thus found himself in a serious *actual* conflict that illustrates the point he and Franck want to make about the need to condone violations. Perhaps Annan made the wrong decisions, but he did what the UN Charter required him to do.

However, this view is also mistaken. The actions Dallaire urgently wanted UNAMIR to undertake clearly would not have violated Article 2(4) of the Charter, because they would have constituted an intervention by the UN itself, not by a member state.

Would Dallaire's proposed actions – confiscating arms and protecting the informant in January, protecting endangered Rwandan civilians in April – have violated Article 2(7) of the UN Charter, which forbids the UN to intervene in matters essentially within the domestic jurisdiction of any state? The UNAMIR force was established on the recommendation of the UN Secretary-General by Security Council Resolution 872 on October 5, 1993, with the consent of both parties to the civil war: the government of Rwanda (headed by President Habyarimana) and the Rwandanese Patriotic Front (RPF). UNAMIR's mission was to help implement the Arusha Peace Agreement concluded on August 4, 1993. Among UNAMIR's official tasks was "to contribute to the security of the city of Kigali inter alia within a weapons-secure area established by the parties in and around the city."[308] The confiscation of weapons about to be distributed to a Hutu militia in Kigali falls squarely within this mission parameter. UNAMIR could not have been charged with intervening in essentially domestic matters for carrying out a mission that was specifically consented to, indeed requested, by both parties to the former civil war and authorized by the UN Security Council.

To be sure, any UN force monitoring the implementation of a ceasefire will sometimes do things that are unwelcome to one side or the other. But both sides understood and agreed to this when requesting the mission. I conclude that the UN had no legal reason to stop the actions Dallaire had proposed to take in January (and later). These actions were blocked not by a strict reading of the UN Charter, nor by a veto in the Security Council, but solely at Kofi Annan's discretion.

By the time the last crucial exchange of cables took place (April 9, 1994), the situation in Rwanda had deteriorated dramatically. On April 6, a plane carrying Rwanda's President Habyarimana and Burundi's President Ntaryamira was shot down on its approach into Kigali airport, killing all on board. Mass killings of Tutsis and moderate Hutus started immediately after the crash, producing a *daily* death toll of about 10,000 and resulting in the murder of over 10 percent of Rwanda's population within three months. Quite apart from Rwanda's prior consent to the UNAMIR mission, such mass killings are not matters essentially within its domestic jurisdiction. By acceding, on April 16, 1975, to the 1948 *Convention on the Prevention and Punishment of the Crime of Genocide*, Rwanda had itself affirmed that genocide "is a crime under international law."

Article 1 of this convention states: "The Contracting Parties confirm that genocide, whether committed in time of peace or in time of war, is a crime under international law which they undertake to prevent and to punish." It is arguable, then, that the UN, and the members of its Security Council in particular, had a legal and moral *duty* to stop the genocide, which they could have done quite easily.[309] This, at least, is the plain meaning of the text, as any ordinary person would understand it – whatever governments and their diplomats and international lawyers may tell us to the contrary after the fact. A good case can be made, then, that the situation in April 1994 was the very contrary of what Kofi Annan and Thomas Franck suggest. International law did not merely permit a UN use of force to stop the genocide – it actually *required* all parties to the *Genocide Convention* to work toward and to give material support to such UN action.

Only this plain reading of international law as *requiring* intervention can explain why the lawyers of the US State Department were worried and why the Clinton administration went to such extraordinary lengths to suppress any use of the word "genocide" (see endnote 306). And this plain reading also explains why the US, the UK, France, and UN officials were so reticent about sharing their information about the situation with other UN Security Council members. When they finally understood, late in April, what was happening in Rwanda, some of the non-permanent members (Argentina, Czech Republic, New Zealand, and Spain) pushed hard for re-expanding UNAMIR peacekeeping operations, which on April 21 had been reduced to 270 soldiers by unanimous Security Council Resolution 912. Madeleine Albright considerably delayed this re-expansion of UNAMIR,[310] but Resolution 918, authorizing a new force strength of 5,500, was finally adopted unanimously on May 17 – too late materially to affect the situation in Rwanda, where the battlefield victories of the RPF were slowly bringing the genocide to a halt.

My reason for reviewing the Rwandan genocide is in part, of course, to do my little bit – against the far more visible efforts by Annan, Clinton, and Albright[311] – to preserve awareness of how these 800,000 horrible deaths were facilitated. If conscientious citizens do not learn from this case, there is little hope that genocides will be effectively prevented or stopped in the future.

A review of the Rwanda genocide may seem tangential to Franck's paper. How important is it to show that one of his examples is ill-chosen because of the great distance between what really happened and Annan's offensive hypothetical? Let me explain why I think it is important.

8.3 Humanitarian heroes fettered by legal niceties?

There are, as I have stated, two quite distinct kinds of reasons the US and its allies might have for not wanting to take international law too literally. Reasons of the first kind – call them humanitarian – derive from their moral commitments: the rules of international law constrain how they may aid and protect foreigners in mortal danger. Reasons of the second kind – call them self-interested – derive from what is euphemistically called their national interest: the rules of international law often constrain these governments in their pursuit of their security and foreign-policy objectives. Selective subversion of the rules – especially those constraining the use of military force – would benefit them by reducing these constraints. To be sure, such subversion might also encourage other states to use military force more freely. But the US (with its NATO and other military allies) has managed to increase its military and economic dominance so much that a subversion of the constraints on the conduct of states is bound to benefit it on balance. It has far more to gain from its own freer use of military force world-wide than it has to lose from a freer use of military force by other, regional powers (China, Russia, India, Indonesia, etc.) in their own areas. In most cases, in fact, it can effectively deter or contain any unwelcome freer use of force by others.

It can hardly be surprising that those who favor subverting the legal rules against the use of force – or the replacement of the existing "idiot rules" by "sophist rules"[312] – emphasize humanitarian over self-interested reasons. And in a world full of humanitarian disasters, these reasons do indeed deserve careful attention. However, these reasons must be judged by the correct criterion. The question is not: what additional human suffering *could* the US and its allies avert if international law gave them a freer hand to use military force abroad? Rather, the correct question is: what additional human suffering *would* the US and other states avert *and produce* if international law gave them a freer hand to use military force abroad? Annan's hypothetical bears on the first, irrelevant question. The actual story of the Rwandan genocide bears on the second, highly relevant question.

Annan and Franck make the plea that we should not be too attached to legal niceties when there are humanitarian heroes out there – statesmen willing and able to mobilize their peoples to sacrifice blood and treasure to free others from mortal danger. I agree wholeheartedly. And yet, this conditional injunction is quite irrelevant so long as its antecedent is false. There are no such humanitarian heroes out there. Minor exceptions aside, the people who govern us and determine our foreign policy and the people they appoint to run the UN show monstrous indifference to mortal dangers encountered by those who are not citizens of our countries. The Rwanda episode shows this. The French made clandestine deliveries of heavy weapons (some of which were confiscated by UNAMIR) and provided military training to the Rwandan army in early 1994.[313] In June and July of 1994, the French conducted a military "Operation Turquois" which rescued the genocidal Rwandan government from total military defeat at the hands of the RPF by establishing a safe area, in which the slaughter of Tutsis continued for a time, and by evacuating various leading figures of the genocide to the Democratic Republic of Congo.[314] The Belgians recalled their UNAMIR contingent as the genocide began, abandoning 2,000 to certain slaughter (see endnote 304). The US tried hard to suppress the word "genocide" and to reduce UNAMIR's cost and troop strength. Kofi Annan shackled UNAMIR in accordance with US preferences, instructing it to protect only "foreign nationals." And our governments still hold Rwanda responsible for servicing Western loans that enabled the murderous Habyarimana regime to arm and organize its supporters for genocide.[315]

Now one may well think that the genocide in Rwanda posed an unusually difficult challenge, as the political costs of involvement were not clearly foreseeable and potentially considerable (as illustrated by the botched US operation in Somalia the year before). But other chapters (especially 2, 3, and 7) in this book cast considerable doubt on the hypothesis that the affluent Western states and, in particular, their governments, foreign ministers, diplomats, and international negotiators are significantly motivated by humanitarian concerns. The best explanation of why our states did nothing to stop the genocide, and in fact facilitated the slaughter by undermining UNAMIR at every turn, is that we, as states, do not care about what happens to people in Rwanda and, for that matter, to poor people outside our own Western circle.

There are no humanitarian heroes among those who exercise power in our names. This is why we are treated to a purely *hypothetical* example. This imagined case appeals irresistibly to the good sense and morality of any person whose humanity has not been thoroughly corrupted. Yes of course, we exclaim, the law (and much else) may and *must* be set aside to save 800,000 people from being hacked to death merely because they are Tutsis or want to live in peace with them. But when the lesson is accepted and the plain meaning of the Charter set aside as unworthy of defense, it is not the good sense of Thomas Franck and us citizens that will fill the vacuum. Rather, outcomes will then be determined by the "good sense" of those whose humanity *has been* corrupted through their ascent to national office, through their power, and through the adversarial character of their role: by the good sense of people like Clinton, Albright, and Annan, who enabled the genocide in Rwanda, by the good sense of people like George W. Bush, Dick Cheney, and Donald Rumsfeld, who use the language of human rights and liberation to justify interventions aimed at enhancing US control of the world's oil reserves.[316]

A study of the overt and covert violence such politicians have employed – and regularly rationalized as humanitarian – in the period since World War II, say, cannot sustain the belief that their forceful interventions do more good than harm.

And there is a further important reason against giving them a freer hand. As smaller states feel increasingly threatened, they will redouble their efforts to protect themselves by acquiring nuclear arms and comparable weapons of mass destruction. (The world has paid a high price for the US "victories" in Afghanistan and Iraq, as these involved accepting Pakistan and India as nuclear powers.) There is decisive moral reason, then, to oppose the suggestions by Annan and Franck in favor of supporting respect for the plain meaning of the UN Charter.

8.4 The jurying model

Franck, by contrast, approves and encourages an increasingly significant role of the UN Security Council in determining whether particular violations of international law matter and, if so, how much:

> In situations of armed intervention, representatives argue the validity of facts alleged by those initiating recourse to force, assess the proportionality of the action taken in relation to the evidence of extreme necessity, and debate the motives of the parties to the dispute. Eventually, they decide. Sometimes – more like a grand jury – they decide not to take any action. Does the record of this process demonstrate a credible assay at institutional "jurying" sufficient to justify the codification of exceptions to article 2(4) of the Charter? Probably not. On the other hand, the process, as it has developed in the practice of the Security Council, may embody elements of another jurying function: applying the law – or selectively *not* applying it – in such a way as to narrow the gap between the strictures of strict legality and the importunings of popular moral intuition.[317]

Is such "jurying" by governments, as exemplified in the UN Security Council, a promising model for how to reconcile the law with "widely shared moral values"?[318]

Franck is right to stress that it is very important that states should have the assurance that claims they make by appeal to international law will be fairly adjudicated. But I am far more skeptical than he is about "jurying" by governments. The basic dilemma I see is this. Fairness centrally requires an adjudication process that is unaffected by power differentials among the disputants.[319] Domestic juries come close to this ideal: jurors have no outside relationship with the parties appearing before them prior to or after their verdict, and their deliberations are not affected by power differentials among themselves.[320] A jury of states lacks all of these features and is highly susceptible to undue influence by the strong.

To be sure, there can be credible jurying – resulting in a morally plausible assessment of a rule violation – within the Security Council and the General Assembly when nothing much is at stake for the great powers. The removals of Idi Amin and Emperor Bokassa are examples of this. But as great-power stakes rise, so do the discrepancies between the jury's reaction on the one hand and facts and morality on the other. For a full decade after Pol Pot's genocidal regime had been overthrown by Vietnamese forces, his Khmer Rouge – still active and posing a threat within Cambodia – retained Cambodia's seat at the UN. This was achieved by intense lobbying by the Reagan and Thatcher governments, which also got Cambodia barred from all international trade and communications agreements and cut off from all development aid through the UN and its agencies (such as the WHO), even while Pol Pot's forces received UN World Food Program aid (as well as considerable financial support from the US).[321]

Or consider Franck's report that "[b]enign silence greeted . . . America's air strike against the Sudan [on August 20, 1998] . . . after the destruction of US embassies in Dar-es-Salaam and Nairobi [on August 7, 1998] by the forces of Osama bin-Laden."[322] Perhaps there was indeed such silence in the deliberative forums of the UN. At least the US easily managed to block a UN investigation of the destroyed Al-Shifa pharmaceutical plant in Khartoum, which it claimed was producing nerve gas and other chemical or biological weapons.[323] But was benign silence justified? The evidence to date overwhelmingly suggests that the Al-Shifa pharmaceutical plant – not to speak of the nearby sugar and candy factory that was also hit and destroyed – produced no weapons of any sort and also had no ties to Al Qaeda or any other terrorist organization. Sued by Al-Shifa's owner, Saleh Idris, for return of $24 million of his money frozen by the US Treasury Department, the US had every opportunity to make its case in court.[324] Instead, the US authorized the full and unconditional release of Idris's assets just before the deadline set by the court (May 3, 1999). The US has made no effort to make good for the destruction of the factory or for the severe shortages this destruction has caused. (The Al-Shifa plant covered most of the pharmaceutical needs of the Sudanese people and their livestock.) The case does not reveal, then, an "increasingly credible capacity for fact-finding"[325] or an "innate human receptivity to moral considerations"[326] in those who participate in the relevant deliberations at the UN.

Let me give one last example of jurying under pressure, with something at stake for a great power. When Yemen voted, in 1990, against UN Security Council Resolution 678 authorizing the attack on Iraq, a senior American diplomat, caught on an open microphone, told the Yemeni ambassador: "That will be the most expensive 'no' vote you ever cast." The US stopped $70 million in aid to Yemen; other Western countries, the IMF, and World Bank followed suit. Saudi Arabia expelled some 800,000 Yemeni workers, many of whom had lived there for years and were sending urgently needed money to their families.[327] Similar pressure was later brought to bear on Ecuador and Zimbabwe as they joined the Security Council at the beginning of 1991. And similar pressure was brought to bear on Security Council members in the winter of 2002–3, when the US was once again seeking support for resolutions on Iraq.[328] When much is at stake for a great power, then weaker states are anything but "largely unencumbered."[329] Rather, they are subject to extremely heavy pressures and inducements from stronger states to vote "the right way."

So long as states are self-interested and very unequal in power, the outcomes of any realistically conceivable jurying process will reflect the existing power imbalance. Any such process will be unfair, though it may also of course involve a heavy dose of fairness rhetoric. In the present era, this unfairness benefits especially the US, which, through arm-twisting of and side payments to jury members, as well as through the threat of marginalizing the jury by non-compliance, can generally get the verdicts it wants.

To be sure, the US and Britain failed to win Security Council authorization for their 2003 invasion of Iraq. This may be adduced to show that jurying can work. In Franck's words:

> the Security Council, however obsolete its composition, does work. When only 4 of its 15 members were willing to approve our invasion of Iraq, the Council was working exactly as intended. It sent us a clear message that, if there were indeed weapons of mass destruction in Iraq, they could be found and dismantled by the most intrusive system of international inspections ever devised. Nothing found by the invading forces in Iraq has proven this wrong. The system also cautioned us that the world could not tolerate one powerful nation unilaterally determining when to occupy another nation and reorganize its society. It warned that thousands, perhaps hundreds of thousands, of innocents might be sacrificed at the altar of such unipolar ambitions. And it expressed skepticism at the unilateralists' claim that America could succeed in imposing its democracy on the Shiites and Sunnis of the Middle East as it had once done in Shinto Japan.[330]

Yes, the Security Council acted well in refusing to authorize this invasion by its most powerful member. And yet, it quickly fell into line, cooperating with the invader, giving moral support and recognition to the new Iraqi authorities installed by the US, condemning any resistance to the occupation, and urging everyone to help clean up the mess.[331] Appealing to Franck's view that "the mildness of its disapprobation of India's [unauthorized and illegal] intervention in the civil war leading to the creation of Bangladesh" reflected the Security Council's appreciation of the moral legitimacy of India's 1973 intervention, the Bush administration can thus argue that the mildness (or rather *absence*) of Security Council disapprobation of the unauthorized and illegal 2003 invasion of Iraq reflects its appreciation of the (even greater) moral legitimacy of this US invasion. Yet it is rather obvious that the lack of disapprobation of the 2003 invasion of Iraq has little to do with its moral legitimacy, and much with the need to maintain good relations with the world's overwhelmingly dominant military and economic superpower (not to speak of the veto powers wielded by the US and UK).

The kind of jurying Franck approves and encourages is not then of much help for bridging the gap between law and widely shared moral values. The reason is that the interests and conduct of the strongest members of the jury diverge far more from widely shared moral values than the text of the UN Charter. Preserving Cambodia's seat at the UN for the genocidal Khmer Rouge was not required by morality or by the UN Charter, but by the interests of the US and UK governments. Ever-expanding settlements in the territories occupied by Israel violate international law and widely shared moral values, yet are nonetheless condoned by the UN Security Council, its earlier resolutions (242 and 338) notwithstanding. The destruction of the Al-Shifa plant violated international law, and widely shared moral values demand that US claims about it being a chemical weapons factory should be investigated; but at the UN such an investigation was rejected and the episode passed over in "benign silence."

My judgment is not that in UN Security Council jurying, when the stakes are high, the moral values of a few strong states prevail over the moral values of the rest. The moral values of the developed West also militate against seating the Khmer Rouge, against Israel's settlement policy, and against the refusal to investigate the Khartoum bombing. What prevails in such cases is the proclaimed national interest of the strongest states as defined by their political and business elites.

8.5 How to think about improving the international legal order

Let me close with a general, more philosophical thought. Normative discussions of humanitarian intervention often suffer from a lack of clarity concerning what exactly is being debated. This happens, because the questions posed – such as, "Under what conditions is humanitarian intervention legitimate?" – look deceptively simple and yet can be interpreted in several different ways. The various questions produced by these interpretations do not merely have different answers. They may raise quite different normative and empirical issues and may therefore require diverse investigations and reflections.

Let me here focus just on the most important ambiguity. It concerns the status of the criterion for judging whether any humanitarian intervention is justified. In thinking about moral justification, we might look for the *ideal criterion* that (as it were) God should use in assessing military interventions. Here God is conceived as a distant observer who, at the end of history perhaps, judges all that happens, but whose judgments are unknown and inconsequential and thus have no effect on the course of history. Alternatively, we might be thinking about the criterion we would want to be in public use: enshrined in international law, appealed to by states, by the UN Security Council, and by other international agencies, and prevalent in world public opinion. Such a *public* criterion may well have a strong feedback effect on the course of history by influencing what military interventions are undertaken and how they are justified and conducted. And it makes sense, therefore, that certain exceptions that we think God would recognize should nonetheless be kept out of this public criterion when including them would, through false appeals, do much more harm than good.[332]

Against this background, my response to Franck is this. A literal reading of the UN Charter is indeed a poor criterion for God to use as the basis for judging, at the end of time, the conduct of politicians. But the rules of the Charter were never meant for this role. They were meant to be plausible rules by which fallible and corrupt politicians would be called to account by their foreign peers as well as by their compatriots and the media. If we take this to be their purpose, then the analogue to section 3.02 of the US *Model Penal Code* which Franck cites for emulation – "Conduct that the actor believes to be necessary to himself or another is justifiable, provided that . . . the harm or evil sought to be avoided by such conduct is greater than that sought to be prevented by the law defining the offense charged"[333] – is a recipe for disaster. In the international arena, even as Franck envisions it, there is no effective court in which a state would have to show that it sincerely and reasonably believed that its conduct would avoid more harm than it produced. With such a rule, then, the say-so of the strong prevails. This is good for the US, and for Russia and China perhaps. But it adds insult to injury for the weak by covering with a veneer of legal legitimacy the military interventions and threats thereof they so often suffer.

International relations are characterized by great inequalities of power, great moral corruption of those in power (in the poor countries no less than in the rich), high stakes, and the absence of effective mechanisms of binding adjudication. In such a context especially, the optimal public rules are not ones that instruct agents to do what they believe is optimal or ones under which a military operation becomes legitimate merely because it is approved by some group of governments.

I conclude that marginalizing international law in favor of Security Council jurying is a terrible idea and a terrible reality – considerably worse, in the world as it is, than maintaining respect for the plain meaning of the UN Charter.

Still, even strict adherence to the Charter is hardly ideal, and so we should ask whether there is a *superior* alternative that is both feasible and reachable from where we are.

Progress requires reform on two fronts. Most importantly, we need on the international level an effective judicial organ for the authoritative interpretation and adjudication of international law – in real time if needed. Only judges, who have tenure and a secure commitment to international law and to the UN, and who must explain and justify their decisions in writing, can possibly render verdicts that are largely unencumbered by the distribution of power. And even this is doubtful in situations where they have reason to believe that a great power will, in response to an unwelcome verdict, simply withdraw from international legal adjudication altogether.[334] In such a situation, judges may feel that the law is best served by bending it in favor of the powerful in order to keep them on board.

If the authoritative interpretation and adjudication of international law were in the hands of an effective and reliable judicial organ capable of quick decisions, then it would make sense to contemplate revisions to the UN Charter that, in particular, broaden the conditions under which military interventions are permitted. Appropriately revised rules might envision that states may conduct a military intervention against a country so long as two conditions are both satisfied:

1 This Court has found that genocide or other crimes against humanity are being perpetrated in the country or that this country poses a
serious security risk to others or fails to comply with its obligations
under the *Treaty on the Non-Proliferation of Nuclear Weapons* or
similar legal constraints governing weapons of mass destruction.

2 The military intervention has not been forbidden either by the UN Security Council or by a supermajority of the UN General Assembly.

This proposal has some chance of solving the problems Franck finds in the strict application of the present UN Charter text. It enables states to respond forcefully to grave crimes and dangers abroad. And it does not subject such a response to a veto by any one permanent member of the UN Security Council. Although it relaxes the constraints on the use of military force in this way, the proposal also provides three powerful safeguards against abuse: The decision about whether a *casus belli* exists is made by a judicial body on the basis of a non-political evidence assessment that must be justified in writing. The authority to make war pursuant to such a court decision can be rescinded by either the Security Council or by a supermajority of the General Assembly – also on political grounds, because they prefer the intervention to be undertaken under UN auspices, for example, or because they believe an intervention to be counterproductive or excessively dangerous.

This proposal, too, faces serious problems. Its practicability requires that great powers do not withdraw from or violate the rules or threaten to do so in order to bend the judges to their will. This in turn requires that their own populations develop a serious commitment to international law, so that a government that quits or violates the regime would incur a substantial loss in domestic legitimacy. This goal seems far off.[335]

Difficult also is the task of reaching detailed agreement on such a revision of the UN Charter. The fundamental dilemma is that, to be fair, rules and their adjudication must treat disputants evenhandedly, without fear or favor induced by power differentials among them. But stronger parties have prudential incentives to hold out for rules and adjudication procedures that favor themselves over weaker parties. This in turn gives the weaker parties incentives to accede to such an unfair regime, because they have far more to lose than the strongest do from the absence or erosion of rules and of authoritative adjudication.

In a world of enormous inequalities in power, there exist then strong prudential pressures against the creation of fair rules and adjudication procedures – pressures toward a regime that is officially rigged in favor of the more powerful states (by giving them veto powers, as in the UN Security Council, or extra votes, as in the World Bank and IMF) and that, even insofar as it is facially neutral, is tilted toward the strong in its application. (Security Council jurying as endorsed by Franck displays both these features as exemplified by great-power vetoes, on the one hand, and by arm-twisting and side payments, on the other.)

It seems unlikely that these pressures can be overcome in the near future, which will be dominated by the US as sole superpower. There may be a better chance by mid-century, when China will be a substantial counterweight to the US and may give the US more of a prudential reason to allow a genuine rule of law to emerge on the international level. At least until then, the humanitarian concerns Franck so eloquently invokes are unlikely to have much influence on state conduct unless there is a substantial moralization of the citizenries of the developed countries.

9

Creating Supranational Institutions Democratically: Reflections on the European Union's "Democratic Deficit"

9.0 Introduction

There are two distinct democratic deficits in the emerging European Union. On the one hand, ordinary citizens of the EU have very little meaningful influence on the political decisions made in their name by the centralized organs and agencies, such as the European Commission, the Council of Ministers, and the European Parliament. Having produced some public expressions of discontent and alienation ("Euro-fatigue"), this problem has been discussed quite extensively, and various proposals have been made by politicians, Eurocrats, and academics for how EU institutions can be made more user-friendly. This elite debate highlights the second problem: ordinary citizens of the EU have had very little meaningful influence on the designing of the emerging European institutions, which have been shaped and modified by a small politico-bureaucratic elite. And this elite decides, quite undemocratically, what sorts of democratizing modifications they are going to implement in order to reduce public hostility to their opaque and undemocratic rule. This chapter addresses only this second democratic deficit in institutional designing.[336]

Some terminology may help clarify the issue. By a *political* decision, I mean any legislative, executive, judicial, or administrative decision that is authoritative for (or within) some comprehensive social system (such as a city, province, state, association of states, etc.). We can then define a sequence of *types* of political decisions.[337] By *everyday* or *first-order* political decisions, I mean any political decisions that are *not* about political decision-making, i.e. not about where, how, when, and by whom political decisions are to be made.[338] By *second-order* political decisions, I mean any political decisions that are about first-order political decision-making, i.e. about where, how, when, and by whom everyday political decisions are to be made. *Third-order* political decisions are then decisions about second-order political decision-making, and so on up. The two democratic deficits I have introduced at the beginning can now be clarified as follows. The first democratic deficit concerns the lack of democratic participation in first-order political decision-making for the EU. Here one is looking for appropriate second-order political decisions that would make the political institutions of the EU more democratic. The second democratic deficit concerns the lack of democratic participation in second-order political decision-making for the EU. This chapter focuses on this second democratic deficit, seeking appropriate third-order political decisions that would make the ongoing *shaping* of the EU's political institutions more democratic.[339]

9.1 The Maastricht verdict of the German Constitutional Court

To help clarify the issues involved, let us briefly examine the German Maastricht Verdict, which is the most elaborate official attempt to date to show the compatibility of European integration with the principle of democracy. The German Constitutional Court was asked to judge the constitutionality of Germany's ratification of the *Maastricht Treaty*[340] and of various related amendments to Germany's *Basic Law*.[341] The 1992 *Maastricht Treaty* is the defining document of the modern European Union. It transformed the bond among European countries from a traditional, narrow economic community into a wide-ranging political union establishing a common foreign policy, common citizenship, and multinational financial policy instruments (eventually the Euro). It involved an unprecedented transfer of power from sovereign national governments to international bodies, and, naturally, was fiercely contested at the time. The German Maastricht Verdict encapsulates the struggle within that country over accession to the treaty.

Of the various constitutional challenges that two separate complainants raised in the German Constitutional Court against the treaty, only one need interest us here.[342] This challenge invokes the democracy requirements of Articles 20 and 38 of the *Basic Law*, whose relevant passages read as follows:

> All state authority emanates from the people. It is exercised by the people in elections and referenda and through special legislative, executive, and judicial organs.[343]

> The deputies to the German Bundestag are elected in universal, direct, free, equal, and secret elections. They are representatives of the whole people, not bound by orders and instructions, and subject only to their conscience.[344]

The challenge is that these requirements[345] rule out the kind of transfers of sovereign powers from organs of the Federal Republic to organs of the European Union that are specifically envisioned in the *Maastricht Treaty* and specifically authorized through the new amendments[346] of the *Basic Law*.

The German Constitutional Court found this challenge admissible only insofar as it appeals to Article 38 and only insofar as it challenges the ratification of the *Maastricht Treaty* (171).[347] These findings are strange and convenient. The first finding is strange, because Article 38 alone (detached from Article 20) would seem to have no relevance to the case at all, while Article 20 (even without Article 38) would seem to be highly pertinent.[348] The first finding is convenient, because Article 20 belongs to the immutable core of the *Basic Law* which must not even be touched ("berührt") through changes in the *Basic Law*, let alone be altered or revoked.[349] The second finding is convenient, because, having found the challenge to the constitutional changes inadmissible, the Court could then liberally appeal to the new constitutional provisions in defense of the constitutionality of ratification of the *Maastricht Treaty* (e.g., pp. 182, 208, 211f.).

The Court responded elaborately (pp. 181–212) to the narrow challenge it found admissible. It laid down that, to be constitutional, transfers of tasks and powers from the Bundestag must not empty out citizens' capacity through elections to legitimate and to influence the exercise of state authority (181–7; cf. also 155, 171f.). The Court clarified this requirement by drawing out some of its implications – among them the following four:

1 The German Bundestag must retain tasks and powers of substantial weight (p. 186).

2 The Federal Republic must retain the power to renounce membership in the European Union and to reject further steps toward integration (p. 190; cf. pp. 203f.).

3 As the tasks and powers of the European Union expand, there is a growing necessity ("wächst die Notwendigkeit") that citizens be able to legitimate and influence the exercise of sovereign powers not merely through their national parliaments but also through a European parliament (p. 184).[350]

4 So long as it is mainly by electing the German Bundestag that German voters are exercising their right to participate in the democratic legitimation of the institutions and organs that exercise sovereign powers, any powers transferred elsewhere must be sufficiently determinate ("hinreichend bestimmbar") to make clear what tasks and powers have been transferred (pp. 187f.).

The Court then concluded that the European Union constructed by the *Maastricht Treaty* does, for now, satisfy its requirement as specified.

One can find fault with this reasoning in two ways. On the one hand, one may claim that the European Union does not – by design or as a matter of practical politics – satisfy the Court's requirement. In this vein, Gustavsson argues persuasively that it would be very difficult in practice for the German Bundestag to renounce membership in the European Union and that the European Central Bank will not be subject to any national or European democratic control.[351] On the other hand, one may criticize as too weak the requirement laid down by the Court, on the ground that it permits German citizens to become, to a substantial extent, subject to governmental organs and agencies over which they can exercise no meaningful democratic control.

As discussed thus far, the Maastricht Verdict is concerned with (what I have called) the first democratic deficit: with the undemocratic character of the emerging European Union. Let us now look at the Court's response to the second democratic deficit: the undemocratic nature of Germany's accession to the European Union. The Court rejected this challenge as inadmissible on the basis of an exceedingly brief half-page argument (p. 180) that lacks even a rudimentary understanding of the challenge. This is surprising, because the Court does a rather better job in summarizing this challenge (pp. 169f.) as follows. The *Maastricht Treaty* ought not to have been ratified without legitimation by the German people (p. 170). By expanding the tasks and competencies of the European Union, the (German) legislature is arrogating to itself powers that belong solely to the people as the subject of constitutive power (p. 169). What is being challenged here is evidently not the constitutionality of what the *Maastricht Treaty* will bring about. For the result of this treaty is that the German legislature will have *reduced* powers – hardly a case of "arrogating powers to itself." What is being challenged, rather, is the German legislature's arrogating to itself the power (or "meta-power") of transferring some of the powers vested in it by the German people to other agencies of its choice. This challenge appeals to the immutable principle of Article 20(2): since all state authority emanates from the people, its elected representatives are not entitled to institute deep changes in how the people exercise their power without securing the people's consent.

To see the force of this challenge, imagine for a moment a slightly different scenario. Imagine that the Bundestag (with consent by the Bundesrat) had altered the *Basic Law* so as to convert Germany into a British-style parliamentary system with winner-takes-all electoral districts and a hereditary monarch. The German Constitutional Court could probably comfortably defend the revised *Basic Law* (the *result* of the alteration) as consistent with its immutable core. But could it defend *the alteration itself* as effected by a legislature that leaves the people – from whom all state authority supposedly emanates – no legal way of blocking it? That such a dramatic change would be unconstitutional is particularly probable in light of the fact that Article 20(2) specifically provides for democratic participation by the people to be exercised not merely through elections, which (directly or indirectly) determine the composition of the legislative, executive, and judicial organs, but also through referenda.[352]

The German Constitutional Court wholly missed the point and construed the objection as arguing that the immutable core of the *Basic Law* can be changed only through a referendum. To this absurd objection the Court responded, predictably, that this core cannot be changed at all and that the absence of a referendum is therefore irrelevant. The amendments and German membership in the Maastricht Union are either consistent with the immutable core (and then beyond the need for a referendum) or inconsistent with it (and then beyond rescue through a referendum). True enough. But this does not answer the challenge to the constitutionality of the *adoption* of the amendments and the *accession* to the Maastricht Union, both of which were effected by elected politicians alone, without the people's consent.[353]

I conclude that, through its Maastricht Verdict, the German Constitutional Court has colluded with the German legislature in undermining the democratic powers that the immutable core of the *Basic Law* has reserved to the German people. This undermining has two aspects. First, important sovereign powers are, and will be, exercised over the German people by organs of the EU which lack democratic accountability. The undemocratic exercise of such sovereign powers – the first democratic deficit – plainly touches, and indeed violates, the principle that all state power emanates from the people. Second, important changes in how the German people are governed have been effected without the consent of the German people. Such undemocratic transformations – the second democratic deficit – also touch, and indeed violate, the principle that all state power emanates from the people. They do so in just the same way as the *Ermächtigungsgesetz* of the German Reichstag had done in 1933.[354]

One might think that the end of European unification is grand enough to justify the means, which is a violation of the plain meaning of the immutable democracy requirement of Article 20(2). I believe, however, that this means was not necessary to achieve that noble goal. The first democratic deficit was avoidable in that democratic accountability of the relevant organs of the EU to the German people could have been assured by giving real oversight powers to a European parliament. This possibility is quite evident. It is much harder to show that the second democratic deficit was also avoidable. Of course, prospective member states could have held national referenda, and some of them did, about whether or not to join up. But such referenda give the people only a simple binary choice. Was it possible to do better – to afford the people a meaningful role in designing European institutions? The remainder of this chapter seeks to make a start in this direction.

9.2 Why the people allegedly cannot play a role in shaping political institutions

It is a favorite view among politicians and experts that a democratic shaping of political institutions is impossible, and that they themselves are therefore called upon to do the job. Three main arguments are offered for this alleged impossibility. The first claims that the creating of new political institutions is unlikely to be accomplished if the people are allowed to debate and decide about competing proposals. In this vein it is said that the United States would never have come into being if the small elite group gathered at the Philadelphia Constitutional Convention of 1787 had not decisively exercised a self-proclaimed authority to set aside the Articles of Confederation. James Madison, under the pseudonym of Publius, defended this decision as follows: "[S]ince it is impossible for the people spontaneously and universally to move in concert towards their object . . . it is therefore essential that such changes be instituted by some *informal and unauthorized propositions*, made by some patriotic and respectable citizens."[355] I will argue that, if the integration of Europe were indeed the people's object, they could move toward this object – though perhaps not "spontaneously." I also believe that a better European Union would have emerged, and more quickly, if the people had been allowed a greater role. We will be better able to evaluate these claims after I have laid out some proposals for the democratic designing of (democratic) political institutions.

The second argument affirms that there is, for societies under given historical conditions, only one best – fully just and optimally efficient – scheme of political institutions. It matters that this scheme be approximated as closely as possible; and experts will be much better able to accomplish this task than ordinary people (whose views on everyday political issues may of course be sought, once fully just political institutions are in place). This claim seems rather implausible in view of the large variety of democratic political institutions that have evolved in this world to date. To be sure, all of these democratic orders have flaws and many have great faults indeed. Still, correcting such faults and flaws will hardly lead to convergence on one best option, or even a few, for a given set of historical conditions. It is rather implausible, for example, that there is one best form and degree of political decentralization for the states of contemporary Europe – so that the political systems of Switzerland, Germany, Britain, and France, say, all ought to be reformed toward this correct point in the multidimensional (de-)centralization space. It is even more implausible that there should be but one correct composition and structure for a European Union. Justice and efficiency do constrain the structure of democratic institutions, of course, but they also leave important parameters undetermined. And these, at least, should be settled democratically, or so I will argue.

The third argument asserts that the very idea of a democratic shaping of political institutions is deeply incoherent. Designing political institutions democratically presupposes that we already have democratic political institutions governing the design process. But this leads either into a vicious circle (the design is to be produced by the very procedures it is yet to design) or to an infinite regress (political procedures$_1$ are to be designed pursuant to democratic procedures$_2$ which are to be designed pursuant to democratic procedures$_3$ which are to be designed . . . ad infinitum).

In response, I propose to halt the regress on the third level. It is current practice that national politicians and experts shape the EU's political institutions (which may then allow the citizens of the EU a certain measure of participation). My proposal provides that national politicians and experts should instead design a procedure that allows EU citizens a certain measure of participation in designing the political institutions of the EU. That is to say, the contribution of politicians and experts to the designing of Europe's political institutions should be confined mainly to third-order political decisions. I say "mainly" for two reasons. Experts and politicians are also citizens, and thus entitled to participate with the rest of us in second-order political decision-making. Moreover, by designing the process of second-order political decision-making, such politicians and experts will invariably frame our options and set our agenda in certain ways that are bound to affect the outcome. The key remedy to this problem would seem to be transparency. In contrast to the current second-order decision-making elite negotiating behind closed doors, I propose a third-order decision-making elite whose deliberations and decisions are fully public.

I claim two main advantages for my proposal in comparison to current practice: it gives ordinary citizens an important role in shaping the political institutions of the emerging European Union, while current practice gives them essentially no role at all.[356] This advantage is evident. And third-order decisions, being at two removes from everyday politics, are more likely than second-order decisions to elicit principled reflections and arguments from the politicians and experts charged with making them (especially if their deliberations and decisions are required to be fully public). This advantage is not obvious, and I will therefore try to show how we can begin to think about third-order decisions in a principled way.

This project requires me to switch gears. So far, I have proposed that the role of politicians and experts be confined mainly to third-order political decisions. Now I will imaginatively assume this role of a third-order political decision-maker in order to show how genuinely democratic second-order decision-making can be made possible. I will address this question not in a political way – asking how we might now make the best of an unhappy status quo – but philosophically: asking how EU institutions could have been shaped democratically from the beginning. This question is important not only for philosophy, but also for other regional or global integration projects that might look at the EU as a model. The implications of my ideas for where the EU should go from here are, in any case, relatively straightforward, and I will say something about this topic toward the end.

9.3 The constitutive features of the Union

The constitutive features of a union such as the EU may be grouped under three headings: domain, scope, and procedures. The *domain* of the EU is the spatio-temporal extension of its jurisdiction, which may be defined in terms of its member states, in terms of its territory, and/ or in terms of its citizens. The *scope* of the EU is the extent of its decision-making powers, which may be defined in terms of the kinds of issues over which it has jurisdiction. The *procedures* of the EU are the ways in which it exercises its powers, its ground rules, which define its various legislative, executive, judicial, and administrative organs, agencies, and offices, including how these are staffed and what powers and duties are attached to them.

Our task is to show how a democratic specification of these features is possible. This task runs into the theoretical difficulty presented by the third argument above. It must somehow be settled *who* is going to participate in this democratic specification and also *how* this democratic specification is going to take place – that is to say, we must find a way of settling the analogues of *domain* and *procedures* on the next higher level. Moreover, we must also structure the democratic specification in such a way that the participants – the potential citizens of the EU – face a manageable menu of choices. This task is made considerably more difficult by the fact that persons' preferences concerning the three topics are likely to be interdependent. There is interdependence within each topic: You may believe that Poland should be a member only if Hungary is (domain), or you may approve of a democratically constituted European parliament only if it is checked by a strong European executive (procedure). There is also interdependence across topics. Whether you believe that the populations of smaller countries should have extra weight in democratic procedures may depend on the domain and/or the scope of the EU. Whether you believe that the EU should have an integrated military may depend on the EU's composition and/or on what procedures would govern its common defense policy. Whether you believe that the Eastern European countries should be members of the EU may depend on the EU's scope and procedures. These interdependencies count against the idea of scheduling democratic decisions about the various features one by one, because the outcome of such a sequence of decisions would be likely to depend quite heavily on the order in which the decisions were presented. Yet, it is also impossible to present the decisions together, because the number of meaningfully distinct options would be quite unmanageable: Theoretically, there are several billion ways of determining just the composition of the EU, even if we arbitrarily limit the set of possible members to states that occupy some soil on the European continent. (With 35 such states, the number of possible EU compositions is close to 2^{35} or about 34,000,000,000.) This number must be multiplied with possible settlements for the scope features and the resulting product multiplied again with possible settlements for the procedures features. It may well seem that such enormous complexities require extended face-to-face negotiation among a few political principals supported by their bureaucratic and academic experts – that any hope for a democratic shaping of a European Union is entirely unrealistic.

Still, there are ways of coping with the difficulties and complexities. My proposal is to structure the second-level democratic decision-making into three stages. In Stage One, the citizens of potential member states participate in determining the most basic features of the EU – in particular, its scope. In Stage Two, the citizens of potential member states vote on the composition (domain) of the European Union. In Stage Three, the citizens of the EU participate in determining the remaining features of the EU – its procedures, mainly, and also the remaining questions of scope.

9.3.1 Stage One: the democratic determination of basic scope

The scope of the EU, simply put, answers the question what first-order political decisions the EU will be in charge of. To render this question manageable for democratic decision-making, we may try to employ three simplifications. The first simplification divides the universe of everyday political decisions into fields or kinds. The second simplification selects those kinds of everyday political decisions which, insofar as they are to be made at the EU level at all, should be made there in a way that is binding on all member countries. The third simplification endorses a principle of subsidiarity which provides that kinds of everyday political decisions are to be allocated to the EU level only insofar as they have a significant impact on persons in more than one member state.[357]

The second simplification calls for some comment. The key idea is that there are fields of political decision-making in which some or all member states can decide to cooperate without thereby affecting the basic structure of the EU. Education policy may be one example. In order to construct a functioning EU, we need not decide beforehand whether there will be an integrated educational policy. The following seven-paragraph excursus will explain the point in some detail, using educational policy as the example.

Excursus: fields of discretionary centralization

Suppose that the composition of the EU is already fixed and that the citizens of the EU at large favor a centralized European education system, while the French prefer to retain exclusive control over educational institutions on French soil. Which democratic preference should prevail? In this case, it seems reasonably clear that the preference of the French should prevail. It is instructive to examine the grounds for this result. The structure of educational institutions has a very significant influence on the development of culture within their reach. And it is among the deepest interests of persons to be able to live in a cultural context in whose evolution they can participate and in which they can feel at home. Unwelcome interference with the French education system through Europe-wide regulations would therefore impose very considerable costs upon the French.[358]

On the other side of the ledger, the possible second-order decision by the French to run their own national education system would impose some burden on the rest of the Union, as it would be somewhat harder for non-French EU citizens to gain the requisite qualifications for working and studying in France. But this fact would not give the French an unfair competitive advantage, because French citizens would be similarly handicapped in their efforts to study or work in one of the other EU countries. In fact, the cost to the French might be greater, if other EU countries decided to integrate their education systems even without the French. Non-French EU citizens could then easily move to study or work in most other EU countries, while French citizens could not easily move to any.

The subject matter of education has given us a model decision on the third level (where the allocation of powers to make everyday decisions is settled). Let us call this the *discretionary model* (or *DM*). *DM* provides that the citizens of each nation decide whether everyday decisions about matters of kind X should be made exclusively by themselves for their own country alone or on a higher level by and for a larger electorate.

Some special features of *DM* call for further comment. One is that *DM* allows for asymmetry, as some EU members may choose to participate in a larger integrated education system while others do not. Such asymmetries are, I believe, perfectly feasible and have worked well elsewhere. The Canadian province of Quebec, for example, has opted out of a variety of Canadian federal programs (e.g. the Canadian pension scheme).[359] The United Nations system contains a considerable number of major semi-independent "specialized agencies" participation in which is optional for UN member states.[360]

DM might follow these real-world examples in allowing the basic features of a possible integrated education system to be determined at the center. The EU would decide to offer its members the option of joining the EU education scheme (EUES), perhaps requiring some supermajority for entry and/or exit in order to avoid the cost of frequent switching. Member states could then decide whether to join this and similar schemes through a single national referendum.[361]

When membership has been settled, everyday decisions within the EUES should then be made democratically by the citizens of EUES member states. The citizens of EU countries that have declined to join the EUES are not entitled to participate. They might nonetheless be granted some non-voting representation in the interest of keeping all educational decision-makers well informed about educational policies within the entire EU.

More complex asymmetries might arise, if several groups of EU countries wanted to build different integrated education systems. (Imagine a North-Eastern one, including Austria, Denmark, Finland, Germany, the Netherlands, and Sweden; and a South-Western one, including Belgium, France, Italy, Luxembourg, Portugal, and Spain). *DM* should allow for this possibility, I believe, just as it allows for the possibility of fewer than two countries deciding to join the EUES. In fact, the two possibilities are quite similar. When there are two major supranational education systems within the EU's domain, then neither of them can lay claim to being *the* European system (or EUES). The similarity is then that in both cases the emergence of the EUES is prevented by the overall outcome of the democratic second-order decisions reached within each of the member states.

The subsidiarity principle limits the potential scope of the EU by shielding from its jurisdiction any issues that can be handled better, or as well, at the national level. The discretionary model further limits the potential scope of the EU by leaving under the jurisdiction of its member states various issues on which any subset of them can opt to coordinate or cooperate without unfair harm to the rest. The primary task of Stage One is then to identify and allocate the basic fields of everyday political decision-making that *neither* are shielded by the subsidiarity principle *nor* fit the discretionary model. Let me propose, in a preliminary way, that these fields are the following eight:

(A) *Basic Rights*: Should the EU be in charge of formulating and enforcing a single catalogue of basic rights for all citizens of the EU?

(B) *Economic Justice*: Should there be an EU-wide system of taxes and subsidies designed to eradicate poverty (and perhaps also roughly to equalize standards of living within the EU)?

(C) *Intra-EU Migration*: Should there be one single EU-wide regime governing EU citizens' options for residing, working, studying, and vacationing in EU countries other than their own?

(D) *Intra-EU Trade and Investment*: Should there be one single EU-wide regime governing the flow of goods and capital across the internal borders of the EU?

(E) *EU Financial System*: Should there be a single EU currency whose supply is centrally controlled by an EU central bank?

(F) *EU Environmental Policy*: Should there be an integrated environmental protection regime, formulated and enforced at the EU level?

(G) *EU Security Cooperation*: Should there be an integrated EU defense force politically controlled by the EU executive?

(H) *EU Foreign Policy*: Should there be a unified EU foreign policy in charge of, in particular, negotiating treaties and maintaining diplomatic relations with non-EU countries, regulating temporary and permanent migration (including asylum) into the EU, formulating and administering unified EU economic policies concerning trade and investment across EU borders, representing the citizens of the EU in international organizations and at international conferences, and responding in behalf of the EU citizenry to special events (wars, natural catastrophes, etc.) outside the EU?[362]

My proposal of these eight fields is illustrative and preliminary, because more thorough reflection and discussions might well show that some of these fields should be consolidated or subdivided, or that some further fields should be added or some listed fields deleted (to be handled, perhaps, according to the discretionary model).[363]

Once the list of fields is finalized, the corresponding list of binary questions can be presented to the citizens of the prospective member states for their judgment. Each prospective citizen of the EU is asked to answer about eight straightforward yes/no questions on the understanding

(i)   that the citizens of each country will have a chance to reject membership in the EU through a referendum at Stage Two;

(ii) that fields of first-order political decision-making allocated to the EU will still be subject to the subsidiarity principle, so that countries – and, indeed, provinces and towns – would, for example, be free to formulate basic rights or economic-justice targets that go beyond those set by the EU (cf. endnote 362); and

(iii) that the powers reserved to the EU will be transferred carefully and gradually, once appropriate EU procedures will have been put in place.

After tabulating the results of the poll separately for each country, the outcome of Stage One can be represented in a two-dimensional grid, whose vertical axis lists the populations of the prospective member states and whose horizontal axis lists the eight fields with the corresponding binary questions. Each box within the grid might contain a percentage figure that represents the proportion of yes votes received by a particular question in a particular prospective member state.

9.3.2 Stage Two: the democratic determination of the domain

It is possible, of course, that the judgments returned by the people are highly unsystematic. It is much more likely, however, that these answers would cluster in such a way that some national populations would be more pro-EU than others across most fields and some fields would elicit more approval for centralization across the prospective

EU populations. The main trade-off will then be one between scope and domain: the more fields of first-order political decision-making are included in the scope of the EU, the fewer states are likely to decide to join up. The results of the Stage One poll can help decide how this trade-off might best be made. Countries whose preferences are strongly anti-EU compared to the average should be dropped from consideration, with the understanding that they might join later. And fields with regard to which there was low approval for centralization even in the remaining countries should also be dropped, again with the understanding that they might be added later on. This procedure shrinks the grid in both dimensions, leaving a core of at least moderately pro-EU countries as well as a core of fields that were approved for centralization by most of these countries. Looking at this core grid, we may find that most of the remaining countries are likely to approve the list of the remaining fields, if this list were presented as a package deal. Should this not appear likely (from the Stage One approval figures), then the least approved field(s) may have to be dropped in order to arrive at a plausible package. This package can then be presented to all prospective member states (the full initial list) for a simple binary referendum: "Do you approve of your country joining an EU whose scope is defined by the following fields?"

Things may become a little more complicated at Stage Two, because a country's decision about joining the EU may depend on the decisions made by other countries. Perhaps the Portuguese want to join only if Spain also joins, or only if Iceland does not join, or only if the EU will have some critical minimum size. These problems might be solved by holding the referenda in some appropriate order or by adding a suitable conditional to some countries' referenda ("Do you approve of your country joining an EU whose scope is defined by the following fields, provided that . . . ?"). If there are enough such interdependencies of preferences, or if approvals of fields are not strongly clustered, then it is possible for a plurality of unions to emerge from the set of potential member states. Politicians actually produced such a plurality after World War II with the formation of the EEC, EFTA, and COMECON. Though much less likely, it is possible for democratic decisions to produce a similar result.

This is how it might happen. Suppose that the pro-EU core countries by and large prefer the scope of the EU to include the field of economic justice, but that the more affluent countries of Western Europe want to join such a union only if it excludes the poorer countries of Eastern Europe, which are equally pro-EU and equally in favor of including economic justice in the EU's scope. Under these circumstances, two separate unions might emerge. But it would be preferable, I think, to try other resolutions first. The Western countries might approve the package deal because they care a great deal about achieving a wider centralization in other fields ((A), (F), (H)) or because they are confident that they can use their influence within the EU to define the goal of economic justice modestly or to set a slow pace toward this goal. I believe that some such resolution would probably work in contemporary Europe, and I will thus set the problem aside.

Stage Two fixes then the domain of the EU to be created by producing democratic commitments from some of the European countries to participate in the formation of an EU, whose scope is defined at least vaguely in terms of general fields of centralized political decision-making.

9.3.3 Stage Three: the democratic determination of the procedures

The democratic determinations of Scope and Domain are easier than that of Procedures, where we are faced with a multidimensional array of innumerable options. This complexity must be reduced by politicians and experts to a few main options, or to a few straightforward and mutually independent issues, which can then be submitted to the EU electorate.

This reduction of complexity can start out from the idea that, while the features of Scope and Domain raise entirely new institutional questions, our questions with regard to Procedures are close analogues to ones that already have answers on the state level. To be sure, these answers vary from state to state. Still, the democratic procedures practiced in the EU member states will turn out to have a great deal in common, and reproducing these common features, at least, on the EU level would presumably be widely approved by the EU electorate.

Among the most important common features are the following:

1 The powers of government are separated into three largely independent branches: Legislative, Executive, and Judiciary.
2 The main legislative organ is an assembly or parliament, directly elected by the entire electorate whose votes have approximately equal weight.
3 Candidates for parliament are nominated by political parties, which compete with one another by formulating alternative political programs (and by fielding alternative candidates).

4 At least half of all parliamentary seats are tied to electoral districts and filled by the candidates winning a plurality of votes in such districts. Thus, every locale within the domain has a personal representative in parliament.

5 Parliament has the authority to pass and rescind laws as well as the authority to block or approve appropriations.

6 The main executive organ is a cabinet, consisting of the heads of various ministries – whose functions may coincide roughly with those fields from among (B) through (H) that were approved in Stages One and Two – and chaired by a prime minister.

7 The cabinet is bound by the laws and appropriations passed by parliament and can be dismissed by parliamentary decision (which may require a supermajority).

The existing EU fulfills only some of these features, and with respect to features (5)–(7) departs quite dramatically from the procedures practiced in its member states. The present European Parliament is weak and the governments of member states have substantial powers to block concerted action at the EU level. These governments argue that they must have these powers because they are, after all, democratically elected to represent their constituencies while decision-making at the EU level has only very weak democratic legitimacy (conferred by those EU citizens who have chosen to take part in EU parliamentary elections). But the question is, whose fault is this? The very governments who have denied the EU citizenry a chance to approve (or disapprove) political decision-making on the EU level are now adducing the lack of such approval as a justification for the extraordinary blocking powers they claim. On my proposal, EU-wide collective decision-making would have been explicitly sanctioned by the electorates of the member states, and there would then be no more reason for special veto powers than there is on the national level – if Scotland lacks the power to block British policies or legislation, why should Britain have the power to block EU policies and legislation?

I have proposed one method of reducing complexity in Stage Three: present to the EU citizenry the option of reproducing for the EU the procedural features that its member states share in common. Here is another proposal that would reduce complexity a good deal further. This proposal provides that Stage Three be split into two phases. The first phase is mainly concerned with the constitution of the European legislature, with how its members are elected and how it operates once it is constituted. It will be relatively easy, for politicians and experts, to develop a few main options or a few straightforward and mutually independent questions for this limited subject matter. These options or questions can then be submitted to an EU-wide referendum, and an EU parliament can then be constituted pursuant to the winning procedures. The parliament so constituted could then, in the second phase, work out a proposal, or a few, concerning the precise structure of judicial and executive organs and the precise relations between the three branches of government.[364] When this work is completed, the EU electorate would, once again, have the last word – approving the parliament's proposal, or one of them, or else rejecting it (them) and requiring the parliament to rework it (them) for resubmission.

Since I am proposing to leave the work of the second phase to the EU parliament, let me here say no more about it (though I might have some further ideas, of course, about how members of parliament ought to proceed). But I should say just a little more about the first phase of Stage Three. I understand the fundamental idea of democracy as the moral imperative that political institutions should maximize and equalize citizens' ability to shape the social context in which they live. Let me here leave aside two obvious questions about this imperative. What is its weight in relation to other moral requirements and desiderata? And how should we trade off the two maximands stipulated within the imperative? I will briefly focus, instead, on the idea of political equality. This idea should be understood as requiring, I believe, that it be possible for all social groups of any kind (and especially for minorities) to gain something approaching proportional representation in the legislature. Ideally, any group that constitutes n percent of the electorate should be able to determine the composition of n percent of the legislature.[365] Of course, it is up to the members of the group whether they, or some of them, choose to form a coalition for the purpose of filling a proportionate number of parliamentary seats. But the political process should be so designed that, if (some or all) members of a group choose to form such a coalition, they should be able to send a proportionate number of representatives to the legislature.

This ideal strongly favors institutional designs that involve proportional representation or multi-delegate constituencies. It is much harder to approximate the ideal in a system with winner-takes-all territorial electoral districts – as exemplified in the US and Great Britain – because one must then engage in a highly deliberate, and thus often divisive ("gerrymandering"), shaping and reshaping of electoral districts on the basis of elite anticipations of what groups voters will particularly wish to identify with. Forming a legislature through random sampling is likewise a bad way of implementing the ideal, because most persons do not want to be legislators and would not be good at it anyway (though random sampling might work better than the status quo in many so-called democracies, where legislative corruption is endemic).[366]

I have space to address only two obvious objections to this argument. One opposes the idea of equal treatment for groups of all different kinds. Yes, if gypsies or Italians strongly desire parliamentary representation in proportion to their numbers, they should be able to achieve this goal. But what reason is there to make the same demand with respect to all ethnic, religious, linguistic, lifestyle groups and even with regard to geographically completely dispersed groups such as dentists, dog-lovers, stamp collectors, war widows, socialists, and Porsche drivers? My answer is that some of these imagined possibilities are, for now, quite unrealistic. For the foreseeable future, a just political process may well produce parliamentary representatives of national, ethnic, and religious groups; but it will not produce parliamentary representatives of Porsche drivers and stamp collectors. But I think it is important that this divergence should occur because of the distribution of deep identifications among the citizenry and not because the structure of the political process advantages citizens with some types of deep identifications over citizens with other types of such identifications. If enough citizens share a certain identification and are willing to form a coalition for the sake of securing representation for themselves in the legislature, then they should be able to gain such representation, irrespective of the type of their identification (and of whether they are geographically concentrated or dispersed). If, for some as yet quite unimaginable reason, citizens did develop a desire to be represented in parliament as drivers of a particular type of car, they should be able to implement this desire. This equal treatment of diverse deep identifications is, I believe, required by the ideal of political equality.

The other objection points to the need for a functioning legislature. If parliament is often dysfunctional because it contains too many oddball parties and groupings (late Weimar Republic, present-day Poland), then it will not maximize citizens' ability to shape the social context in which they live. This is why, in many social systems, the ideal will not be attainable *fully*, even with the help of fancy(ful) computer systems. But this problem does not require discriminations among types of groups, because there are neutral ways of reducing the number of represented groups. A society could, for instance, require a minimum number of votes (as exemplified by the German 5 percent hurdle) for parliamentary representation, with the threshold set only as high as necessary to ensure its objective.

9.4 Concluding remarks

It will surely be said that the procedure sketched in this chapter is excessively cumbersome and greatly overtaxes the interest and abilities of the average European. My response is that, if it does, the reason is not any genetic liability of the average European, but the simple fact that Europeans, and citizens generally, have never yet been allowed truly meaningful political participation. They have been excluded from such participation by their rulers: by politicians and judges, for whom democracy seems to have nothing to do with people shaping their own social environment. I am fully convinced that European citizens, if allowed a say, would rise to the occasion, would deliberate carefully about the options presented to them and make good decisions. The project of the EU presents an excellent opportunity for attempting a democratic shaping of democratic political institutions, because there is no pressing emergency demanding quick and decisive action.[367] The European elite has wasted much time on intransparent horse-trading and inefficient bickering. It would have been much better to spend this time on public deliberation and a gradual and careful shaping of our future political institutions, which could have given the EU the kind of birth that we and our progeny would have been able to look back upon with pride. In any case, it is worth reiterating that the complexities involved in my proposal are by no means unmanageable. Citizens would be called upon to participate in about five decisions: the poll about the scope of the projected EU at Stage One, a possible referendum about fields of discretionary centralization, the referendum about the domain of the EU at Stage Two, the referendum about the legislative institutions of the EU in the first phase of Stage Three, and the referendum about the judicial and executive institutions of the EU in the second phase of Stage Three.[368]

It may also be asked: what is the point of discussing how things should have gone, given that things have already transpired quite differently? To this question, I have three answers. My discussion is relevant to the attitude we should take toward the existing EU institutions and to those who have been shaping and are continuing to shape them. Pointing out the opportunities they foreclosed should make us more skeptical about their projects and intentions. My discussion is also relevant to the question where we should go from here. The EU is by no means finished yet, and while some of the roads I have sketched may now be closed for good, others are still open. Thus it is quite possible to submit future changes in the scope of the EU to a referendum, for example, or to reshape the European Parliament so that it accords better with what I have called the fundamental idea of democracy. My discussion is also relevant, finally, to future integrative enterprises in other parts of the world, or even in the world at large. Given the ever-increasing incidence of externalities across national borders, significant supranational integration seems a practical necessity.

Notes

1 In Pogge, *World Poverty and Human Rights*, p. 104, I described such a monument. Built to resemble the Vietnam War Memorial, and listing the names of all those who have died from poverty-related causes since the end of the Cold War, this black granite wall would have to be 480 miles long, stretching from Detroit to New York, perhaps, or from Rome to Vienna. Between the appearance of that book and this later one, my imaginary wall will have grown another 60 miles or so – half a mile per week.

2 Wealth data, for the year 2000, are from Davies et al., *The World Distribution of Household Wealth*, Appendix 1, table 10a. Income data, for the year 2002, were kindly provided by Branko Milanovic (World Bank) and are on file with the author (see below sect. 5.4, table 5.7). Global inequality has sharply increased further in the period leading up to the global financial crisis toward the end of 2008, though accurate figures are not yet available.

3 We should remember, however, that many people in Germany and the occupied territories, like Oskar Schindler, managed – on their own and without taking excessive risks – to protect victims of the violence.

4 This latter death toll is thought to be about 200 million, including 17 and 60 million deaths in World Wars I and II (the concentration camps and gulags included), 30 million deaths in Mao's Great Leap Forward (1958–61), 20 million deaths due to repression under Stalin, 9 million deaths in the Russian civil war (1917–22), 8 million deaths from King Leopold II's brutal exploitation of the Congo Free State (1886–1908), and 6 million deaths in the Korean and Second Indochina (Vietnam) wars.

5 FAO, "1.02 Billion People Hungry"; WHO and UNICEF, *Progress on Drinking Water and Sanitation*, pp. 30 and 7.

6 Fogarty International Center, "Strategic Plan."

7 UN-Habitat, *The Challenge of Slums*, p. vi; UN-Habitat, "Urban Energy."

8 UNESCO Institute for Statistics, "Literacy Topic."

9 See ILO, *End of Child Labour*, p. 6.

10 In 2004, there were about 59 million human deaths. The main causes highly correlated with poverty were (with death tolls in thousands): diarrhea (2,163) and malnutrition (487), perinatal (3,180) and maternal conditions (527), childhood diseases (847 – measles accounting for about half), tuberculosis (1,464), malaria (889), meningitis (340), hepatitis (159), tropical diseases (152), respiratory infections (4,259 – mainly pneumonia), HIV/AIDS (2,040) and sexually transmitted diseases (128) (WHO, *Global Burden of Disease*, table A1, pp. 54–9). To be sure, some deaths from these causes would still have occurred even in the absence of poverty. But these are greatly outnumbered by the contribution that poverty makes to deaths from globally common causes such as cancer, cardiovascular disease, traffic accidents, and violence. It is likely then that rather more than one third of all human lives are substantially shortened by severe poverty.

11 Karwal, *At General Assembly Event.*

12 UNDP, *Human Development Report 2003*, pp. 310–30; UNRISD, *Gender Equality*; Social Watch, *Unkept Promises.*

13 See Chen and Ravallion, "The Developing World Is Poorer than We Thought," p. 45. The World Bank's poverty lines are discussed in depth in chs 3 and 4.

14 Calculated from data supplied by Branko Milanovic (World Bank). See also below sect. 3.4, table 3.4.

15 Data from 2002, supplied by Branko Milanovic (World Bank). Using exchange rate conversion, the top decile had 71.1 percent of global household income versus 0.26 percent for the bottom decile. For more comprehensive data, including from earlier years, see below sect. 5.4, table 5.7, and Milanovic, *Worlds Apart*, pp. 107–8.

16 Davies et al., *World Distribution of Household Wealth*, Appendix 1, table 10a. Many economists find such comparison misleading, claiming that they should instead be made in terms of PPPs, which would reduce these ratios by a factor of about 2.5 (using the new PPPs for 2005, discussed in sect. 4.2 below). However, actual exchange rates are the more appropriate measure for assessing the influence (bargaining power and expertise) that parties can bring to bear. Actual exchange rates are also the appropriate measure for assessing the avoidability of poverty. For comparing standards of living, going exchange rates are indeed inappropriate. But general-consumption PPPs are also problematic for the assessment of very low incomes because the consumption expenditure pattern of the very poor differs greatly from the pattern of international

consumption expenditure on which PPPs are based. This issue receives detailed discussion below in ch. 4.

17 Milanovic, *Worlds Apart*, p. 108.

18 Ibid., see also below sect. 5.4, table 5.7.

19 Sect. 5.4, table 5.6.

20 The European Union, and supranational organizations more generally, are the subject of ch. 9.

21 Rawls's views on the (purely) domestic sources of deprivations are the subject of sect. 2.2.

22 This insight is encapsulated in the remarkable Article 28 of the 1948 *Universal Declaration of Human Rights*, which I discuss in detail in sect. 2.1.

23 Rawls, *Law of Peoples*, p. 37.

24 See Pogge, *World Poverty and Human Rights*, chs. 4 and 6 for a fuller discussion.

25 These points are widely acknowledged by mainstream economists and top officials of the international financial institutions. See, for example, the speech of former World Bank Chief Economist Nick Stern, "Dynamic Development." He stated that in 2002 the rich countries spent about $300 billion on export subsidies for agricultural products alone, roughly six times their total development aid. He said that cows receive annual subsidies of about $2,700 each in Japan and $900 in Europe – far above the annual income of most human beings. He also cited protectionist anti-dumping actions, bureaucratic applications of safety and sanitation standards, and textile tariffs and quotas as barriers to poor country exports: "Every textile job in an industrialized country saved by these barriers costs about 35 jobs in these industries in low-income countries." Stern was especially critical of escalating tariffs – duties that are lowest on unprocessed raw materials and rise sharply with each step of processing and value added – for undermining manufacturing and employment in poor countries, thus helping to "confine Ghana and Côte D'Ivoire to the export of unprocessed cocoa beans; Uganda and Kenya to the export of raw coffee beans; and Mali and Burkina Faso to the export of raw cotton." Full elimination of agricultural protection and production subsidies in the rich countries would raise agricultural and food exports from low and middle-income countries by 24% and total annual rural income in these countries by about $60 billion (about three-quarters of the global poor live in such rural areas) (World Bank, *Cutting*).

26 For 2008, the OECD reports ODA of $119.8 billion (OECD, *Development Aid*), with about $12 billion of this spent on "basic social services" (UN, *Millennium Development Goals Indicators*). For additional detailed aid statistics, see also Shah, *US and Foreign Aid Assistance*.

27 De Córdoba and Vanzetti, "Now What?," table 12, p. 28, calculate annual welfare gains of $135.3 billion for the less developed countries. Cline, *Trade Policy and Global Poverty*, calculates $86.51 billion (table 4.1, p. 180) and, if the dynamic effect on productivity growth is included,

$203 billion (in 1997 dollars, p. 255) associated with a poverty reduction somewhere in the vicinity of 500 million people (table 5.3, p. 252, as slightly revised in a subsequent "Technical Correction to the First Printing"). The World Bank, *Global Economic Prospects 2002*, pp. 168–78, had earlier estimated a poverty reduction of 320 million. Both estimates rely on a definition of poverty in terms of $2.00 PPP 1993, as explained in ch. 4 below.

28 In Thailand, Sanofi-Aventis sold its cardiovascular disease medicine Plavix for 70 baht ($2.20) per pill, some 6000% above the price at which the Indian generic firm Emcure agreed to deliver the same medicine (clopidogrel). See Oxfam, "Investing for Life."

29 For further details, see Hollis and Pogge, *Health Impact Fund*, and subsequent discussion papers available at www.healthimpactfund.org.

30 For a more elaborate discussion of this objection, see Pogge, *World Poverty and Human Rights*, ch. 5.

31 I discuss the problem of terrorism and the "war on terror" in ch. 7.

32 See sect. 1.4 above.

33 With the word "uncompensated," I mean to exempt people like Oskar Schindler (as depicted in Spielberg's movie). Through his manufacturing activities and tax payments, Schindler cooperated in imposing the social institutions and policies of Nazi Germany. But doing this allowed him to compensate (more than adequately) for his contributions to harm through protection efforts for its victims. His conduct complied with the negative duties imposed on him by the human rights of the victims of the Third Reich – no less fully than if he had left Germany. In fact, Schindler did much better by these victims than he would have done by emigrating.

34 The word "reasonably" is meant to acknowledge not merely the limits of human foresight, but also the possibility that the institutional reduction of human-rights deficits might sometimes have high costs in terms of culture, say, or the natural environment. It is best to avoid the claim that human rights must never give way in such cases – certainly in our world, where human rights could be largely or fully realized through institutional reforms that would not entail such high costs.

35 The next three sections are adapted from a longer essay: Pogge, "Severe Poverty as a Human Rights Violation." UNESCO's permission for this adaptation is gratefully acknowledged.

36 Rawls, "Law of Peoples," p. 77.

37 Rawls, *Law of Peoples*, p. 108.

38 Ibid., pp. 37–8, 106–20.

39 World Bank, *World Development Report 2009*, p. 353.

40 Ibid.

41 For a brief, accessible account with examples, see Peterson, "American Sugar Policy." See also endnote 25.

42 The content and impact of TRIPS, noted in ch. 1, are discussed in UNDP, *Human Development Report 2001*, ch. 5; Correa, *Intellectual Property Rights*; Juma, "Intellectual Property Rights"; Watal, "Access to

Essential Medicines"; Pogge, *World Poverty and Human Rights*, ch. 9; Hollis and Pogge, *Health Impact Fund*; Consumer Project on Technology, *CPTech's Page on Intellectual Property Rights*; and World Trade Organization, *TRIPS Material on the WTO Website*.

43 See Reddy and Barry, *International Trade and Labor Standards*.

44 See Pogge, *World Poverty and Human Rights*, p. 131.

45 See Kar and Cartwright-Smith, *Illicit Financial Flows*, pp. iv, 10–11. See also Baker, *Capitalism's Achilles Heel*.

46 See Bennett, *The Act Itself*, for discussion.

47 By "WTO globalization" I mean the kind of globalization that has been pushed by the United States during the last three decades or so, as most clearly manifested in the WTO regime. In the debates about its pros and cons, we should always remember that globalization could have been organized quite differently and could be substantially restructured even now.

48 I explore this question in chs. 3 and 4.

49 See Pogge, "Severe Poverty as a Violation of Negative Duties," pp. 55–8.

50 See National Park Service, *Jim Crow Laws*.

51 See Pogge, *World Poverty and Human Rights*, pp. 143–5.

52 Pogge, "Severe Poverty as a Violation of Negative Duties," p. 61, and cf. endnote 34 on my use of the word "reasonably."

53 Pogge, *Realizing Rawls*, pp. 49–50

54 Karwal, *Call for Equity and Action*.

55 In the middle of the nineteenth century, Great Britain and other Western powers prosecuted a series of "opium wars" against China. The first invasion was initiated in 1839 when Chinese authorities in Canton (Guangzhou) had confiscated and burned opium brought in illegally by foreign traders (Schaffer Library of Drug Policy, *Short History of the Opium Wars*).

56 See Cohen, *History, Labour, and Freedom*, pp. 262–3.

57 For a good start toward such a theory, see Parfit, *Reasons and Persons*, ch. 3.

58 See Pogge, "Severe Poverty as a Violation of Negative Duties," pp. 63–4.

59 The *Convention* came into effect in February 1999 and has been widely ratified since; see www.oecd.org/home.

60 In the United States, the post-Watergate Congress sought to prevent the bribing of foreign officials through its 1977 *Foreign Corrupt Practices Act*, passed after the Lockheed Corporation was found to have paid – not a modest sum to some third-world official, but rather – a $2 million bribe to Prime Minister Kakuei Tanaka of powerful and democratic Japan. Not wanting its firms to be at a disadvantage vis-à-vis their foreign rivals, the US was a major supporter of the *Convention*, as was the non-governmental organization Transparency International, which helped mobilize public support in many OECD countries.

61 Pieth and Ivory, "Honest Corporations."

62 UNDP, *Human Development Report 2007/2008*, pp. 278–80.

63 Lam and Wantchekon, "Dictatorships," p. 31.
64 Ibid., p. 35. See also Wantchekon, "Why Do Resource Dependent Countries Have Authoritarian Governments?."
65 UNDP, *Human Development Report 2007/2008*, pp. 291–3, four rightmost columns.
66 The number of Chinese living below $2.50 per day (2005 purchasing power in the US) has reportedly declined by 36% or 364 million between 1984 and 2005 (Chen and Ravallion, "Developing World," table 7, p. 45).
67 Thanks to the end of the Cold War, military expenditures worldwide have declined from 4.7% of aggregate GDP in 1985 to 2.9% in 1996 (UNDP, *Human Development Report 1998*, p. 197) and to about 2.5% or $1,339 billion in 2007 (SIPRI, "SIPRI Yearbook 2008," p. 10.). Today, this global peace dividend is worth nearly $1,200 billion annually.
68 The World Bank Food Index fell from 139.3 in 1980 to 100 in 1990 and then to 90.1 in 2002. These statistics are published by the World Bank's Development Prospects Group. See World Bank, *Global Economic Prospects 2004*, p. 277. Food prices have risen substantially in 2006–8 (FAO, "The Number of Hungry People Rises").
69 See Pogge, *World Poverty and Human Rights*, ch. 6, for ideas about how to modify the international resource and borrowing privileges. See also Wenar, "Property Rights and the Resource Curse."
70 See Pogge, *World Poverty and Human Rights*, ch. 8, proposing a Global Resources Dividend as such a compensation scheme.
71 Their current governmental effort amounts to $12 billion (2006) in official development assistance (ODA) for basic social services (UN, *Millennium Development Goals Indicators*; accessed June 26, 2009). Private and corporate gifts sustain additional efforts at poverty eradication, primarily through international NGOs and international agencies such as UNICEF and the World Food Program.
72 See ch. 3 below.
73 UNDP, *Human Development Report 2002*, p. 202.
74 For the latest ODA statistics, see OECD, *Development Aid*. Data about recipients (available at OECD, QWIDS) show that Iraq received one-fifth of all ODA in 2005.
75 See Pogge, *World Poverty and Human Rights*, ch. 8. Amazingly, $300 billion is only 0.6% of the global product or 0.8% of the combined GNI of the affluent countries (World Bank, *World Development Report 2009*, p. 353) – considerably less than the annual US military budget (Center for Defense Information, *What Is the "Defense" Budget?*) or the annual "peace dividend" the affluent countries are reaping from the end of the Cold War (see endnote 67).
76 This point has been emphasized by Derek Parfit.
77 *UN Millennium Declaration*, Article 19. This *Declaration* was unanimously adopted without vote by the UN General Assembly on 8 September 2000. The six goals stated in Article 19 of the *Declaration* were subsequently reformulated as eight goals.

78 UNDP, *Human Development Report 1997*, pp. 5, 238.
79 *Rome Declaration on World Food Security*. The US instantly issued an "Interpretive Statement" to the effect that "the attainment of any 'right to food' or 'fundamental right to be free from hunger' is a goal or aspiration to be realized progressively that does not give rise to any international obligations." See ibid., Annex II to the Final Report of the World Food Summit.
80 See UN Population Division, *World Population Prospects*, for comprehensive population statistics.
81 Chen and Ravallion, "The Developing World Is Poorer than We Thought," table 7, p. 44.
82 Ibid., calculated by interpolation.
83 UN Population Division: *World Population Prospects* (accessed 12/22/09). Chen and Ravallion seem to have used slightly different population statistics, but this does not materially affect the calculations.
84 *UN Millennium Declaration*, Article 19.
85 See for instance UN, *Millennium Development Goals Report 2008*, p. 6.
86 Ibid.
87 UN Population Division, *World Population Prospects* (accessed 12/22/09).
88 UN, *Millennium Development Goals Report 2008*, p. 50.
89 Ibid., pp. 20 and 24.
90 *UN Millennium Declaration*, Article 19, emphasis added.
91 Chen and Ravallion, "The Developing World Is Poorer than We Thought," table 7, p. 44.
92 UN, *Implementation*, pp. 8 and 22.
93 Chen and Ravallion, "The Developing World Is Poorer than We Thought," table 7, p. 44; UN Population Division, *World Population Prospects* (accessed 12/22/09).
94 Chen and Ravallion, "The Developing World Is Poorer than We Thought," table 7, p. 44.
95 Pogge, *World Poverty and Human Rights*, endnote 18.
96 "PPP" stands for "purchasing power parity." Another common expression refers to these internationally comparable units of value as "2005 international dollars." A poor country's currency is usually worth much more in international dollars (i.e. converted at PPPs) than it is worth in ordinary dollars (i.e. converted at the going exchange rate). This is so because and insofar as commodities are cheaper in poor countries than the exchange rate of their currency to the US dollar would suggest.
97 Chen and Ravallion, "The Developing World Is Poorer than We Thought," table 7, pp. 44–5.
98 A minus sign in a cell indicates that the poverty headcount has fallen in the column period relative to the row's poverty line.
99 UNDP, *Human Development Report 1997*, pp. 5, 238. One is reminded of Jay Bybee's definition of torture by reference to death or organ failure – to be discussed in ch. 7 below.

100 Talk of eradication survived from the *Rome Declaration* all the way to current MDG-1 monitoring (UN, *Millennium Development Goals Report 2008*, p. 6).

101 It is possible, though, that the PPPs available for one base year are more reliable than those of another – perhaps on account of participation by more countries or more comprehensive price data. If the 2005 PPPs are better in this respect than the 1993 PPPs, say, then they may indeed support a more accurate picture of the 1981–2005 poverty trend.

102 Chen and Ravallion, "The Developing World Is Poorer than We Thought," p. 2.

103 See Ravallion, Chen and Sangraula, "Dollar a Day Revisited," pp. 6–8, 33–9.

104 Chen and Ravallion, "How Did the World's Poorest Fare?" p. 285. The level chosen was actually $32.74 PPP 1993 per person per month.

105 Ravallion, Datt and van de Walle, "Quantifying Absolute Poverty," pp. 348–9. The level chosen was actually $31 PPP 1985 per person per month.

106 Or $30.42 PPP 1985 per person per month. See Chen and Ravallion, "How Did the World's Poorest Fare?" p. 285, n. 7.

107 See Reddy and Pogge, "How *Not* to Count the Poor," table 3.1, showing that the Bank's replacement of $1.00 PPP 1985 with $1.08 PPP 1993 has lowered the IPL in 77 out of 92 countries and by about 24% on average (11% on a population-weighted basis). The impact of the latest substitution of $1.25 PPP 2005 is analyzed in Reddy, "The Emperor's New Suit." Whenever an IPL is replaced by a new one that involves a different base year, the impact on the corresponding national poverty lines varies from country to country (ch. 4 below explains further why this is so).

108 See Bureau of Labor Statistics, *Consumer Price Index*.

109 Ibid.

110 USDA, *Thrifty Food Plan*, p. 2.

111 See Center for Nutrition Policy and Promotion, *Cost of Food at Home*, using June 2005.

112 For some anecdotal evidence, see also Zimmerman, "Dining on a Dollar a Day."

113 The PPPs the Bank uses for the currencies of the various poor countries is available at World Bank, *World Development Indicators Online*: "PPP conversion factor, private consumption (LCU per international $)." This is based on the 2005 PPP for "individual consumption expenditure by households" as listed in World Bank, *Global Purchasing Power Parities*, table 1, pp. 28–37.

114 Figures based on Chen and Ravallion, "The Developing World Is Poorer than We Thought," pp. 27 and 42–6; World Bank, *Global Purchasing Power Parities*, table 3; and *World Development Report 2007*, p. 289.

115 See Center for Defense Information, *What Is the "Defense" Budget?*.

116 See endnote 10 and more generally sect. 1.1 above.

117 Harrison, "Resource Mobilization," p. 184. See also Harrison, *Economics of World War II*, p. 287 *et passim*.

118 The imagined Roosevelt story is wholly contrary to fact. The actual Franklin Roosevelt was committed to defeating completely, with all deliberate speed, not only the Nazi menace but also extreme poverty worldwide. In his State of the Union Address of January 6, 1941, he set forth as a guiding principle for a post-fascist world – to be attained "in our own time and generation" – "freedom from want, which, translated into world terms, means economic understandings which will secure to every nation a healthy peacetime life for its inhabitants – everywhere in the world."

119 One might think that the pledge of the fictional Roosevelt would have been worse because the harm in question was actively caused in violation of negative duties. But this active harming was done by Germans and their allies, without US involvement. So by doing nothing about it, the US would have violated no negative duties. As I argue in the text, if there is an asymmetry, it goes the other way because the US and other affluent states are actively involved in designing and upholding global institutional arrangements that foreseeably aggravate poverty worldwide (see ch. 2 above). Other things being equal, it is worse actively to contribute to harms that could be avoided at low cost than passively to allow harms that could be averted only at high cost.

120 The predatory fishing practices of heavily subsidized European fleets in West African waters are described, for instance, in Lafraniere, "Europe Takes Africa's Fish."

121 The critique of this chapter can straightforwardly be extended also to the UNDP's Human Poverty Index and Gender Empowerment Measure. I only sketch this extension in the endnotes.

122 Recall how the Thrifty Food Plan maintained by the USDA is taking age into account (see text at endnote 111).

123 See Okin, "Poverty," pp. 284–6, 305. The UNDP's Human Poverty Index (HPI) exemplifies an analogous failure when, like nearly all poverty indices, it delinks the data it employs from the individuals whose data they are, thereby ignoring how poverty is distributed by gender and age. This implies that it does not matter morally or for policy formulation whether poverty is suffered disproportionately by females (or any other salient group). This implication is untenable. A severe disadvantage avoidably suffered by many becomes even more unjust when it is suffered disproportionately by females or by some other disfavored (e.g., ethnic or religious) group. Delinking also implicitly attaches the same significance to any deprivation regardless of who suffers it. This is implausible because human vulnerabilities vary by age and gender. The HPI seeks to circumvent this problem by focusing on aspects of disadvantage that seem to have roughly the same significance for everyone. It thereby systematically ignores deprivations specific to women and girls – e.g. related to pregnancy, giving birth, childcare, household time burdens and sexual violence – for the sake of a false universality.

124　See endnote 113. The Bank has very recently begun to use two PPPs for many of the larger developing countries in order to take account of cost of living differences between rural and urban areas. See the discussion two paragraphs down in the text.

125　Milanovic, "Even Higher Global Inequality," p. 424.

126　Many thanks to Shaohua Chen (World Bank) for explaining to me these new, nationally differentiated PPP conversions. For the Bank's approach to China specifically, see Chen and Ravallion, "China Is Poorer than We Thought," p. 5 *et passim*.

127　World Bank, *Global Purchasing Power Parities*, table 1, pp. 28–37. Drawn from this source, the following table provides, for 88 countries with significant numbers of very poor people, the 2005 PPP for "individual consumption expenditure by households" (PPPiceh), as used in the Bank's poverty count, alongside the 2005 PPP for "food and nonalcoholic beverages" (PPPfnb); both are expressed in local currency units equivalent to one dollar. The next column then calculates the ratio of the two PPPs – showing the extent to which PPPiceh overstates command over food and nonalcoholic beverages, especially in the (mostly African) countries with the highest proportion of poor people. In the case of Nigeria, for example, 78.58 naira are deemed to have, in 2005, the same purchasing power as one dollar in the US. But, in the same year, it took 159.02 naira to buy as much food as one dollar bought in the US. In regard to food prices, individual consumption PPPs thus overstate the purchasing power of the Nigerian naira by a factor of 2.024 or 102%. The 50% figure given in the text is calculated from the (not population-weighted) geometric mean of the ratios in the table, which is 1.496. The arithmetic mean of the ratios is slightly higher at 1.516.

	2005	2005	Ratio		2005	2005	Ratio
	PPPiceh	PPPfnb			PPPiceh	PPPfnb	
Angola	70.50	126.79	1.798	Lebanon	1107.12	1149.93	1.039
Argentina	1.35	1.70	1.259	Lesotho	3.43	5.66	1.650
Armenia	196.19	277.66	1.415	Liberia	0.51	0.89	1.745
Bangladesh	25.49	34.28	1.345	Madagascar	756.38	1367.97	1.809
Benin	275.19	495.42	1.800	Malawi	56.92	100.86	1.772
Bhutan	18.46	25.39	1.375	Malaysia	2.11	2.76	1.308
Bolivia	2.57	3.61	1.405	Maldives	9.74	11.30	1.160
Botswana	3.38	5.43	1.607	Mali	289.68	482.74	1.666
Brazil	1.57	1.69	1.076	Mauritania	125.67	223.16	1.776
Brunei Darussalam	1.08	1.50	1.389	Mexico	7.65	8.16	1.067
Burkina Faso	242.42	388.15	1.601	Moldova	4.83	6.35	1.315
Burundi	447.04	803.65	1.798	Mongolia	522.49	697.10	1.334

	2005	2005	Ratio		2005	2005	Ratio
	PPPiceh	PPPfnb			PPPiceh	PPPfnb	
Cambodia	1615.30	2304.16	1.426	Montenegro	0.50	0.66	1.320
Cameroon	294.50	471.30	1.600	Morocco	5.51	7.82	1.419
Cape Verde	78.17	97.06	1.242	Mozambique	11625.69	18411.54	1.584
Central African Rep.	307.47	566.14	1.841	Namibia	5.06	7.03	1.389
Chad	327.57	597.46	1.824	Nepal	26.47	34.09	1.288
China	4.09	5.52	1.350	Niger	267.33	460.78	1.724
Colombia	1191.74	1738.54	1.459	Nigeria	78.58	159.02	2.024
Comoros	294.41	470.80	1.599	Pakistan	20.71	33.45	1.615
Congo, Dem. Rep.	316.23	542.69	1.716	Paraguay	2127.80	2621.79	1.232
Congo, Rep.	375.57	632.74	1.685	Peru	1.65	2.28	1.382
Cote d'Ivoire	325.81	528.52	1.622	Philippines	24.18	33.60	1.390
Djibouti	107.81	185.37	1.719	Rwanda	236.75	333.21	1.407
Ecuador	0.50	0.66	1.320	Sao Tome and Principe	6363.13	10467.10	1.645
Egypt, Arab Rep.	2.02	3.00	1.485	Senegal	298.24	522.49	1.752
Equatorial Guinea	436.29	736.79	1.689	Serbia	34.31	48.03	1.400
Ethiopia	2.75	4.13	1.502	Sierra Leone	1396.21	2758.54	1.976
Fiji	1.55	1.78	1.148	South Africa	4.57	5.53	1.210
Gabon	443.75	751.51	1.694	Sri Lanka	40.04	59.95	1.497
Gambia, The	10.34	23.21	2.245	Sudan	123.51	209.25	1.694
Georgia	0.78	1.04	1.333	Swaziland	3.73	5.64	1.512
Ghana	4475.82	8920.97	1.993	Syrian Arab Republic	24.65	28.17	1.143
Guinea	1479.57	2947.16	1.992	Tajikistan	0.93	1.39	1.495
Guinea-Bissau	284.28	461.33	1.623	Tanzania	482.45	793.51	1.645
Hong Kong, China	7.24	8.82	1.218	Togo	282.26	506.06	1.793
India	15.60	21.13	1.354	Tunisia	0.70	1.01	1.443
Indonesia	4192.83	5817.59	1.388	Turkey	1.00	1.29	1.290
Iran, Islamic Rep.	2714.82	5664.83	2.087	Uganda	744.62	1040.09	1.397
Iraq	639.87	820.45	1.282	Venezuela	1251.12	1833.68	1.466
Kazakhstan	64.96	71.24	1.097	Vietnam	5919.89	8352.05	1.411
Kenya	32.68	54.14	1.657	Yemen, Rep.	91.06	114.72	1.260
Kyrgyz Republic	13.00	18.69	1.438	Zambia	2830.33	3930.78	1.389
Lao PDR	3741.62	5999.52	1.603	Zimbabwe	47952.42	70339.25	1.467

128 This is also proposed by Deaton and Dupriez, "Global Poverty," where the Indian rupee is chosen as base currency.

129 Reddy and Pogge, "How *Not* to Count the Poor," table 3.1.

130 Ibid.

131 For example, in 1999, applying its method with its $1 PPP 1985 IPL, the Bank reported that in 1993 sub-Saharan Africa and Latin America had poverty rates of 39.1% and 23.5%, respectively. In 2000, applying the same method with its $1.08 PPP 1993 IPL, the Bank reported that these same regions in the same year (1993) had poverty rates of 49.7% and 15.3%, respectively. Compare World Bank, *World Development Report 1999/2000*, p. 25, with World Bank, *World Development Report 2000/2001*, p. 23.

132 One further empirical reason for questioning the Bank's optimism about the decline in poverty derives from the evolution of the number of chronically undernourished people as tracked by the UN Food and Agriculture Organization. This number – stated as "more than 800 million" in the *Rome Declaration* – has now crossed the 1 billion mark for the first time in human history (FAO, "1.02 Billion People Hungry"). The number of those who experience hunger intermittently is substantially larger. The reduction of hunger is the second target within MDG-1.

133 Sen, "A Decade of Human Development," p. 22, where Sen identifies himself as the father and principal author of the HDI. See also Sen, *Development as Freedom*, pp. xvi, 79, 318f., n.41,

134 A country's education score is a weighted average based on its adult literacy rate (two-thirds weight) and its primary, secondary and tertiary school enrollment rate (one-third weight).

135 All indices used by the UNDP are explained in a technical note in UNDP, *Human Development Report 2007/2008*, pp. 355–61.

136 The harmonic mean of two numbers, a and b, is $2/(\frac{1}{a} + \frac{1}{b})$. Thus the harmonic mean of 6 and 12 is $2/(\frac{1}{6} + \frac{1}{12}) = 8$.

137 If the population is not half female and half male, then the calculation becomes a bit more complex. Every GDI component is then calculated as the *weighted* harmonic mean of the male and female subscores – just like the corresponding HDI score would be the *weighted* arithmetic mean of these two scores.

138 Some of the following criticisms, and others, are fruitfully discussed in a special issue of the *Journal of Human Development* 7/2 (2006): 145–290, edited by Stephan Klasen.

139 Remarkably, the GDI defines gender parity in life expectancy as attained when female life expectancy is 5 years above male. It thus penalizes a society in which life expectancy is 26 for males and 30 for females for disadvantaging its *females*. The GDI thereby encourages such a society to shift resources from males to females in order to approach the ideal five year difference. Sen has not explained how this is supposed to be consistent with his capability approach which conceives equality as requiring that those who are worse endowed by nature ought to have

additional resources so that they attain the same level of freedom to function. For some discussion of this issue, see Klasen, "UNDP's Gender-related Measures" and Geske Dijkstra, "Towards a Fresh Start."

140 The UNDP's Human Poverty Index also has this same problem.

141 This point alludes to the UNDP's Gender Empowerment Measure (GEM), designed to complement the GDI. The GEM displays a marked elite bias, giving no weight to female participation in grass-roots organizations or in lower levels of the formal or the informal economy, nor to the avoidance of marginalization, social exclusion and entrapment in stultifying or hazardous work (Klasen, "UNDP's Gender-related Measures"; Cueva, "What is Missing?"). Another serious failing of the GEM is its lack of conceptual clarity. Its first two components (parliamentary seats, senior positions in the economy and the professions) relate to the relative shares of females and males, while the third component relates to levels of income. As a result, a poor country cannot return a high GEM score, even if it minimizes gender-based inequality. The GEM also suffers because the required data are not available in many countries and the index is of very little practical value to policy-makers. I am grateful to Kieran Donaghue for discussion of the GEM.

142 Fractiles are segments – of equal but unspecified size – of some population whose members are ordered by some measure or other characteristic. These segments might be percentiles, ventiles, deciles, or quintiles, for example, each respectively comprising one hundredth, twentieth, tenth, or fifth of this population.

143 *The Economist*, "An Alternative View," by permission.

144 There are a fair number of countries whose economic trajectory looks more impressive in GDP than in GNI terms. Much of the growth in Chile, Nigeria, Equatorial Guinea, Congo Republic, Angola and Mozambique, for instance, has benefited foreigners. See World Bank, *World Development Indicators Online* (accessed July 6, 2009).

145 Ibid. (accessed June 23, 2009). This database does not provide inflation-adjusted GNI data. Nonetheless, the ratios of these nominal $-figures (in the right-hand column) are comparable across years.

146 Calculated by dividing the two residuals: (world GNI minus high-income country GNI) divided by (world population minus high-income country population). Data from World Bank, *World Development Indicators Online* (accessed June 23, 2009).

147 Derived from table 1 in the World Bank's *World Development Reports* for the years 1982, 2002, 2007, and 2009 respectively, which use then current foreign exchange rates to convert into dollars. Again, the ratios among these nominal $-figures are comparable across years.

148 See, for example, Danaher, *50 Years Is Enough*; Pogge, *World Poverty and Human Rights*; Singer, *One World*; Stiglitz, *Globalization and Its Discontents*; Monbiot, *Manifesto for a New World Order*.

149 World Bank, *World Development Indicators Online* (accessed June 23, 2009).

150 See UNU-WIDER, *World Income Inequality Database.*
151 Tax Foundation, "Fiscal Facts," table 5.
152 World Bank, *World Development Report 2009*, pp. 352–3.
153 UNDP, *Human Development Report 2007/2008*, table 15, p. 281, as updated from World Bank, *World Development Indicators Online* (accessed June 23, 2009).
154 Saez and Piketty, "Income Inequality in the United States . . . Updated to 2007," table A3. Ibid., table 1 decomposes the 16% average per capita household income growth during the last US economic expansion (2002–7), showing that the top 1% enjoyed real growth of 62% while the remaining 99% of the population had 7% growth. The top 1% captured 65% of the real per capita growth of the economy. In the preceding expansion under Clinton (1993–2000), the top percentile captured 45% of the real per capita growth of the US economy.
155 World Bank, *World Development Report 2009*, pp. 352–3.
156 UNDP, *Human Development Report 2007/2008*, table 15, pp. 282–4, as updated from World Bank, *World Development Indicators Online* (accessed June 23, 2009).
157 Distributing each country's entire GNI over its ten deciles, my calculations of the bottom decile absolute share ignore that a large fraction of GNI goes for government expenditures. My figures therefore substantially exceed both the average income and the average consumption expenditure of the poor.
158 Unlike the previous table for affluent countries, where economic position was calculated giving equal weight of one half to the relative and absolute shares of the poor, this table for poorer countries gives three quarters weight to the absolute and one quarter weight to the relative share of the poor. As a consequence, the figures under "economic position" are not comparable across tables. Moreover, problems with the use of general consumption PPPs in assessing consumption expenditures of very poor households (see sect. 4.2 above) suggest that even within this table comparisons in the second, fourth and fifth columns should be made with caution.
159 World Bank, *World Development Indicators 2009*, table 2.9, pp. 72–4.
160 Chen and Ravallion, "The Developing World Is Poorer than We Thought," table 7, pp. 44–5.
161 Figures in the second column are calculated by dividing each year's GNI (in current yuan) by China's population that year, then using China's GDP deflator to convert into constant 2005 yuan, then dividing by China's 2005 PPP (individual consumption expenditure by households: 4.09 yuan to the US dollar). Pre-2004 data in the third column are from Reddy and Minoiu, "Chinese Poverty" (based on World Bank data). The third-column entry for 2004 is from World Bank, *World Development Indicators 2008*, table 2.8, p. 68. The World Bank has recently published dramatically lower Chinese income inequality estimates for 2005 – World Bank, *World Development Indicators 2009*, table 2.9,

p. 72 – and withdrawn the earlier estimates from its *World Development Indicators Online*. Unfortunately, this does not reflect a change in the situation of the Chinese poor, but methodological revisions, including the new 37% revaluation of the value of rural household spending (discussed in sect. 4.2 above). While such a modification can be appropriate in a poverty measurement exercise, it is highly questionable in the measurement of intra-national inequality. People must often choose where to live on the basis of where they can afford to live. Compare the Qiu family which, owing to its tight budget, lives far outside the city and commutes in to work, with the similar Wang family which, on a 37% larger budget, can afford to live in the city within walking distance of the workplace. Looking at this situation, the Bank judges that there is no real income inequality because the Wangs live at a location where prices are 37% higher. But this overlooks the fact that the Qius live at a much less desirable location. The Wangs could also live in the countryside, but they happily pay extra to live in the city. The Qius would also happily pay extra to live in the city, if only they had the money.

162 Because assessments of China's PPP vary widely and because general household consumption PPPs are, at any rate, a poor indicator of what basic necessities the poor can buy (sect. 4.2 above), figures in the fourth and fifth columns are only roughly comparable to those in the corresponding columns of the preceding table.

163 UNDP, *Human Development Report 2007/2008*, pp. 282–4. No such high decile inequality ratio would, of course, be recorded by the Bank, whose new method of measuring inequality (endnote 161) has already reduced China's decile inequality ratio from 22 (2004) to 13 (2005).

164 The number of people outside China living below $2.50 PPP 2005 per day has reportedly risen from 1,744 million in 1981 to 2,031 million in 1990 and to 2,439 million in 2005 (calculated from Chen and Ravallion, "The Developing World Is Poorer than We Thought," table 7, p. 45).

165 World Bank, *World Development Indicators Online* (accessed July 8, 2009), dividing for each year "household final consumption expenditure, PPP (constant 2005 international $)" by "population, total."

166 World Bank, *PovcalNet* (accessed June 17, 2007, and July 9, 2009, to calculate data for the middle and right columns, respectively); full calculations are on file with the author. The middle-column data are published in Pogge and Moellendorf, *Global Justice: Seminal Essays*, p. xvi. Part of the explanation for the divergence appears to be that the Bank now attributes greater purchasing power to money spent by rural households (Chen and Ravallion, "The Developing World Is Poorer than We Thought," pp. 8–11). This modification disproportionately raises the consumption (measured in 2005 international dollar) attributed to lower percentiles where rural households are overrepresented. This raising effect is smaller for earlier years because many early surveys did not keep track of household location. This leads to a merely apparent improvement in the condition of the poor in (at least) Argentina, Brazil,

Bolivia, Cambodia, Chile, China, Colombia, Ecuador, Pakistan, Peru, Thailand, and Uruguay and thus to an understatement of the increase in global inequality (which, of course, was not meant to be measured by the povcal exercise). Again, many thanks to Shaohua Chen (World Bank) for explaining the method.

167 This conclusion is supported by the work another World Bank researcher, Branko Milanovic, has done on the global income distribution. See above, text at endnotes 17–18.

168 World Bank, *World Development Indicators 2008*, table 2.8, p. 68.

169 Data kindly supplied by Branko Milanovic (World Bank). The terminology of ventiles, deciles, and quintiles is explained in endnote 142.

170 See Davies et al., "World Distribution of Household Wealth," appendix 1, table 10a. PPP conversions probably overstate the true purchasing power of the poor, because PPPs are calculated as a kind of weighted average price ratio, weighting all commodities according to their prominence in international consumption expenditure. Services and other non-tradables raise the assessed purchasing power of poor countries' currencies far above their exchange rate. But the cheapness of services is no boon to the local poor who must concentrate their meager funds on a narrow band of basic necessities, which are not as much cheaper in poor countries as PPPs would suggest. For full elaboration of this and related points, see the fifth problem discussed in sect. 4.2 above and, further, Reddy and Pogge, "How *Not* to Count the Poor."

171 The example shows a mathematical point: given large inequality, variations in how growth is distributed have a much greater impact on the poor than on the rich. It is also worth noting the impact of the choice on economic (and hence also social and political) inequality. While Path One would reduce the income inequality ratio between the two groups from 33:1 (2002) to a still huge 26:1 (2020), Path Two would further increase this inequality ratio to 37:1.

172 Sen, "Population: Delusion and Reality," was among the first to bring this causal relationship to popular attention. There is now abundant empirical evidence across regions and cultures, showing that, when poverty declines, fertility rates also decline sharply. Wherever people, especially women, have gained access to contraceptives and associated knowledge and have gained some assurance that their children will survive into adulthood and that their own livelihood in old age will be secure, they have substantially reduced their rate of reproduction. We can see this in the dramatic declines in total fertility rates (children per woman) in areas where poverty has declined. In the past 55 years, this rate has dropped from 5.67 to 1.68 in East Asia, for instance, and from 3.04 to 1.46 in Portugal and from 3.18 to 1.79 in Australia. In economically stagnant poor countries, by contrast, there has been little change over the same period: total fertility rates went from 5.50 to 5.36 in Equatorial Guinea, from 7.11 to 6.52 in Mali, from 8.12 to 7.19 in Niger, and from 6.09 to 6.47 in Sierra Leone (UN Population Division, *World Population*

Prospects: The 2008 Revision, accessed June 15, 2009). The correlation is further confirmed by synchronic comparisons. Currently, the total fertility rate is 4.63 for the 50 least developed countries versus 1.60 for the more developed regions, and 2.45 for the remaining countries (ibid.) The complete list of national total fertility rates also confirms a strong correlation with poverty and shows that already some 80 of the more affluent countries have reached total fertility rates below 2 (CIA, *Country Comparison: Total Fertility Rate*, accessed June 15, 2009), foreshadowing future declines in population. Taken together, these data provide overwhelming evidence that poverty reduction is associated with large fertility declines.

173 Dworkin, *Life's Dominion*.

174 Dworkin specifically mentions in this vein Tribe, *Abortion* and Rosenblatt, *Life Itself*. Though he makes serious efforts to incorporate the European (mainly British) political experience, his discussion is nevertheless strongly focused on the United States, and particularly on the period since the Supreme Court, in *Roe v. Wade* (1973), affirmed a woman's constitutional right to choose an abortion during the first six months of her pregnancy. I follow Dworkin in discussing the abortion controversy primarily within this context, while sharing his view that the issues are relevantly similar in many other countries.

175 Dworkin, *Life's Dominion*, p. 9.

176 Ibid., pp. 106, 172.

177 Ibid., p. 151.

178 Ibid., p. 155.

179 Ibid., p. 109.

180 Cf. ibid., pp. 164f.

181 Dworkin himself opposes such a waiting period as unduly coercive (ibid., pp. 173f.). But I think he would hold that the restructured pro-life view he outlines could plausibly permit (or even require) it. He is taken to task for this in Stroud, "Dworkin and *Casey* on Abortion."

182 Dworkin, *Life's Dominion*, p. 20.

183 The three analogues clearly show that Dworkin cannot establish the crucial link to toleration merely through rhetorical questions like the one cited in the text ("whether a state can impose the majority's conception of the sacred on everyone"), or: "Does a decent government attempt to dictate to its citizens what intrinsic values they will recognize, and why, and how?" (ibid., p. 117). We do dictate in just this way when we outlaw animal sacrifices, multiple marriages, and pedophile relations desired by both the minor and his or her parents.

The analogues show something else as well. Dworkin argues that women must be legally free to have an abortion, for "if a majority has the power to impose its own views about the sanctity of life on everyone, then the state could *require* someone to abort, even if that were against her own religious or ethical convictions" (ibid., p. 159). But this is plainly false. Our widely shared belief that the state may *prohibit* animal sacrifices, polygamy, and pedophilia surely does not entail that the state may also *require* them.

184 Cuomo's argument was presented in a 1984 speech at Notre Dame University in Indiana, which is reprinted as Cuomo, "Religious Belief." Rawls's argument was developed around the same time and is now comprehensively restated in Part II of Rawls, *Political Liberalism*. Dworkin cites both arguments with approval (Dworkin, *Life's Dominion*, pp. 31 and 252, n.13, respectively).

185 Esp. Dworkin, *Life's Dominion*, pp. 156ff.

186 Both kinds of doubt are raised, for example, in Greenawalt, *Religious Convictions and Political Choice*. See also Galston, "Neutral Dialogue."

187 Thomson, "Abortion," p. 14.

188 This argument is roughly parallel to how the constraint could be adduced – now to universal acclaim – in favor of women's suffrage: The burden of proof is to be placed on those favoring *un*equal moral status. This line of thought has considerable force, I believe, against Dworkin's argument, which assigns an inferior moral status to a human fetus, a status that is gradually elevated as the human and natural "investment" in it becomes more substantial (Dworkin, *Life's Dominion*, pp. 91–100). It has no force, however, against libertarian proponents of legalized abortions – discussed below – who concede that a human fetus has the same moral status as a human being already born.

189 Thomson, "Abortion," p. 12

190 Dworkin, *Life's Dominion*, pp. 13f. Attentive readers may question my use of Dworkin's data, given their age. But respected polling organizations have found that opinions about the laws governing abortion remain remarkably stable over time (see American National Election Studies, "Abortion (2), by Law 1980–2004," and additional sources at www.themonkeycage.org/2009/05/has_the_public_become_more_opp.html). For ease of comparison with the original, I rely on the 1990s figures Dworkin cites.

191 36.8% agree that "abortion is just as bad as killing a person who has already been born, it is murder" and 11.5% agree that "abortion is murder, but it is not as bad as killing someone who has already been born."

192 Dworkin, *Life's Dominion*, p. 14.

193 Estimating on the basis of the poll findings I have cited, this percentage would be at least: $(48.3\% - 10\%) \div 48.3\%$, and at most: $(60\% - 7\%) \div 60\%$.

194 This, of course, is the Catholic position. See Fisher, "Pope Reaffirms View."

195 Thomson, "A Defense of Abortion." Dworkin briefly mentions Thomson's view en passant (Dworkin, *Life's Dominion*, pp. 54, 249, n.4), but does not engage with its substance.

196 The doctrine of self-defense limits the right to life so that one may kill another when this is necessary to protect oneself against a threat he poses, even through no fault of his own. A woman may therefore cause the death

of her fetus when it threatens her survival (or perhaps merely her health), even if this fetus has a right to life. The doctrine of double effect limits the right to life so that one may perform an action that one foresees will result in the death of an innocent human being, if this death is not intended either as an end or as a means and if the good the action will produce cannot be attained at lesser cost and is sufficiently large to balance the evil of the death foreseen. Aiming to preserve the life (or perhaps merely the health) of a pregnant woman, her doctor may therefore take necessary measures that will foreseeably result in the death of her fetus. Although these two ways of incorporating exceptions into the standard pro-life position go back at least to Aquinas, Dworkin mentions neither. Both doctrines are discussed in Grisez, *Abortion* and in Donagan, *The Theory of Morality*, sects. 3.3 and 5.3. See also Anscombe, *Ethics, Religion, and Politics*, pp. 54–81, and Foot, "Problem of Abortion."

197 Thomson's argument seems quite safe in Anglophone legal systems and moral thought, which require persons to act as "Good Samaritans" only in exceptional circumstances. Thus Donald Regan argues quite convincingly that the finding in *Roe v. Wade* could plausibly be defended on equal protection grounds: It is unfair to impose upon pregnant women Good-Samaritan requirements far more stringent than those imposed on other persons (Regan, "Rewriting *Roe v. Wade*"). Societies shaped by continental European jurisprudence, by contrast, tend to conceive the right to life as imposing stronger positive duties, whose cost-thresholds may lie above the cost of an unwanted pregnancy. In such contexts Thomson's conclusion may then not be compatible with assigning to a human fetus as much of a right to life as to human beings already born.

198 We have seen how either of these views can be combined with the belief that abortion may or should be legally permitted in certain exceptional circumstances.

199 For example, someone concerned to mitigate global poverty may face the question of whether she can do this most effectively by doing volunteer work abroad, by going into politics, by writing a book, by becoming a fund-raiser, or by accumulating a lot of wealth for future donations.

200 See sects. 1.1 and 1.2 for details on the extent and gravity of world poverty. On children specifically, many details are provided in UNICEF's annual State of the World's Children reports, available at www.unicef. org/sowc. Every year some 1.8 million children die from simple diarrhea, which could be cured with a 20-cent oral rehydration pack, and some 2 million die of pneumonia and 420,000 of measles, both also easily curable, WHO, *Global Burden of Disease*, p. 72, table A5. Further detailed statistics can be found in the UNDP's annual Human Development Reports. Of course, there may be some minor disputes about the exact numbers. But they do not matter. The numbers I provide in the text would have to be wildly off for my argument to be affected.

201 The straightforward binary choice I am entertaining in this paragraph is a simplification, because one might be active in both causes. The

arguments to come might then be taken to show only that one should allocate more effort to one cause than to the other. I leave this complication aside, partly to save space and partly because morally active persons tend plausibly to concentrate their efforts on one cause.

202 This epistemic principle probably does not hold quite across the board. In particular, it may not hold when there is some negative logical or causal connection between what people believe about some proposition and the truth value of this proposition itself. A classic example is the so-called contrarian school of stock market prognosis: If most large investors are convinced that the stock market is about to rise, then (so contrarians believe) the stock market is likely to go down. The optimists, after all, are presumably already heavily invested in stocks. So future demand for stocks must come from non-optimists who are turning more optimistic. A large proportion of optimists is then a bad sign: It shows that there are few investors left who still might turn more optimistic; and it also shows that there are many investors who could turn more pessimistic. In the case of abortion, this limitation of the epistemic principle does not apply. There is no good reason for believing that an *increase* in the number of serious persons taking one side of the abortion debate makes it *less* likely that this side has it right.

203 The US Supreme Court verdict in *Roe v. Wade* is no permanent victory, because it can be overturned by the same court through the votes of new judges appointed by Republican Presidents. Such an overturning would be no permanent victory either, because the US Congress would then come under pressure to take compensatory action and the battle would also be carried into state legislatures, where new anti-abortion laws would need to be passed. The hope of settling the matter through a constitutional amendment seems extremely unrealistic at this point; and even such an amendment could be overturned again. The 18th amendment to the US constitution, outlawing alcohol consumption, was adopted in 1920 and overturned in 1933 through the 21st amendment.

204 A proponent of permissive abortion laws might present the following counterargument: "Perhaps, if we allowed abortion to be outlawed, much moral effort would be freed up for other causes. But the "moral case load" would dramatically increase as well. There would be large numbers of additional babies born unwanted and into the worst of social circumstances. It is then unlikely that our quitting the abortion battle would enable us significantly to reduce the incidence of moral evils." I won't here go into the complex empirical issues that a proper evaluation of this counterargument would have to address, because I want to concentrate on formulating the appeal to those on the other side, who believe that abortion should be legally prohibited.

205 This distinction was introduced in Pogge, *Realizing Rawls*, sect. 3. I have since revised my view about its moral significance.

206 See Pogge, "Three Problems," sect. V, for a detailed discussion.

207 For the distinction between design and implementation priorities, see Pogge, *Realizing Rawls*, p. 127.

208 I interpret the notion of responsibility this objection appeals to in objective terms: One bears more responsibility as one's conduct is more seriously wrong. Saying that we are responsible for global poverty means then that we act wrongly in upholding the social institutions that produce it. Any subjective notion of responsibility as guilt or blameworthiness is thus left aside. But let me say that objective responsibility entails subjective responsibility only under certain conditions, such as the absence of genuine and excusable factual and moral error.

209 It could easily be challenged – for example by the claim that, when two persons together murder a third, the moral responsibility of each of the two is as weighty as that of a single murderer would be. I am not trying to resolve this issue here, but merely responding to an objection in its own terms. For a sophisticated, if preliminary, treatment of moral mathematics, see Parfit, *Reasons and Persons*, ch. 3.

210 Our global economic order is upheld and enforced chiefly by the "G-7" countries: the US, Japan, Germany, the UK, France, Italy, and Canada, whose combined GNIs are 57% of the global product. The US population constitutes about 42% of that of the G-7. For all high-income countries, their combined GNI amounts to 75% of the world total, and the US population share shrinks to 29%. (These 2007 population and GNI figures are from World Bank, *World Development Report 2009*, table 1, pp. 352–3.) So it seems fair to suppose, in the spirit of the suggested moral mathematics, that each advantaged US citizen – however this group is defined – bears about a three times larger share of responsibility for the US abortion problem than for the global poverty problem. In fact, this seems generous in view of the predominance of the US in world affairs.

211 The latest figure released by the Centers for Disease Control and Prevention is 820,151 for 2005; see Gamble et al., "Abortion Surveillance – United States, 2005," table 1. Admittedly, the true number is higher, because some abortions are performed unofficially – through a high dose of some widely available birth control pill, perhaps, or through a dose of privately imported RU-486. This is irrelevant, however, because outlawing abortions will not reduce (but rather increase) the number of such unofficial abortions.

212 In making this rough calculation, I have ignored two important factors that would greatly strengthen my response to the objection. First, one can reasonably hold against an institutional scheme only *avoidable* deaths. What matters is how many *more* deaths it produces than its best feasible institutional alternative. Through feasible institutional reforms we can probably eradicate deaths due to global poverty much more fully than deaths due to abortion, as outlawing abortion would increase the number of illegal abortions. Our responsibility for US abortion deaths is then significantly less than, and our responsibility for global poverty deaths about the same as, I am suggesting in the text. Second, the

catastrophe of global poverty does not manifest itself in deaths alone. It affects billions of people who chronically suffer grievous deprivation. By upholding global institutions that produce massive poverty, we are responsible also for a great deal of suffering on the part of those who, for the time being, manage to survive. Permissive abortion laws, by contrast, produce little serious harm beyond the deaths they engender.

My response to the objection can easily be extended to citizens of any rich country smaller than the US – one with a tenth of the US population, say. An advantaged person in this country bears the same share of responsibility for the global poverty problem as an equally advantaged person in the US and a roughly ten times larger share of responsibility for the national abortion problem, whose magnitude is, however, only roughly one tenth of that in the US.

213 I ignore complications arising from the fact that persons may live away from their home country, temporarily or permanently. In such cases, the assigned responsibility for their security and welfare is shared between their fellow-nationals and fellow-residents.

214 For a more extensive argument to this conclusion, see Pogge, *World Poverty and Human Rights*, ch. 3. I point there to the counterproductive incentives provided by a conception of justice whose basic requirements on social institutions can be weakened or evaded through the introduction of national borders. These incentives may well have played a role in the decolonization movement of the 1960s and in the South African homelands policy. Even if not: That a moral conception provides such incentives – whether they affect conduct or not – should make us suspicious of this conception.

215 For some idea of the effects of such fluctuations, and for the notion of exchange entitlements, see Sen, *Poverty and Famines*.

216 One such mechanism, involving a fair sharing of the benefits of deep-sea mining "to benefit all peoples, with special regard for the least developed countries," was to have been part of the *Law of the Sea Treaty*. It was killed, however, with the acquiescence of other rich countries, by the Clinton Administration. Other mechanisms that have been proposed are a Tobin Tax (Tobin, "A Tax on International Currency Transactions") and a Global Resources Dividend. See Pogge, *World Poverty and Human Rights*, ch. 5, esp. p. 131, and ch. 8.

217 "At least," because such a partial program could concentrate on those measures, projects, and policies that are most effective. It is likely that (beyond some threshold) intelligent efforts to combat global poverty will have declining marginal effectiveness. The "earlier" efforts can focus on situations where destitute persons are geographically concentrated and easy to reach, and where it does not take much to help them become self-sufficient.

218 I have also assumed that the death of an unborn human being due to abortion – no matter how early the stage of pregnancy – is morally equivalent to the death of a child or adult due to starvation. I have

assumed this, because this is what many who have joined the battle against abortion believe. But those who find merit in my *argument from doubt*, or those who believe that the extreme, drawn-out suffering involved in disease or starvation makes such a death significantly worse, may conclude that we should give precedence to the struggle against global poverty, even if we could save an equal number of lives in either cause.

219 There is one kind of battle related to the topic of global poverty that exists quite independently of my appeal. There are those (myself included) who believe that we should, as a nation, devote ourselves to initiating the kinds of institutional reforms in our world economy that are necessary to eradicate global poverty. And there are others who believe we ought not so to commit ourselves (perhaps because such reforms, by diminishing the gap between rich and poor in the world, would reduce our standard of living – or, by lessening the dependence of the poor upon the rich, reduce our political clout.) This, again, is a disagreement about a question that must and will be answered, one way or another, in each nation. And so, if there are significant forces on both sides, this disagreement may spawn political battles over whether this or that developed country shall be committed to the struggle against global poverty. But such battles are much less divisive than the abortion battle. Our opponents are not saying that our objectives are morally wrong (as is the case on both sides of the abortion battle). They are not even denying that our objectives are morally worthy. They are merely arguing that it is morally permissible to slow down or abandon the pursuit of these objectives on account of countervailing considerations that they deem to be morally significant as well. Also, such battles do not pose anything like the same threat to the standing of morality in our culture.

220 It might do wonders, also, for the moral ties between nations. The relations between Japan, the US, and the Europeans – often strained by selfish and petty intergovernmental bickering over trade matters – could certainly benefit from the experience of collaboration on a moral program. And such a program would also do much to initiate trust and friendship between the peoples of the developed and the less developed countries.

221 To be sure, other terrorist attacks have occurred since then. But here I focus on terror attacks that have either taken place on the territory of Western, developed countries (e.g., Sept. 11) or were apparently directed primarily at Westerners (e.g., Bali). Despite some early reports to the contrary, it is unclear whether the Mumbai attacks of Nov. 26–29, 2008 were targeted specifically at Westerners; out of some 164 people killed, 14 were Western citizens. See Crumley, "The Mumbai Attacks" and Bagchi, "26 Foreigners Killed."

222 See Frank, "Funding the Public Health Response," arguing that recent shifts of public funds into counter-terrorist efforts have a large negative impact on morbidity and mortality from natural disasters and common

medical conditions, and Wilson and Thomson, "Deaths from International Terrorism."

223 Global Fund to Fight AIDS, "Current Grant Commitments."
224 Belasco, *Cost of Iraq.*
225 This is not a pitch for censorship, of course, but for responsible and intelligent journalism and reporting.
226 A considerable diversity of Western responses should, however, be noted. See Haubrich, "Civil Liberties in Emergencies."
227 Rawls, *Theory of Justice*, sect. 9.
228 Later, Voinarovski declares with respect to the planned assassination of Admiral Dubasov, the Governor-General of Moscow, that "if Dubasov is accompanied by his wife, I shall not throw the bomb" (Camus, *The Rebel*, p. 140; Spence, *Boris Savinkov*, pp. 45f.). Savinkov similarly opposes an attempt to kill Dubasov on the St. Petersburg–Moscow Express on the ground that "if there were the least mistake, the explosion could take place in the carriage and kill strangers" (Camus, *The Rebel*, p. 140). Later, when escaping from a Czarist prison, the same Savinkov reportedly "decides to shoot any officers who might attempt to prevent his flight, but to kill himself rather than turn his revolver on an ordinary soldier" (ibid.).
229 Pogge, "Historical Wrongs," sect. 2.2.
230 Bin Laden, Interview with *Daily Ummat.*
231 Quran 5:32.
232 In the formulation of Blackstone, *Commentaries on the Laws of England*, Book IV, p. 352.
233 On September 22, 2001, George W. Bush waived the so-called Pressler Amendment, which had blocked most military and economic aid to Pakistan on account of this country's nuclear weapons program. See Norris et al., "Pakistan's Nuclear Forces, 2001."
234 It might be objected that the possibility of error might not be a serious possibility in some cases. In the case of Moses, perhaps, when God appeared to him, or in the cases of Jesus or Mohammad or even their immediate followers or disciples. It is well to recall then that Mohammad, the final prophet according to Islamic teaching, lived some 1400 years ago. So the possibility of errors in understanding the Divine will as revealed by Muhammad is certainly a real possibility in our time, as the diversity of schools and interpretations amply confirms. Exempting oneself from this possibility would be to claim (contrary to Islamic teaching) the status of prophet for oneself or for some contemporary from whom one is receiving direct instruction.
235 See, for example, Abou El Fadl, "Islam and the Theology of Power."
236 Pogge, "Justice," sect. 5, first hypothesis.
237 Rawls, *Political Liberalism*, lecture 4.
238 In 2005, the FBI issued 47,221 national security letter (NSL) requests requiring businesses to turn over private data about their customers. The Justice Department's public report stated that the FBI issued 9,254 NSL

requests in calendar year 2005. "The number of NSL requests we identified significantly exceeds the number reported in the Department's first public annual report on NSL usage, issued in April 2006, because the Department was not required to include all NSL requests in that report" (Department of Justice, "National Security Letters," p. xix). See also ACLU, *Hundreds of New Documents.*

239 Maguire and Lines, "Exclusive"; and CNN, *Critique of Worldwide Media Coverage.* The US had bombed Al Jazeera stations twice before – Kabul in 2001 and Baghdad in 2003 – killing one reporter.

240 See Dehghanpisheh et al., "Death Convoy of Afghanistan," reporting on the surrender at Konduz of November 25, 2001; Physicians for Human Rights, *Preliminary Assessment of Alleged Mass Gravesites*, and the documentary film *Afghan Massacre*, directed by Jamie Doran.

241 Reitman, "UN Probes Claims," McCarthy, "US Afghan Ally," and Lasseter, "Afghan War-Crimes Evidence Removed."

242 But see Risen, "US Said to Have Averted Inquiry."

243 Filipov, "Warlord's Men." The rapes targeted the Pashtun community from which the Taliban had derived much of their political support.

244 North, "Dostum Gets Afghan Military Role"; Filkins, "Afghan Leader." On the evolution of the situation in Afghanistan generally, see reports by Amnesty International (www.amnestyusa.org/countries/afghanistan/reports.do) and Human Rights Watch, *Fatally Flawed*; "Killing You is a Very Easy Thing for Us"; "Enduring Freedom"; *Afghanistan: Killing and Torture.* See also Uranium Medical Research Center, *UMRC's Preliminary Findings*, foreseeing "a potential public health disaster for Afghanistan" from massive coalition use of non-depleted uranium in bombs and missiles.

245 Coalition personnel took hundreds of photographs and video clips of the abuses they inflicted on their captives; the most horrific ones were never published, but shown at closed hearings to members of the US Congress. See Wilkinson, "Photos Show Dead Iraqis"; Mackay, "Iraq's Child Prisoners," reporting more than 100 children in coalition custody, subjected to rape and torture; Pearlstein and Patel, *Behind the Wire*; Human Rights Watch, *Leadership Failure* and "US Operated Secret 'Dark Prison'"; Amnesty International, *United Kingdom Human Rights* and *Beyond Abu Ghraib*; Schmitt and Marshall, "Task Force 6–26." In addition to such widespread recreational torture, there were more official torture sessions, which, as recently emerged, were videotaped by the CIA. This videotaping was kept secret from the Sept. 11 Commission, whose chairmen now feel betrayed by the CIA (Mazzetti, "9/11 Panel Study Finds that CIA Withheld Tapes"). At least a few hundred hours of these video recordings were destroyed in 2005 despite several court orders requiring such evidence to be preserved (Apuzzo, "Judge Wants Details on Destroyed CIA Videotapes").

246 Maze, "Rise in Moral Waivers." In 2006, 20% of army recruits, over 50% of marine recruits, 18% of navy recruits, and 8% of air force recruits

needed moral waivers to enlist (Baldor, "Military Grants More Waivers").

247 Some tens of thousands of private security contractors have enjoyed official immunity from prosecution in Iraqi courts (under Order 17, passed by the US-led Coalition Provisional Authority in 2004) and de facto immunity in US courts. Such contractors working for Blackwater have killed dozens of unarmed and non-threatening civilians, and contractors employed by Titan and CACI were prominently involved in the Abu Ghraib abuses, including the rape of a minor in the presence of US military personnel. See Human Rights First: *Private Security Contractors at War*. The US Congress finally curtailed the de facto immunity of contractors in October 2007. The Iraqi government has moved a few weeks later to end their official immunity. See the Human Rights Watch Q&A *Private Military Contractors and the Law*.

248 The highest-ranking officer convicted was an army captain found guilty of kicking detainees and of staging a mock execution. He was sentenced to 45 days in jail. See Eric Schmitt, "Iraq Abuse Trial." See also the chapter on investigative failures in Human Rights Watch, *By the Numbers*.

249 Human Rights Watch, *Leadership Failure*; *"No Blood, No Foul"*; and, especially, Jaffer and Singh, *Administration of Torture*.

250 MSNBC, *Hardball: Tactics of Interrogation*.

251 Lasseter, "America's Prison for Terrorists."

252 UN, *Human Rights Experts Issue Joint Report*. The ICRC has been visiting Guantánamo Bay since January 2002, accompanied by efforts of the American Red Cross to appease its more blindly patriotic US donors: "It seems a horror to many Americans that anyone – especially the Red Cross – would be interested in the welfare of the Afghan war detainees being held by the US military in Guantánamo Bay, Cuba. However, it is our very own government that requested the International Committee of the Red Cross (ICRC) to visit with the detainees" (since removed from the Red Cross's website, but archived at Project to Enforce the Geneva Conventions, *Why the Red Cross Is Visiting Detainees in Guantanamo Bay*). ICRC visits take place on the understanding that its reports remain confidential and are conveyed only to select US authorities. One such report was leaked. Its contents are described in Lewis, "Red Cross Finds Detainee Abuse." See also Glaberson, "Red Cross Monitors Barred."

253 Center for Constitutional Rights, *Report on Torture* and *Detention in Afghanistan*; Begg and Brittain, *Enemy Combatant*. See also the extensive testimony of Jumah al-Dossari in Amnesty International, *USA: Days of Adverse Hardship*, and Sydney Morning Herald, "The David Hicks Affadavit."

254 See Wiser, "Torture Question."

255 *Hamdan v Rumsfeld*, pp. 50–1.

256 Ibid., pp. 5, 59–62.

257 Ibid., p. 67.

258 *Military Commissions Act of 2006*.

259 Greenhouse, "Justices, 5–4, Back Detainee Appeals."

260 Amnesty International, *United States of America/Yemen*. See also Benjamin, "Inside the CIA's Notorious 'Black Sites.'"

261 See "United Kingdom" in Amnesty International, *Report 2005*.

262 See Bybee, *Standards of Conduct*, pp. 19–20.

263 Ibid., p. 46.

264 See Levin, *Legal Standards*, n. 8.

265 Text of the *Geneva Conventions* at: www.icrc.org/Web/Eng/siteeng0.nsf/html/genevaconventions.

266 John Yoo, a major contributor to the Levin memo, provided this defense on May 2, 2005 (Yoo, "Human Rights"). In its Article 4, the *Fourth Geneva Convention* specifies that "persons protected by the Convention are those who, at a given moment and in any manner whatsoever, find themselves, in case of a conflict or occupation, in the hands of a Party to the conflict or Occupying Power of which they are not nationals" – excepting only "Nationals of a state which is not bound by the Convention."

267 Ross and Esposito, "CIA's Harsh Interrogation Techniques Described." These techniques were used and refined by the Nazi Gestapo, and waterboarding was a technique commonly used by Pol Pot's Khmer Rouge in Cambodia.

268 BBC, *File on 4: Rendition*. Cf. Levy and Scott-Clark, "One Huge US Jail": "Robert Baer, a CIA case officer in the Middle East until 1997, told us how it works. 'We pick up a suspect or we arrange for one of our partner countries to do it. Then the suspect is placed on civilian transport to a third country where, let's make no bones about it, they use torture. If you want a good interrogation, you send someone to Jordan. If you want them to be killed, you send them to Egypt or Syria. Either way, the US cannot be blamed as it is not doing the heavy work'."

269 See Commission of Inquiry into the Actions of Canadian Officials in Relation to Maher Arar, *Report*. In another case, a British resident was rendered by the CIA to Morocco for 18 months of torture (including cutting of his genitals with a razor blade). He was then flown to Guantánamo Bay, where he continued to be confined without charge or trial until February 23, 2009. See Robert Verkaik, "CIA Photos."

270 See CBC News, "US Won't Change Policy on Deportations to Third Countries."

271 See Lewis, "Man Mistakenly Abducted by CIA."

272 On June 26, 2004, White House, "Bush Commemorates UN Day."

273 A secret poll conducted in Iraq for the UK Ministry of Defense and later leaked to the media found that "forty-five per cent of Iraqis believe attacks against British and American troops are justified – rising to 65 per cent in the British-controlled Maysan province; 82 per cent are 'strongly opposed' to the presence of coalition troops; less than one per cent of the population believes coalition forces are responsible for any improvement in security; 67 per cent of Iraqis feel less secure because of

the occupation; 43 per cent of Iraqis believe conditions for peace and stability have worsened; 72 per cent do not have confidence in the multi-national forces" (Rayment, "Secret MoD Poll").

274 CBS, *60 Minutes: Punishing Saddam*.
275 Mohamed Rashed Daoud al-'Owhali, who was given a life sentence for his involvement in the 1998 bombing of the US Embassy in Nairobi. See Hirshkorn, "Bomber's Defense."
276 Albright, *Madam Secretary*, p. 275.
277 See Campaign Against Sanctions on Iraq, *Starving Iraq*, table 7, for a tabulation of the various estimates.
278 Garfield, interview by *Columbia News*.
279 See PBS Frontline, "Debate Over U.N. Sanctions," also reporting Garfield's earlier estimate that the sanctions had killed 227,713 children in the 91 months from August 1990 until March 1998.
280 Quoted in Pilger, "Squeezed to Death."
281 Ibid.
282 See von Sponeck, *A Different Kind of War*.
283 Burghardt's reasons (described in Arnove, "Sanctions on Iraq") are more fully articulated in her essay, "The Humanitarian Situation in Iraq."
284 "The Pentagon . . . has no plans to determine how many Iraqi civilians may have been killed or injured or suffered property damage as a result of US military operations in Iraq" (Graham and Morgan, "US Has No Plans to Count Civilian Casualties"). Jack Straw, UK Secretary of State for Foreign and Commonwealth Affairs, concurred, stating that "in the conditions that exist in Iraq . . . it would be impossible to make a reliably accurate assessment . . . of the overall civilian casualties" and that, in any case, the UK has no obligation under international humanitarian law to make such an assessment (Straw, written ministerial comment). No credible unofficial figures exist for the civilian death toll in Afghanistan. Some of these deaths get a tiny notice in the papers, such as this one:

> *Coalition airstrike kills 9 in Afghanistan*
> A coalition airstrike hit a home in Afghanistan's Kapisa province, killing nine members of a family, Deputy Gov. Sayad Mohammad Dawood Hashimmi said. The military said two bombs hit a compound that armed militants were seen moving into after a rocket attack on a US base. "These men knowingly endangered civilians by retreating into a populated area," said Army Lt. Col. David Accetta, a military spokesman (*USA Today*, "Coalition Airstrike").

Unofficial tallies of civilian deaths in Iraq record about 100,000 reported deaths since the 2003 invasion with the assumption that the true number is considerably larger (www.iraqbodycount.org). A recent survey estimates 654,965 excess civilian deaths between March 18, 2003, and June 2006 (with a 95% confidence interval of 392,979 to 942,636), including 601,027 deaths from violence. See Burnham et al., "Mortality," p. 1426. This survey was roundly rejected by the US and UK governments, but found to be well grounded in internal communications within the UK government. See Bennett-Jones, "Iraqi Deaths Survey 'Was Robust'."

285 Stiglitz, *Globalization and Its Discontents.*

286 See Correa, "Implications of Bilateral Free Trade Agreements"; Correa, "Public Health"; and Pogge, *World Poverty and Human Rights*, ch. 9.

287 Warrick and DeYoung, "Obama Reverses Bush Policies."

288 Priest, "Bush's 'War' on Terror."

289 The articles of Chapter VII of the UN Charter authorize the UN Security Council to take forceful action in response to any "threat to the peace, breach of the peace, or act of aggression" (Article 39, cf. Article 42).

290 Franck, "Legality and Legitimacy," p. 143.

291 Ibid.

292 United States, "National Security Strategy," pp. 6, 15–16. National Security Presidential Directive 17. There is also a classified version of the latter document.

293 Annan, "Two Concepts of Sovereignty."

294 Franck, "Legality and Legitimacy," p. 144.

295 Ibid., p. 145.

296 See Gourevitch, *We Wish to Inform You*; UN, *Report of the Independent Inquiry*; Des Forges, *Leave None to Tell the Story*; OAU, *Rwanda: The Preventable Genocide*; Power, "Bystanders to Genocide."

297 For the full text of this fax, see PBS Frontline, "Warning That Was Ignored." It is clear from the record that the governments of the US, France, and the UK, as well as the UN, had received abundant independent information about the planning and build-up toward genocide. This information was not made available either to Dallaire or to other members of the UN Security Council.

298 Security Council Resolution 872 (October 5, 1993), which initiates UNAMIR. The Kigali weapons-secure area had in fact been established on December 24, 1993. UN Department of Peacekeeping Operations, *UNAMIR Background Document.*

299 The two cited messages were sent on January 10 and 11. See UN, *Report of the Independent Inquiry*, p. 11.

300 Des Forges, *Leave None to Tell the Story*, under "Warnings," (available at www.hrw.org/reports/1999/rwanda/Geno4-7-01.htm).

301 UN, *Report of the Independent Inquiry*, p. 19.

302 These last two historical hypotheticals do not entail, and are not meant to suggest, that Annan's conduct was motivated by a desire to promote his career. The materials I have read do not, in my view, support a confident judgment of this question one way or the other.

303 UN, *Report of the Independent Inquiry*, p. 69.

304 Security Council Resolution 912, 21 April 1994. At this time, UNAMIR's actual troop strength was already down to 1,515. In accordance with the plan revealed by the informant, troops of the Rwandan Presidential Guard had beaten ten Belgian soldiers to death on April 7, 1994, and had thereby achieved their purpose of inducing Belgium to pull out its

contingent (on April 14). Withdrawing toward the airport, the Belgians left behind about 2,000 civilians, who had found refuge in the Official Technical School (ETO) that the Belgian contingent was occupying in Kigali. Most of these civilians were murdered immediately after the Belgians abandoned the ETO on April 11. By April 25, UNAMIR's troop strength was down to 503 (Power, "Bystanders to Genocide"). Dallaire nonetheless managed to protect some 25,000 Rwandans throughout the following weeks.

305 On the TV program *Nightline*, May 4, 1994: "Here you have a real genocide, in Kigali." Cited in UN, *Report of the Independent Inquiry*, p. 70.

306 Ronayne, *Never Again?* pp. 174–5. The *New York Times* reports: "One document, dated May 1, 1994, summarizes a meeting of several unidentified officials who were analyzing the Rwanda situation. The meeting ends with a warning against branding the massacres genocide. 'Be careful,' the document reads. 'Legal at State was worried about this yesterday. Genocide finding could commit USG to actually "do something."' 'Legal' refers to the legal adviser at the State Department and USG is the United States government" (Lewis, "US Knew"). The prohibition on using the word "genocide" is manifested in the contorted answers various spokespersons for the US State Department provided to questions about the applicability of the word. Having evaded the question on April 28 and May 11, spokespersons later (May 25, June 10) said that they had been given "guidance" to speak of "acts of genocide," prompting a reporter to ask "How many acts of genocide does it take to make genocide?" See PBS Frontline, "One Hundred Days of Slaughter."

307 Cf. US Department of State, "Clinton Administration Policy." Even after the catastrophe in Rwanda, the US continued its battle to reduce the UN budget and its own share thereof, targeting peacekeeping operations in particular. As part of this effort, it refused for years to pay its dues and ended up owing the UN about $2 billion. The effort paid off. Christmas 2000, the richest country on earth with 31.8% of global GDP that year (UNDP, *Human Development Report 2002*, pp. 190–3) had its share of the UN budget reduced from 25 to 22% and its share of the peacekeeping budget from 30 to 27%. The total savings for the US: about half a dollar annually per citizen. Crossette, "After Long Fight."

308 Security Council Resolution 872 (October 5, 1993). Also relevant is "Operational Directive No. 02: Rules of Engagement" (Interim), File No. 4003.1, of November 19, 1993, extensively cited in Des Forges, *Leave None to Tell the Story*. She describes this document, which is not publicly available, as follows:

> The first paragraph of the document indicates that these Rules of Engagement "are drafted by the Force, but are approved by the UN and may only be changed with UN authority." . . . Although the document was marked "interim," it was accepted by UN headquarters in New York and

was not amended by it. It was circulated to the member states that provided troops to UNAMIR and was in effect at the time of the genocide. (Des Forges, *Leave None to Tell the Story*, under "Choosing War," available at www.hrw.org/reports/1999/rwanda/Geno1-3-11.htm)

The UNAMIR mandate permitted the peacekeepers to use force in self-defense, which was defined as including "resistance to attempts by forceful means to prevent the Force from discharging its duties under the mandate of UNAMIR." They were allowed to use their weapons "to defend themselves, other UN lives, or persons under their protection against direct attack" and, even more broadly, they were directed to use armed force "when other lives are in mortal danger." In addition, the strong language of Paragraph 17 of the Rules of Engagement specified that the force was "morally and legally obligated" to "use all available means" to halt "ethnically or politically motivated criminal acts" and that it "will take the necessary action to prevent any crime against humanity." (Ibid., under "Ignoring Genocide," available at www.hrw.org/reports/1999/rwanda/Geno15-8-01. htm)

309 In 1994, the UN Security Council consisted of Argentina, Brazil, China, Czech Republic, Djibouti, France, New Zealand, Nigeria, Oman, Pakistan, Russia, Rwanda, Spain, United Kingdom, and the United States. Three of these states – Djibouti, Nigeria, and Oman – were not parties to the *Genocide Convention*, and may therefore have been legally free to oppose UN action. Still, had the other 12 states done what they had committed themselves to doing, they would have declared the situation in Rwanda a threat to the peace (under Article 39 of the UN Charter) and would have stopped the genocide.

310 Cf. PBS Frontline, "One Hundred Days of Slaughter." After the vote was finally taken, on May 17, Albright testified on Capitol Hill: "Emotions can produce wonderful speeches and stirring op-ed pieces. But emotions alone cannot produce policies that will achieve what they promise. If we do not keep commitments in line with capabilities, we will only further undermine U.N. credibility and support. . . . ultimately, the future of Rwanda is in Rwandan hands" (ibid.).

311 Years later, when Gourevitch's account of the genocide was making headlines, Clinton pretended he had no clue about it and wrote little notes to his advisors: "Is what he is saying true?" and "How did this happen?" In March of 1998, speaking at Kigali airport to genocide survivors, he said: "We come here today partly in recognition of the fact that we in the United States and the world community did not do as much as we could have and should have done to try to limit what occurred" (Power, "Bystanders to Genocide"). Kofi Annan apparently liked this formulation, saying on the 10-year anniversary of the start of the genocide: "I believed at that time that I was doing my best. But I realised after the genocide that there was more that I could and should have done to sound the alarm and rally support" (*BBC News*, "UN Chief's Rwanda Genocide Regret"). Promoted to Secretary of State, Madeleine Albright said in response to

the publication of OAU report, *Rwanda: The Preventable Genocide*: "I followed instructions because I was an Ambassador, but I screamed about the instructions that I got on this. I felt that they were wrong and I made that point, but I was an Ambassador under instructions." Interview on ABC's *This Week*.

312 Franck, "Legality and Legitimacy," p. 149.

313 Des Forges, *Leave None to Tell the Story*, under "Chronology" (available at www.hrw.org/reports/1999/rwanda/Geno4-7-01.htm), and under "French Support for Habyarimana" (available at www.hrw.org/reports/1999/rwanda/Geno1-3-11.htm).

314 Ibid.; cf. PBS Frontline, "One Hundred Days of Slaughter."

315 "Perhaps there was no better reflection of the world's shabby treatment of post-genocide Rwanda than the matter of the debt burden incurred by the Habyarimana government. The major source of the unpaid debt was the weapons the regime had purchased for the war against the RPF, which had then been turned against innocent Tutsi during the genocide. . . . incredibly enough, the new government was deemed responsible for repaying to those multilateral and national lenders the debt accrued by its predecessors. The common-sense human assumption that Rwanda deserved and could not recover without special treatment and, that the debt would have been wiped out more or less automatically, had no currency in the world of international finance. Instead of Rwanda receiving vast sums of money as reparations by those who had failed to stop the tragedy, it in fact owed those same sources a vast sum of money." OAU, *Rwanda: The Preventable Genocide*, sects. 17.30 and 17.33. As the report recounts, the leading sellers of arms into Africa are the US, Russia, China, and France. Weapons sales to the developing world at large for the 1994–2001 period (in 2001 dollars) amounted to $60 billion from the US, $40 billion from Russia, $25 billion from France, $8 billion each from China and the UK, $5 billion from Germany, and $20 billion from the rest of Europe. Grimmett, *Conventional Arms Transfers*.

316 If US leaders really cared about human rights and liberation, they would show some interest in Burma, whose population, twice that of Iraq, has long suffered under a brutal and widely hated military junta. Toppling the junta and letting Aung San Suu Kyi take power in Burma would be vastly easier and cheaper than the US operation in Iraq. Aung San Suu Kyi won 82% of parliamentary seats in the 1990 national elections, which the junta permitted but then refused to recognize. Since that time, her movements have been tightly restricted by the junta, which has also committed massive atrocities against the Burmese population. The junta's abuses are amply documented in ongoing reporting by Amnesty International and Human Rights Watch, in the *Report of the Special Rapporteur on the Situation of Human Rights in Myanmar, Paulo Sérgio Pinheiro*, and in the *Burma Human Rights Yearbooks* (www.burmalibrary.org/show.php?cat=2252&lo=d&sl=0).

317 Franck, "Legality and Legitimacy," pp. 150–1.

318 Ibid., p. 145.
319 But see Gauthier, *Morals by Agreement* for the opposite view of what fairness is.
320 Still, existing domestic jurying is hardly ideal. Significant distortions may be introduced, for example, by how much the contending parties spend on their legal teams, jury selection specialists, and expert witnesses.
321 Franck acknowledges that the UN has not "acted wisely" in this case. In mitigation, he points out: "That Vietnam's use of force violated the Charter text is beyond question" (Franck, "When, If Ever," p. 65). I disagree. Preceding the invasion, the Khmer Rouge regime had made many significant military incursions into Vietnamese territory that it claimed as its own. So there is a self-defense argument here. For the assessment of this argument it may also be relevant that the Khmer Rouge had killed two million Cambodians, committing a genocide that no other country was willing to stop. The Vietnamese had compelling reason to believe that this regime constituted a very serious danger.
322 Ibid., p. 62. Readers will recall that this air strike was timed to coincide with Monica Lewinsky's second and final day of grand jury testimony. See *Houston Chronicle*: "Clinton: A Story Unfolds."
323 This was after a 10-minute discussion in the UN Security Council meeting of August 24, 1998, during which the US claimed that the Sudanese might tamper with the evidence. *BBC News,* "No UN Action." The US did not explain how the Sudanese could remove all chemical traces from a site that had been hit by thirteen cruise missiles and was continuously open to international journalists.
324 It is said that doing so would have compromised US intelligence sources. However, proof of chemical or biological weapons production could have been obtained through an examination of the factory site after its destruction. Despite US opposition to such an examination, soil samples from the site were examined by three European laboratories and the Manchester engineering firm Dames and Moore, under the overall supervision of Professor Thomas Tullius, chairman of Boston University's department of chemistry. No evidence of suspicious chemicals was found (Rouhi, "Analytical Credibility," pp. 37ff.). A 300-page report by Kroll Associates (January 1999, commissioned by Idris) reaches the same conclusion (Henry L. Stimson Center, "US Case"). The fact that the US blocked an official investigation of the site suggests that its intelligence services expected such a search to turn up nothing.
325 Franck, "Legality and Legitimacy," p. 152.
326 Ibid., p. 147.
327 Cf., e.g., Urbina, "UN Resolution: Dangerous Ambiguity."
328 Hoyos and Beattie, "Nations Ponder."
329 Franck, "Legality and Legitimacy," p. 152.
330 Foreign Policy Association/Princeton Town Hall Meeting, "Transcript of Remarks by Thomas Franck."
331 Cf. Security Council Resolutions 1483, 1500, 1511, and 1546.

332 A public criterion for judging military interventions, if it itself is to be judged in part at least by its effects, requires a meta-criterion in the background for assessing alternative candidate public criteria by how well each would work in the world as it is. This model is exemplified by Rawls, who proposes his two principles of justice as a public criterion of justice which is justified against other candidate public criteria by reference to its expected relative impact on the fulfillment of citizens' higher-order interests. Cf. Rawls, *Justice as Fairness*, pp. 18–19, 42–3, 192. This sort of instrumentalization could be carried one step further: A theorist may think that she should base her public advocacy not on the quality of the effects of the various candidate public criteria ("I should advocate whatever criterion is such that its general acceptance would have the best effects"), but on the quality of the effects of her own advocacy. For example, if she believes that C_1 would be the best public criterion but that only C_2 and C_3 stand any chance of adoption, she would then throw her full support behind C_2 in order to defeat the even worse C_3, while ignoring C_1 which, if it came into the discussion, would only divide and dilute the political forces opposed to C_3.

333 Franck, "Legality and Legitimacy," p. 146.

334 As the US did in 1986 when it withdrew its acceptance of compulsory jurisdiction of the International Court of Justice and, defying its verdict, continued to support the Nicaraguan contras.

335 No substantial loss of internal legitimacy seems to have occurred when the US, in 1986, quit the compulsory jurisdiction of the International Court of Justice over the case brought by Nicaragua or when the US enacted the *American Servicemembers' Protection Act* (colloquially known as the "Hague Invasion Act"), under which "The President is authorized to use all means necessary and appropriate to bring about the release of any [covered United States persons, covered allied persons, and individuals detained or imprisoned for official actions taken while the individual was a covered United States person or a covered allied person, and in the case of a covered allied person, upon the request of such government] who is being detained or imprisoned by, on behalf of, or at the request of the International Criminal Court." US citizens also strongly supported the 2003 invasion of Iraq, despite the fact that the US and the UK failed (by a very large margin) to obtain UN Security Council authorization.

336 Castiglione, "Contracts and Constitutions," pp. 61–3, distinguishes three democratic deficits. The first is a democratic deficit in the narrow sense: "strictly speaking, 'democratic deficit' denotes the lack of input which directly representative institutions, namely the European Parliament, have in the legislative activity of the Union." The second is the "federal deficit": "on the one hand many of the institutions of the Union . . . have an intrinsic federal nature . . . , while on the other the main political actors, the national governments, tend to maintain the political process in a state of ambiguity so that they can play the system

according to their own contingent interests." The third is a "constitutional deficit," which "refers to the way in which the political-administrative élite of the Union has systematically underplayed the constitution-making processes which have progressively transformed the European Community into a de-facto polity, and to the general lack of awareness and debate on constitution-making as a process intrinsic to the formation of a political community." My topic corresponds to Castiglione's constitutional deficit, though my effort will be in a more normative and constructive vein.

337 I use the word "type" in allusion to Bertrand Russell's theory of types, though my use of the term can surely be grasped without an understanding of this theory.

338 I do not pretend that this distinction is entirely clear cut. One can quibble over whether the decision about the dress code for judges, or about a new air conditioning system for parliament, is or is not *about* political decision-making in the relevant sense. I will proceed on the assumption that the distinction is clear enough for present purposes.

339 Some rudimentary proposals have been made in this direction by others. Weale, for example, has proposed that a European federal constitution should receive a "democratic baptism" through a European constituent assembly. See Weale, "Democratic Legitimacy," pp. 90–4.

340 The *Maastricht Treaty* was adopted on February 7, 1992. The Bundestag voted for ratification (with 543 of 568 valid votes) on December 2, 1992; the Bundesrat (unanimously) on December 18, 1992. German ratification became effective on December 31, 1992. The German Bundestag is the lower house of parliament, whose members are chosen in nationwide elections. The Bundesrat is the upper house, whose members are appointed by the governments of the German provinces ("Länder").

341 These amendments entered into force on December 25, 1992, after the Maastricht votes of Bundestag and Bundesrat. The *Basic Law* (*Grundgesetz*) functions as the German constitution.

342 The remaining challenges were ruled inadmissible by the Court.

343 Article 20(2): "Alle Staatsgewalt geht vom Volke aus. Sie wird vom Volke in Wahlen und Abstimmungen und durch besondere Organe der Gesetzgebung, der vollziehenden Gewalt und der Rechtsprechung ausgeübt." All translations from the German are my own.

344 Article 38(1): "Die Abgeordneten des Deutschen Bundestages werden in allgemeiner, unmittelbarer, freier, gleicher und geheimer Wahl gewählt. Sie sind Vertreter des ganzen Volkes, an Aufträge und Weisungen nicht gebunden und nur ihrem Gewissen unterworfen."

345 Which the Court obfuscatingly conflates into "the democracy principle" (cf. endnote 351).

346 Most important is the addition of Article 23(1), whose second sentence reads: "The Federal Republic may for this purpose [the realization of a united Europe] transfer sovereign powers by law with the consent of the Bundesrat." ("Der Bund kann hierzu [zur Verwirklichung eines vereinten

Europas] durch Gesetz mit Zustimmung des Bundesrates Hoheitsrechte übertragen.")

347 All page references in the present section refer to the official text of the Court's verdict in *Entscheidungen des Bundesverfassungsgerichts*, vol. 89, pp. 155–213.

348 The Court itself recognizes this (pp. 181, 182; cf. 187) by construing the narrow challenge it deems admissible as implicitly invoking Article 20.

349 Article 79(3). Article 38 does not belong to this core, and the legislature could thus defeat successful legal challenges based on this Article simply by amending it.

350 A growing necessity is, of course, an oxymoron. Presumably, the Court wanted to say that, at some point in the integration process, the European Parliament would have to be given real powers while avoiding to say anything further about when this point would be reached.

351 Gustavsson, "Defending the Democratic Deficit." Gustavsson nicely stresses how the Court itself felt compelled to acknowledge that the European Central Bank involves a "modification" of the democracy principle: "This limitation of the democratic legitimation emanating from the voters in the member states touches the democracy principle, but, as a modification of this principle authorized in the second sentence of Article 88 of the *Basic Law*, it is nevertheless consistent with Article 79(3) of the *Basic Law*" (p. 208). ("Diese Einschränkung der von den Wählern in den Mitgliedstaaten ausgehenden demokratischen Legitimation berührt das Demokratieprinzip, ist jedoch als eine in Art. 88 Satz 2 GG vorgesehene Modifikation dieses Prinzips mit Art. 79 Abs. 3 GG vereinbar.") One needs many years of conditioning through legal training to be able to see this as anything but a flagrant breach of the *Basic Law*: Article 79(3) expressly declares inadmissible any legal changes that touch the requirement that "all state power emanates from the people." The German Constitutional Court admits that it is sanctioning a limitation of the people's power that touches and modifies the democracy principle. But it sees no inconsistency with Article 79(3). Why not? Because the second sentence of Article 88 authorizes the modification. But wait! This sentence was newly added at the time of the ratification of the *Maastricht Treaty* and was itself under challenge in this very legal case. More importantly, this sentence cannot possibly make a difference to whether or not a modification is consistent with Article 79(3). For modifications of the democracy principle that do not violate Article 20 are consistent with Article 79(3) even without any help from Article 88. And with regard to modifications that do violate Article 20, the fact that they are authorized by Article 88 – far from showing the constitutionality of the modification – shows the unconstitutionality of the authorization! Insofar as an article of the *Basic Law* authorizes measures that violate the immutable core of the *Basic Law*, it can have no legal force at all.

352 Oddly, the word "Abstimmungen" here is often translated as "voting." But this is a mistake. To be sure, any *Abstimmung* is an instance of voting.

But the word "Abstimmung" does not cover the kind of voting that takes place in regular elections ("Wahlen"). The reference to *Abstimmungen* thus clearly envisions voting activities other than elections – namely referenda ("Volksabstimmungen").

353 The Court is remarkably alert to potential conflicts between the interests of the people and those of their elected representatives – when doing so serves the Court's argumentative objectives. Thus the Court justifies the planned European Central Bank by pointing out that "the autonomous vesting of most tasks of monetary policy in an independent central bank detaches the exercise of sovereign powers of the state from direct national or supranational parliamentary responsibility, in order to withdraw monetary matters from the reach of interest groups and holders of political office concerned about re-election" (p. 208).

354 This "Enabling Law" (officially entitled the *Law to Remedy the Distress of the People and the Nation*) was a constitutional amendment adopted by both houses of the German parliament which, initially for a period of four years, conferred legislative powers to the existing executive headed by Chancellor Adolf Hitler.

355 Rossiter, *The Federalist Papers*, p. 253. This passage is from *The Federalist* No. 40, written by James Madison. The surrounding text and Nos. 39 and 43 (likewise by Madison) are also pertinent. See also Ackerman, *We The People*, ch. 7.

356 Citizens can vote for this or that political party in national or European Parliament elections. But the effects of such choices on the shaping of European political institutions – if any – are too remote to be foreseeable. Moreover, citizens cannot reasonably be expected in national elections to choose a party on the basis of its stance on just this one set of issues.

357 On the meaning of "subsidiarity" as enshrined in Article 3b of the *Treaty on European Union*, see for example Blichner and Sangolt, "The Concept of Subsidiarity." The intuitive idea is quite general and thus holds equally well for sub-national levels of decision-making: The point of democratic procedures is to enable persons to participate in shaping the social context that shapes their lives. Insofar as this value is better promoted if we all have rather more influence upon the social context in our own locale than if we all had rather little influence equally spread more broadly, political decision-making should be decentralized – in the limiting case all the way down to the individual.

358 One might well point out that the (partial) loss of a distinctive French culture would impose a significant loss on all Europeans. This loss may here be left aside, however, because it is one that Europeans would be free to take into account, if they were assigned the power to determine educational policy for Europe at large.

359 For more on Canada and asymmetry, see esp. pp. 277–83 of Kymlicka, "Federalism, Nationalism, and Multiculturalism." I take no stance here on Kymlicka's view that the Quebecois are especially entitled to asymmetrical accommodation because they constitute a national minority.

360 Among these are the FAO, ILO, IMF, IMO, UNESCO, WHO, and the World Bank. UNESCO, for example, was abandoned by UN-members Singapore, Great Britain, and the US for long periods, even while it was including non-UN-member Switzerland.

361 This proposal raises various fascinating disaster possibilities in that the preference of one national electorate may depend on the decision of another. If there are strong reasons for believing this, national referenda might be held in the appropriate order. But what if there are cyclical preference dependencies? What if Portugal wants to join if and only if Ireland does and Ireland wants to join if and only if Portugal does not? I doubt these are realistic scenarios and, in any case, I cannot deal with them here.

362 Affirmative answers to (A), (B), (G), or (H) should be understood to mean that the EU would be at least partly in charge. Some additional functions in these fields might remain at the national level (or even below), if this is mandated by the subsidiarity principle.

363 Many less important fields could obviously be added, but I believe that, at Stage One, citizens should focus on the most important issues (*basic* scope) Within the institutional framework of the EU, less important fields can be democratically decided later on – for example, whether there should be an EU-wide police force, an EU-wide vaccination program, EU-wide standards for food and medicine safety and quality, and so forth.

364 One may object to this idea that the parliament will be inclined to give itself excessive powers vis-à-vis the other two branches of government, thus undermining any genuine separation of powers. I do not believe this is a great danger, because many members of the first EU parliament will be plausible candidates for the executive and judicial position they create and circumscribe.

365 It may be thought that this specification still fails to do justice to permanent minorities who, even with a proportionate number of seats in parliament, may still lose on all contested issues. Often, political decentralization, fair-mindedness of the majority, or legislative bargaining (where the majority is sometimes divided) can solve this problem. But I see no plausible institutional solution for cases in which these remedies fail.

366 These matters have been understood and debated for quite a long time – e.g. by Thomas Wright Hill (1821), Thomas Gilpin (1844), and Thomas Hare (1873), all discussed in Beitz, *Political Equality*, ch. 6. Unrepresentative systems can nevertheless survive, of course, if those who stand to lose from reform can use the existing system to block reform.

367 Such emergencies were typically present, of course, during the most important events shaping modern political institutions – in the wake of the French Revolution (with the threat of reactionary intervention) and during the shaping of the United States (with the War of Independence).

368 Insofar as options might have to be resubmitted, more than five decisions might be necessary.

Bibliography

Abou El Fadl, Khaled. "Islam and the Theology of Power." *Middle East Report* 221 (2001): 28–33. www.merip.org/mer/mer221/221_abu_el_fadl. html.

Ackerman, Bruce. *We The People.* Vol. 1, *Foundations.* Cambridge MA: Harvard University Press, 1991.

ACLU (American Civil Liberties Union). *Hundreds of New Documents Reveal Expanded Military Role in Domestic Surveillance.* October 14, 2007. www. aclu.org/safefree/nationalsecurityletters/32145prs20071014.html.

Albright, Madeleine. Interview on ABC's *This Week.* July 9, 2000. usinfo.org/ wf-archive/2000/000710/epf101.htm.

Albright, Madeleine. *Madam Secretary: A Memoir.* New York: Miramax Books, 2003.

American National Election Studies. "Abortion (2), by Law 1980–2004." November 27, 2005. www.electionstudies.org/nesguide/toptable/tab4c_2b. htm.

American Servicemembers' Protection Act. Section 2008 of Public Law 107–201, 116 Stat., 899, 22 U.S.C. 7401 (2002). www.state.gov/t/pm/rls/othr/ misc/23425.htm.

Amnesty International. *Amnesty International Report 2005: The State of the World's Human Rights.* New York: Amnesty International, 2005. www. amnesty.org/en/report/info/POL10/001/2005.

Amnesty International. *United States of America/Yemen: Secret Detention in CIA "Black Sites."* November 8, 2005. web.amnesty.org/library/Index/ ENGAMR511772005.

Amnesty International. *USA: Days of Adverse Hardship in US Detention Camps.* December 16, 2005. web.amnesty.org/library/index/ ENGAMR511072005.

Amnesty International. *United Kingdom Human Rights: A Broken Promise.* February 23, 2006. web.amnesty.org/library/Index/ENGEUR450042006.

Amnesty International. *Beyond Abu Ghraib: Detention and Torture in Iraq.* March 6, 2006. web.amnesty.org/library/index/engmde140012006.

Annan, Kofi. "Two Concepts of Sovereignty." *The Economist.* September 18, 1999. www.un.org/News/ossg/sg/stories/kaecon.html.

Anscombe, Elizabeth. *Ethics, Religion, and Politics. The Collected Philosophical Papers of G. E. M. Anscombe*, vol. 3. Minneapolis: University of Minnesota Press, 1981.

Apuzzo, Matt. "Judge Wants Details on Destroyed CIA Videotapes." *Miami Herald.* January 24, 2008.

Arnove, Anthony. "Sanctions on Iraq: The 'Propaganda Campaign'." *ZNET Daily Commentaries.* April 1, 2000. www.zmag.org/zspace/commentaries/386.

Bagchi, Indrani. "26 Foreigners Killed." *Times of India.* November 30, 2008. www.timesofindia.indiatimes.com/World/USA/26_foreigners_killed_in_terror_attack/articleshow/3774092.cms.

Baker, Raymond W. *Capitalism's Achilles Heel.* Hoboken, NJ: John Wiley & Sons, 2005.

Baldor, Lolita C. Associated Press. "Military Grants More Waivers to Recruits." February 14, 2007. www.palmcenter.org/press/dadt/in_print/military_grants_more_waivers_to_recruits.

Basic Law. *Grundgesetz für die Bundesrepublik Deutschland.* www.bundestag.de/dokumente/rechtsgrundlagen/grundgesetz/index.html.

BBC. *File on 4: Rendition.* Aired February 8, 2005. news.bbc.co.uk/nol/shared/bsp/hi/pdfs/15_02_05_renditions.pdf.

BBC News. "No UN Action on Sudan Missile Attack." August 24, 1998. http://news.bbc.co.uk/1/hi/world/africa/157192.stm.

BBC News. "UN Chief's Rwanda Genocide Regret." March 26, 2004. http://news.bbc.co.uk/2/hi/africa/3573229.stm.

Begg, Moazzam and Victoria Brittain. *Enemy Combatant: A British Muslim's Journey To Guantanamo and Back.* London: Free Press, 2006.

Beitz, Charles. *Political Equality.* Princeton, NJ: Princeton University Press, 1989.

Belasco Amy. *The Cost of Iraq, Afghanistan, and Other Global War on Terror Operations Since 9/11.* Congressional Research Service Report for Congress. Washington, DC: Library of Congress, 2009. www.fas.org/sgp/crs/natsec/RL33110.pdf.

Benjamin, Mark. "Inside the CIA's Notorious 'Black Sites'." *Salon.* December 14, 2007. www.salon.com/news/feature/2007/12/14/bashmilah.

Bennett, Jonathan. *The Act Itself.* Oxford: Oxford University Press, 1995.

Bennett-Jones, Owen. "Iraqi Deaths Survey 'Was Robust'." BBC News. March 26, 2007. http://news.bbc.co.uk/2/hi/uk_news/politics/6495753.stm.

Bin Laden, Osama. Interview with *Daily Ummat* (Karachi). September 28, 2001. Frequently reprinted, e.g. at www.justresponse.net/Bin_Laden1.html.

Blackstone, Sir William. *Commentaries on the Laws of England*. Facsimile of the First Edition of 1765–69. Chicago: University of Chicago Press, 1979.

Blichner, Lars and Linda Sangolt. "The Concept of Subsidiarity and the Debate on European Cooperation: Pitfalls and Possibilities." *Governance: An International Journal of Policy and Administration* 7 (1994): 284–306.

Bureau of Labor Statistics. *Consumer Price Index*. US Department of Labor, 2009. www.bls.gov/cpi (accessed December 23, 2009).

Burghardt, Jutta. "The Humanitarian Situation in Iraq: The Humanitarian Program 'Oil for Food,' and Human Rights." *CSCA Web*. July 2001. www.nodo50.org/csca/english/petxalim-ddhh-eng.html.

Burnham, Gilbert, Riyadh Lafta, Shannon Doocy, and Les Roberts. "Mortality after the 2003 Invasion of Iraq: A Cross-sectional Cluster Sample Survey." *The Lancet*, Volume 368, Issue 9545, Pages 1421–1428, October 21, 2006. www.thelancet.com/journals/lancet/article/PIIS0140-6736(06)69491-9/fulltext.

Bybee, Jay S. *Standards of Conduct for Interrogation under 18 USC sects. 2340–2340A*. Office of Legal Counsel, U.S. Department of Justice. August 1, 2002. http://fl1.findlaw.com/news.findlaw.com/hdocs/docs/doj/bybee80102mem.pdf.

Campaign Against Sanctions on Iraq. *Starving Iraq: One Humanitarian Disaster We Can Stop*. March 1999. www.casi.org.uk/briefing/pamp_ed1.html.

Camus, Albert. *The Rebel: An Essay on Man in Revolt*, trans. Anthony Bower. New York: Vintage, 1956.

Castiglione, Dario. "Contracts and Constitutions." In Richard Bellamy, Vittorio Bufacchi and Dario Castiglione, eds., *Democracy and Constitutional Culture in the Union of Europe*. London: Lothian Foundation Press, 1995.

CBC News. "US Won't Change Policy on Deportations to Third Countries: Ambassador." December 4, 2003. www.cbc.ca/news/story/2003/12/04/cellucci_passport031204.html.

CBS. *60 Minutes: Punishing Saddam*. Aired May 12, 1996.

Center for Constitutional Rights. *Detention in Afghanistan and Guantanamo Bay: Composite Statement of Shafiq Rasul, Asif Iqbal, and Rhuhel Ahmet*. July 26, 2004. www.ccrjustice.org/files/report_tiptonThree.pdf.

Center for Constitutional Rights. *Report on Torture and Cruel, Inhuman, and Degrading Treatment of Prisoners at Guantánamo Bay, Cuba*. July 2006. www.ccrjustice.org/files/Report_ReportOnTorture.pdf.

Center for Defense Information. *What Is the "Defense" Budget?* 2008. www.cdi.org/PDFs/What is the Defense Budget.pdf.

Center for Nutrition Policy and Promotion. *Cost of Food at Home*. United States Department of Agriculture, December 2008. http://www.cnpp.usda.gov/USDAFoodCost-Home.htm.

Chen, Shaohua and Martin Ravallion. "How Did the World's Poorest Fare in the 1990s?" *Review of Income and Wealth* 47 (2001): 283–300.

Chen, Shaohua and Martin Ravallion. "China Is Poorer than We Thought, But No Less Successful in the Fight against Poverty." World Bank Policy Research Working Paper WPS 4621, Washington, DC, 2008. http://econ.worldbank.org/docsearch.

Chen, Shaohua and Martin Ravallion. "The Developing World Is Poorer than We Thought, But No Less Successful in the Fight against Poverty." World Bank Policy Research Working Paper WPS 4703, Washington, DC, 2008. http://econ.worldbank.org/docsearch.

CIA (Central Intelligence Agency). *Country Comparison: Total Fertility Rate.* In *The World Factbook.* 2009. https://www.cia.gov/library/publications/the-world-factbook/rankorder/2127rank.html.

Cline, William R. *Trade Policy and Global Poverty.* Washington, DC: Center for Global Development, 2004.

CNN. *Critique of Worldwide Media Coverage.* Aired November 26, 2005. transcripts.cnn.com/TRANSCRIPTS/0511/26/i_c.01.html.

Cohen, Gerald A. *History, Labour, and Freedom.* Oxford: Oxford University Press, 1989.

Commission of Inquiry into the Actions of Canadian Officials in Relation to Maher Arar. *Report of the Events Relating to Maher Arar: Analysis and Recommendations.* Ottawa: Public Works and Government Services Canada, 2006. www.pch.gc.ca/cs-kc/arar/Arar_e.pdf.

Consumer Project on Technology. *CPTech's Page on Intellectual Property Rights.* n.d. www.cptech.org/ip.

Convention against Torture and Other Cruel, Inhuman or Degrading Treatment or Punishment. Adopted by General Assembly Resolution 39/46 of December 10, 1984. www2.ohchr.org/english/law/cat.htm.

Convention (IV) relative to the Protection of Civilian Persons in Time of War (Fourth Geneva Convention). Geneva, August 12, 1949. www.icrc.org/ihl. nsf/7c4d08d9b287a42141256739003e636b/6756482d86146898c125641e004aa3c5.

de Cordoba, Santiago Fernandez and David Vanzetti. "Now What? Searching for a Solution to the WTO Industrial Tariff Negotiations." In Sam Laird and Santiago Fernandez de Cordoba, eds., *Coping with Trade Reforms: A Developing-Country Perspective on the WTO Industrial Tariff Negotiations.* Basingstoke: Palgrave Macmillan, 2006.

Correa, Carlos M. *Intellectual Property Rights, the WTO and Developing Countries: The TRIPS Agreement and Policy Options.* London: Zed Books, 2000.

Correa, Carlos M. "Public Health and Intellectual Property Rights." *Global Social Policy* 2, no. 3 (2002): 261–78. http://gsp.sagepub.com/cgi/reprint/2/3/261.

Correa, Carlos M. "Implications of Bilateral Free Trade Agreements on Access to Medicines." *Bulletin of the World Health Organization* 84 (2006): 399–404. www.who.int/bulletin/volumes/84/5/399.pdf.

Crossette, Barbara. "After Long Fight, U.N. Agrees To Cut Dues Paid By U.S." *New York Times.* December 23, 2000, p. A1. www.nytimes.com/2000/12/23/world/after-long-fight-un-agrees-to-cut-dues-paid-by-us.html?pagewanted=1.

Crumley, Bruce. "The Mumbai Attacks: Terror's Tactical Shift." *Time.* November 29, 2008. www.time.com/time/world/article/0,8599,1862795,00.html.

Cueva, Hanny Beteta. "What Is Missing in Measures of Women's Empowerment?" *Journal of Human Development* 7, no. 2 (2006): 221–41.

Cuomo, Mario. "Religious Belief and Public Morality: A Catholic Governor's Perspective." In Mario Cuomo. *More Than Words: The Speeches of Mario Cuomo*. New York: St Martin's Press, 1993.

Danaher, Kevin. ed. *50 Years Is Enough: The Case Against the World Bank and the International Monetary Fund*. Cambridge, MA: South End Press, 1994.

Davies, James B., Susanna Sandstrom, Anthony Shorrocks, and Edward N. Wolff. *The World Distribution of Household Wealth*. UNU-WIDER, December 5, 2006. www.iariw.org/papers/2006/davies.pdf.

Deaton, Angus, and Olivier Dupriez. "Global Poverty and Global Price Indexes." Working paper, June 2009, available at www.princeton.edu/~deaton/downloads/Global_Poverty_and_Global_Price_Indexes.pdf.

Dehghanpisheh, Babak, John Barry, and Roy Gutman. "The Death Convoy of Afghanistan." *Newsweek*. August 26. 2002. www.newsweek.com/id/65473.

Department of Justice, Office of the Inspector General. "A Review of the Federal Bureau of Investigation's Use of National Security Letters." March 2007. www.usdoj.gov/oig/special/s0703b/final.pdf.

Des Forges, Alison. *Leave None to Tell the Story: Genocide in Rwanda*. New York: Human Rights Watch, 1999. www.hrw.org/reports/1999/rwanda/index.htm.

Dijkstra, A. Geske. "Towards a Fresh Start in Measuring Gender Equality: A Contribution to the Debate." *Journal of Human Development* 7, no. 2 (2006): 275–83.

Donagan, Alan. *The Theory of Morality*. Chicago: University of Chicago Press, 1977.

Doran Jamie, dir. *Afghan Massacre: The Convoy of Death*. 2002. www.informationclearinghouse.info/article3267.htm.

Dworkin, Ronald. *Life's Dominion: An Argument about Abortion, Euthanasia and Individual Freedom*. London: Harper Collins, 1993.

Economist, The. "An Alternative View: GDP Per Head." March 11, 2004.

Entscheidungen des Bundesverfassungsgerichts, vol. 89: 155–213.

FAO (Food and Agriculture Organization of the United Nations). *The State of Food Insecurity in the World 2008: High Food Prices and Food Security – Threats and Opportunities*. Rome: FAO, 2008.

FAO (Food and Agriculture Organization of the United Nations). "Number of Hungry People Rises to 963 Million." News Release. December 9, 2008. www.fao.org/news/story/en/item/8836/icode/ (accessed January 13, 2010).

FAO (Food and Agriculture Organization of the United Nations). "1.02 Billion People Hungry." News Release. June 19, 2009. www.fao.org/news/story/en/item/20568/icode/ (accessed January 13, 2010).

Filipov, David. "Warlord's Men Commit Rape in Revenge against Taliban." *Boston Globe*. February 24, 2002, p. A1.

Filkins, Dexter. "Afghan Leader Outmaneuvers Election Rivals." *New York Times*, June 24, 2009, p. A1. www.nytimes.com/2009/06/25/world/asia/25karzai.html.

Fisher, Ian. "Pope Reaffirms View Opposing Gay Marriage and Abortion." *New York Times*, March 14, 2007. www.nytimes.com/2007/03/14/world/europe/14vatican.html.

Fogarty International Center for Advanced Study in the Health Sciences. "Strategic Plan: Fiscal Years 2000–2003." Bethesda, Md.: National Institutes of Health, n.d. www.fic.nih.gov/about/plan/exec_summary.htm.

Foot, Philippa. "The Problem of Abortion and the Doctrine of Double Effect." In Philippa Foot, *Virtues and Vices and Other Essays in Moral Philosophy*. Berkeley: University of California Press, 1978.

Foreign Policy Association/Princeton Town Hall Meeting. "Transcript of Remarks by Thomas Franck." May 9, 2003. www.fpa.org/topics_info2414/topics_info_show.htm?doc_id=175569.

Franck, Thomas. "When, If Ever, May States Deploy Military Force Without Prior Security Council Authorization?" *Washington University Journal of Law and Policy* 5 (2001): 51–71.

Franck, Thomas. "Legality and Legitimacy in Humanitarian Intervention." In *Humanitarian Intervention. Nomos*, vol. 47. Edited by Terry Nardin and Melissa Williams. New York: New York University Press, 2005.

Frank, Erica. "Funding the Public Health Response to Terrorism." *British Medical Journal.* 331 (2005): 526–7. bmj.com/cgi/content/full/331/7517/E378.

Galston, William. "Neutral Dialogue and the Abortion Debate." *Report from the Institute for Philosophy and Public Policy* 10 (1990): 12–15.

Gamble, Sonya B., Lilo T. Strauss, Wilda Y. Parker, Douglas A. Cook, Suzanne B. Zane, and Saeed Hamdan. "Abortion Surveillance – United States, 2005." *Morbidity and Morality Weekly Report*, 57, SS13 (2008): 1–32. www.cdc.gov/mmwr/preview/mmwrhtml/ss5713a1.htm?s_cid=ss5713a1_e.

Garfield, Richard. Interview by *Columbia News*. March 3, 2000. www.columbia.edu/cu/news/media/00/richardGarfield/index.html.

Gauthier, David. *Morals by Agreement*. Oxford: Oxford University Press, 1987.

Glaberson, William. "Red Cross Monitors Barred from Guantánamo." *New York Times*, November 16, 2007. www.nytimes.com/2007/11/16/washington/16gitmo.html.

Global Fund to Fight AIDS, Tuberculosis and Malaria. "Current Grant Commitments and Disbursements." October 8, 2009. www.theglobalfund.org/en/commitmentsdisbursements/.

Gourevitch, Philip. *We Wish to Inform You that Tomorrow We Will be Killed With Our Families*. New York: Picador, 1999.

Graham, Bradley and Dan Morgan. "US Has No Plans to Count Civilian Casualties." *Washington Post*. April 15, 2003, p. A13. www.globalpolicy.org/component/content/article/167/35300.html.

Greenawalt, Kent. *Religious Convictions and Political Choice*. Oxford: Oxford University Press, 1987.

Greenhouse, Linda. "Justices, 5–4, Back Detainee Appeals for Guantánamo." *New York Times*. June 13, 2008. www.nytimes.com/2008/06/13/washington/13scotus.html.

Grimmett, Richard F. *Conventional Arms Transfers to Developing Nations*. Washington, DC: Congressional Research Service Report for Congress, August 6, 2002. http://fpc.state.gov/documents/organization/12632.pdf.

Grisez, Germain. *Abortion: The Myths, the Realities, and the Arguments*. New York: Corpus Books, 1970.

Gustavsson, Sverker. "Defending the Democratic Deficit." In Albert Weale and Michael Nentwich, eds., *Political Theory and the European Union: Legitimacy, Constitutional Choice, and Citizenship*. London: Routledge, 1998.

Hamdan v Rumsfeld. 548 U.S. (2006). Majority opinion written by Justice Stevens. www.supremecourtus.gov/opinions/05pdf/05-184.pdf.

Harrison, Mark. "Resource Mobilization for World War II: the USA, UK, USSR, and Germany, 1938–1945." *Economic History Review* 41 (1988): 171–92.

Harrison, Mark, ed. *The Economics of World War II: Six Great Powers in International Comparison*. Cambridge: Cambridge University Press, 2000.

Haubrich, Dirk. "Civil Liberties in Emergencies." In C. Neal Tate. ed., *Governments of the World: A Global Guide to Citizens' Rights and Responsibilities*, 4 vols. Farmington Hills, MI: Macmillan Reference, 2005.

Henry L. Stimson Center. "US Case for Al Shifa Attack Disintegrates." *CBW Chronicle* 3 (February 2000). www.stimson.org/cbw/?sn=cb2001121262.

Hirschkorn, Phil. "Bomber's Defense Focuses on U.S. Policy in Iraq." *CNN International*. June 4, 2001. edition.cnn.com/2001/LAW/06/04/embassy.bombings.02.

Hollis, Aidan and Thomas Pogge. *The Health Impact Fund: Making New Medicines Accessible for All*. Incentives for Global Health: 2008.

Houston Chronicle. "Clinton: A Story Unfolds." n.d.

Hoyos, Carola and Alan Beattie. "Nations Ponder Whether They Can Afford to Oppose US Stance." *Financial Times*. November 7, 2002, p. 7.

Human Rights Documentation Unit of the NCGUB (National Coalition Government of Burma). *Burma Human Rights Yearbooks, 2004–2007*. November 26, 2008. www.burmalibrary.org/show.php?cat=2252&lo=d&sl=0.

Human Rights First. *Private Security Contractors at War: Ending the Culture of Impunity* New York: Human Rights First, 2008. www.humanrightsfirst.info/pdf/08115-usls-psc-final.pdf.

Human Rights Watch. *Fatally Flawed: Cluster Bombs and Their Use by the United States in Afghanistan*. 2002. hrw.org/reports/2002/us-afghanistan.

Human Rights Watch. *"Killing You is a Very Easy Thing for Us": Human Rights Abuses in Southeast Afghanistan*. July 2003. www.hrw.org/reports/2003/afghanistan0703.

Human Rights Watch. *"Enduring Freedom": Abuses by US Forces in Afghanistan.* March 2004. hrw.org/reports/2004/afghanistan0304.

Human Rights Watch. *Afghanistan: Killing and Torture by US Predate Abu Ghraib.* May 20, 2005. www.hrw.org/en/news/2005/05/20/afghanistan-killing-and-torture-us-predate-abu-ghraib.

Human Rights Watch. *Leadership Failure: Firsthand Accounts of Torture of Iraqi Detainees by the US Army's 82nd Airborne Division.* September 2005. hrw.org/reports/2005/us0905.

Human Rights Watch. "US Operated Secret 'Dark Prison' in Kabul." *Human Rights News.* December 19, 2005. hrw.org/english/docs/2005/12/19/afghan12319.htm.

Human Rights Watch. *By the Numbers: Findings of the Detainee Abuse and Accountabililty Project.* April 25, 2006. www.hrw.org/en/reports/2006/04/25/numbers.

Human Rights Watch. *"No Blood, No Foul": Soldiers' Accounts of Detainee Abuse in Iraq.* July 2006. hrw.org/reports/2006/us0706.

Human Rights Watch. *Q&A: Private Military Contractors and the Law.* 2007. www.hrw.org/legacy/english/docs/2004/05/05/iraq8547.htm.

ICCPR (International Covenant on Civil and Political Rights). Adopted by General Assembly Resolution 2200A (XXI) of December 16, 1966. www2.ohchr.org/english/law/ccpr.htm.

ICESCR (International Covenant on Economic, Social and Cultural Rights). Adopted by General Assembly Resolution 2200A (XXI) of December 16, 1966. www2.ohchr.org/english/law/cescr.htm.

ILO (International Labour Organization). *The End of Child Labour: Within Reach.* Geneva: International Labour Office, 2006. www.ilo.org/public/english/standards/relm/ilc/ilc95/pdf/rep-i-b.pdf.

Jaffer, Jameel, and Amrit Singh. *Administration of Torture: A Documentary Record from Washington to Abu Ghraib and Beyond.* New York: Columbia University Press, 2007.

Juma, Calestous. "Intellectual Property Rights and Globalization: Implications for Developing Countries." Science, Technology and Innovation Discussion Paper No. 4. Harvard Center for International Development, 1999.

Kar, Dev, and Devon Cartwright-Smith. *Illicit Financial Flows from Developing Countries 2002–2006.* Washington: Global Financial Integrity, 2008. www.ffdngo.org/documentrepository/GFI%20Report.pdf.

Karwal, Roshni. *At General Assembly Event, a Call for Equity and Action on Development Goals.* UNICEF, 2008. www.unicef.org/policyanalysis/index_45740.html.

Klasen, Stephan. "UNDP's Gender-related Measures: Some Conceptual Problems and Possible Solutions." *Journal of Human Development* 7, no. 2 (2006): 243–74.

Kymlicka, Will. "Federalism, Nationalism, and Multiculturalism." In Dimitrios Karmis and Wayne Norman, eds., *Theories of Federalism: A Reader* (New York: Palgrave Macmillan, 2005).

Lafraniere, Sharon. "Europe Takes Africa's Fish, and Boatloads of Migrants Follow." *New York Times*, January 14, 2008. www.nytimes.com/2008/01/14/world/africa/14fishing.html.

Lam, Ricky and Leonard Wantchekon. "Dictatorships as a Political Dutch Disease." Working Paper 795, Yale University, 1999. www.econ.nyu.edu/user/nyarkoy/wantche1.pdf.

Lasseter, Tom. "America's Prison for Terrorists often Held the Wrong Men." *McClatchy Newspapers*. June 15, 2008. www.mcclatchydc.com/detainees/story/38773.html.

Lasseter, Tom. "As Possible Afghan War-Crimes Evidence Removed, US Silent." *McClatchy Newspapers*. December 11, 2008. www.mcclatchydc.com/227/story/57649.html.

Levin, Daniel. *Legal Standards Applicable Under 18 U.S.C. sects. 2340-2340A.* Office of Legal Counsel, US Department of Justice. December 30, 2004. www.usdoj.gov/olc/18usc23402340a2.htm.

Levy, Adrian and Cathy Scott-Clark. "One Huge US Jail." *Guardian*. March 19, 2005. www.guardian.co.uk/afghanistan/story/0,1284,1440836,00.html.

Lewis, Neil A. "Papers Show U.S. Knew of Genocide in Rwanda." *New York Times*. August 22, 2001, p. A5. http://query.nytimes.com/gst/abstract.html?res=FA0915F63D550C718EDDA10894D9404482.

Lewis, Neil A. "Red Cross Finds Detainee Abuse in Guantánamo." *New York Times*. November 30, 2004, p. A1. www.nytimes.com/2004/11/30/politics/30gitmo.html?ex=1259470800&en=825f1aa04c65241f&ei=5088&partner=rssnyt.

Lewis, Neil A. "Man Mistakenly Abducted by CIA Seeks Reinstatement of Suit." *New York Times*. November 29, 2006, p. A15. query.nytimes.com/gst/fullpage.html?res=9E06E5DD113EF93AA15752C1A9609C8B63.

Mackay, Neil. "Iraq's Child Prisoners." *Sunday Herald* (Glasgow). August 1, 2004. www.globalpolicy.org/security/issues/iraq/attack/law/2004/0801childprison.htm.

Maguire, Kevin and Andy Lines. "Exclusive: Bush Plot to Bomb His Arab Ally." *Mirror*. November 22, 2005. www.mirror.co.uk/news/tm_objectid=16397937&method=full&siteid=94762&headline=exclusive–bush-plot-to-bomb-his-arab-ally-name_page.html.

Maze, Rick. "Rise in Moral Waivers Troubles Lawmaker." *Navy Times*. February 20, 2007. www.navytimes.com/news/2007/02/apWaivedRecruits070213/.

Mazzetti, Mark. "9/11 Panel Study Finds that CIA Withheld Tapes." *New York Times*, December 22, 2007. www.nytimes.com/2007/12/22/washington/22intel.html.

McCarthy, Rory. "US Afghan Ally 'Tortured Witnesses to His War Crimes.'" *Guardian*. November 18, 2002. www.guardian.co.uk/international/story/0,3604,842082,00.html.

Milanovic, Branko. *Worlds Apart: Measuring International and Global Inequality*. Princeton, NJ: Princeton University Press, 2005.

Milanovic, Branko. "Even Higher Global Inequality than Previously Thought: A Note on Global Inequality Calculations Using the 2005 International Comparison Program Results." *International Journal of Health Services* 38, no. 3 (2008): 421–9.

Military Commissions Act of 2006. Public Law 109-366, 120 Stat., 2600. October 17, 2006. www.loc.gov/rr/frd/Military_Law/pdf/PL-109-366.pdf.

Monbiot, George. *Manifesto for a New World Order.* New York: New Press, 2004.

MSNBC. *Hardball: Tactics of Interrogation.* Aired January 16, 2006. www.msnbc.msn.com/id/10895199.

National Park Service. *Jim Crow Laws.* 2006. http://www.nps.gov/malu/forteachers/jim_crow_laws.htm.

National Security Presidential Directive 17 (NSPD 17). Identical to Homeland Security Presidential Directive 4 (HSPD 4). www.fas.org/irp/offdocs/nspd/nspd-17.html.

Norris, Robert, William Arkin, Hans Kristensen, and Joshua Handler. "Pakistan's Nuclear Forces, 2001." *Bulletin of the Atomic Scientists* 58, no. 1 (2002). http://thebulletin.metapress.com/content/485jr988wv3v1551/fulltext.pdf.

North, Andrew. "Dostum gets Afghan Military Role." BBC News. March 2, 2005. http://news.bbc.co.uk/2/hi/south_asia/4308683.stm.

OAU (Organization of African Unity) International Panel of Eminent Personalities. *Rwanda: The Preventable Genocide.* July 7, 2000. www.visiontv.ca/RememberRwanda/Report.pdf.

OECD (Organisation for Economic Cooperation and Development). *Development Aid at Its Highest Level Ever in 2008.* OECD, March 30, 2009. www.oecd.org/document/35/0,3343,en_2649_34487_42458595_1_1_1_1,00.html.

OECD (Organisation for Economic Cooperation and Development). *QWIDS (Query Wizard for International Development Statistics).* 2009. stats.oecd.org/qwids.

Okin, Susan. "Poverty, Well-Being, and Gender: What Counts, Who's Heard?" *Philosophy and Public Affairs* 31, no. 3 (2003): 280–316.

Oxfam. "Investing for Life: Meeting Poor People's Needs for Access to Medicines through Responsible Business Practices." Oxfam Briefing Paper 109, Oxfam, Oxford, UK, November 2007. www.oxfam.org/en/policy/bp109_investing_for_life_0711.

Parfit, Derek. *Reasons and Persons.* Oxford: Oxford University Press, 1984.

PBS Frontline. "One Hundred Days of Slaughter: A Chronology of US/UN Actions." In *The Triumph of Evil.* 1999. www.pbs.org/wgbh/pages/frontline/shows/evil/etc/slaughter.html.

PBS Frontline. "The Warning That Was Ignored." In *The Triumph of Evil.* 1999. www.pbs.org/wgbh/pages/frontline/shows/evil/warning/cable.html.

PBS Frontline. "The Debate Over U.N. Sanctions." In *IRAQ – Truth and Lies in Baghdad.* November 2002. www.pbs.org/frontlineworld/stories/iraq/sanctions.html.

Pearlstein, Deborah and Priti Patel. *Behind the Wire*. New York: Human Rights First, 2005. www.humanrightsfirst.org/us_law/PDF/behind-the-wire-033005.pdf.

Peterson, Matt. "American Sugar Policy Leaves a Sour Taste." *Policy Innovations*, July 8, 2009. www.policyinnovations.org/ideas/commentary/data/000136.

Physicians for Human Rights. *Preliminary Assessment of Alleged Mass Gravesites in the Area of Mazar-I-Sharif, Afghanistan*. Boston and Washington DC, 2002. http://physiciansforhumanrights.org/library/report-prelimass-afghanistan.html.

Pieth, Mark and Radha Ivory. "Do Honest Corporations Stand a Chance?" *Forbes*, January 22, 2009. www.forbes.com/2009/01/22/siemens-compliance-scandal-biz-corruption09-cx_mp_ri_0122siemens.html.

Pilger, John. "Squeezed to Death." *Guardian*. March 4, 2000. www.guardian.co.uk/weekend/story/0,3605,232986,00.html.

Pogge, Thomas. *Realizing Rawls*. Ithaca: Cornell University Press, 1989.

Pogge, Thomas. "Three Problems with Contractarian-Consequentialist Ways of Assessing Social Institutions." *Social Philosophy and Policy* 12 (1995): 241–66.

Pogge, Thomas. "Historical Wrongs: The Other Two Domains." In Lukas Meyer, ed., *Justice in Time: Responding to Historical Injustice*. Baden-Baden, Germany: Nomos, 2004.

Pogge, Thomas. "Severe Poverty as a Violation of Negative Duties." *Ethics & International Affairs* 19, no. 1 (2005): 55–84.

Pogge, Thomas. "Justice." In Donald M. Borchert, ed., *Encyclopedia of Philosophy*, 2nd edn. Farmington Hills, MI: Macmillan Reference, 2006.

Pogge, Thomas. "Severe Poverty as a Human Rights Violation." In Thomas Pogge, ed., *Freedom from Poverty as a Human Right: Who Owes What to the Very Poor*. Oxford: Oxford University Press and UNESCO, 2007.

Pogge, Thomas. *World Poverty and Human Rights: Cosmopolitan Responsibilities and Reforms*, 2nd edn. Cambridge: Polity, 2008.

Pogge, Thomas and Darrel Moellendorf, eds. *Global Justice: Seminal Essays*. St Paul, MN: Paragon House, 2008.

Power, Samantha. "Bystanders to Genocide." *Atlantic Monthly*. September 2001. www.theatlantic.com/issues/2001/09/power.htm.

Priest, Dana. "Bush's 'War' on Terror Comes to a Sudden End." *Washington Post*. January 23, 2009. www.washingtonpost.com/wp-dyn/content/article/2009/01/22/AR2009012203929.html?nav=emailpage.

Project to Enforce the Geneva Conventions, *Why the Red Cross Is Visiting Detainees at Guantanamo Bay*. n.d. (Original posted October 24, 2002). www.pegc.us/archive/Organizations/American_Red_Cross_20021024.txt.

Ravallion, Martin, Shaohua Chen and Prem Sangraula. "Dollar a Day Revisited." World Bank Policy Research Working Paper WPS 4620, Washington, DC, 2008. http://econ.worldbank.org/docsearch.

Ravallion, Martin, Gaurav Datt and Dominique van de Walle. "Quantifying Absolute Poverty in the Developing World." *Review of Income and Wealth* 37 (1991): 345–61.

Rawls, John. "The Law of Peoples." In *On Human Rights: The Amnesty Lectures of 1993*. Edited by Stephen Shute and Susan Hurley. New York: Basic Books, 1993.

Rawls, John. *Political Liberalism*, 2nd edn. New York: Columbia University Press, 1996.

Rawls, John. *The Law of Peoples: With "The Idea of Public Reason Revisited."* Cambridge, MA: Harvard University Press, 1999.

Rawls, John. *A Theory of Justice*, 2nd edn. Cambridge, MA: Harvard University Press, 1999.

Rawls, John. *Justice as Fairness: A Restatement*. Edited by Erin Kelly. Harvard University Press, 2001.

Rayment, Sean. "Secret MoD Poll: Iraqis Support Attacks on British Troops." *Daily Telegraph*. October 23, 2005. www.telegraph.co.uk/news/worldnews/middleeast/iraq/1501319/Secret-MoD-poll-Iraqis-support-attacks-on-British-troops.html.

Reddy, Sanjay. "The Emperor's New Suit: Global Poverty Estimates Reappraised." SCEPA (Schwartz Center for Economic Policy Analysis) Working Paper 2009-11, New School for Social Research, 2009. www.newschool.edu/cepa/publications/workingpapers/SCEPA%20Working%20Paper%202009-11.pdf.

Reddy, Sanjay and Christian Barry. *International Trade and Labor Standards: A Proposal for Linkage*. New York: Columbia University Press, 2008.

Reddy, Sanjay and Camelia Minoiu. "Chinese Poverty: Assessing the Impact of Alternative Assumptions." Working paper, Columbia University, 2007. http://papers.ssrn.com/sol3/papers.cfm?abstract_id=799844.

Reddy, Sanjay and Thomas Pogge. "How *Not* to Count the Poor." In Sudhir Anand and Joseph Stiglitz, eds., *Measuring Global Poverty*. Oxford: Oxford University Press, 2010 (also at www.socialanalysis.org).

Regan, Donald. "Rewriting *Roe v. Wade*." *Michigan Law Review* 77 (1979): 1569–646.

Reitman, Valerie. "UN Probes Claims of Violence against Afghan Witnesses: Reports of Torture and Killings Are Tied to Case of Dead Taliban Fighters." *Los Angeles Times*. November 15, 2002, p. A13.

Risen, James. "US Said to Have Averted Inquiry Into '01 Afghan Killings." *New York Times*. July 10, 2009. www.nytimes.com/2009/07/11/world/asia/11afghan.html?hp.

Rome Declaration on World Food Security. Adopted at the World Food Summit in Rome, November 1996. www.fao.org/wfs.

Ronayne, Peter. *Never Again? The United States and the Prevention and Punishment of Genocide Since the Holocaust*. Lanham MD: Rowman and Littlefield, 2001.

Rosenblatt, Roger. *Life Itself: Abortion in the American Mind*. New York: Random House, 1992.

Ross, Brian and Richard Esposito. "CIA's Harsh Interrogation Techniques Described." *ABC News*. November 18, 2005. abcnews.go.com/WNT/Investigation/story?id=1322866&page=1.

Rossiter, Clinton, ed. *The Federalist Papers*. New York: New American Library, 1961.

Rouhi, Maureen. "Analytical Credibility." *Science Insights* 77, no. 8 (1999): 37. http://osf1.gmu.edu/~sslayden/curr-chem/chem-war/7708scit3.htm.

Saez, Emmanuel and Thomas Piketty. "Income Inequality in the United States, 1913–1998," *Quarterly Journal of Economics* 118 (2003): 1–39, as updated in "Tables and Figures Updated to 2007 in Excel Format," August 2009, available at elsa.berkeley.edu/~saez/.

Schaffer Library of Drug Policy. *A Short History of the Opium Wars*. n.d. http://www.druglibrary.org/schaffer/heroin/opiwar1.htm.

Schmitt, Eric. "Iraq Abuse Trial Is Again Limited to Lower Ranks." *New York Times*. March 23, 2006, p. A1. http://query.nytimes.com/gst/fullpage. html?res=9404E6D71630F930A15750C0A9609C8B63.

Schmitt, Eric and Carolyn Marshall. "Task Force 6–26: Inside Camp Nama; in Secret Unit's 'Black Room,' a Grim Portrait of US Abuse." *New York Times*. March 19, 2006, p. A1. www.nytimes.com/2006/03/19/international/ middleeast/19abuse.html.

Sen, Amartya. *Poverty and Famines*. Oxford: Oxford University Press, 1981.

Sen, Amartya. "Population: Delusion and Reality." *New York Review of Books* 41, no. 15 (1994).

Sen, Amartya. *Development as Freedom*. New York: Anchor Books, 2000.

Sen, Amartya. "A Decade of Human Development." *Journal of Human Development* 1 (2000): 17–23.

Shah, Anup. *US and Foreign Aid Assistance*. Global Issues, April 13, 2009. www.globalissues.org/article/35/us-and-foreign-aid-assistance#ForeignAid NumbersinChartsandGraphs.

Singer, Peter. *One World*. New Haven: Yale University Press, 2002.

SIPRI (Stockholm International Peace Research Institute). "SIPRI Yearbook 2008: Armaments, Disarmaments and International Security: Summary." 2008. yearbook2008.sipri.org/files/SIPRIYB08summary.pdf.

Social Watch. *Unkept Promises*. Montevideo: Instituto del Tercer Mundo, 2005. www.socialwatch.org/node/10021.

Special Rapporteur on the Situation of Human Rights in Myanmar. *Report of the Special Rapporteur on the Situation of Human Rights in Myanmar, Paulo Sérgio Pinheiro*. A/HRC/6/14, December 7, 2007. www2.ohchr.org/ english/bodies/hrcouncil/docs/6session/A.HRC.6.14.doc.

Spence, Richard B. *Boris Savinkov: Renegade on the Left*. Boulder, CO: East European Monographs, 1991.

von Sponeck, Hans. *A Different Kind of War: The UN Sanctions Regime in Iraq*. Oxford: Berghahn Books, 2006.

Stern, Nicholas. "Dynamic Development: Innovation & Inclusion." Speech at the Center for Economic Studies, Ludwig Maximilian University, Munich, Nov. 19, 2002. www.cesifo-group.de/link/ces_ml2002_lecture1. pdf.

Stiglitz, Joseph E. *Globalization and Its Discontents*. New York: W. W. Norton, 2002.

Straw, Jack. Written ministerial comment. November 17, 2004. *Hansard*, 426/57, 2004. www.fco.gov.uk/resources/en/news/2004/11/fco_nst_171104_ strawiraqcasualty.

Stroud, Sarah. "Dworkin and *Casey* on Abortion." *Philosophy and Public Affairs* 25 (1996): 140–70.

Sydney Morning Herald. "The David Hicks Affadavit." December 10, 2004. www.smh.com.au/news/World/David-Hicks-affidavit/2004/12/10/ 1102625527396.html.

Tax Foundation. "Fiscal Facts." July 30, 2009. www.taxfoundation.org/ publications/show/250.html.

Thomson, Judith Jarvis. "A Defense of Abortion." *Philosophy and Public Affairs* 1 (1971): 47–66.

Thomson, Judith Jarvis. "Abortion." *Boston Review*, Summer 1995: 10–14.

Tobin, James. "A Tax on International Currency Transactions." In UNDP, *Human Development Report 1994*, p. 70.

Tribe, Laurence H. *Abortion: The Clash of Absolutes*. New York: W. W. Norton, 1990.

UDHR (Universal Declaration of Human Rights). Approved and proclaimed by the General Assembly of the United Nations on 10 December 1948, as Resolution 217 A (III).

UN. Charter of the United Nations. Signed on 26 June, 1945 at the conclusion of the United Nations Conference on International Organization, and came into force on October 24, 1945. www.un.org/en/documents/charter/index. shtml.

UN. *Report of the Independent Inquiry into the Actions of the United Nations during the 1994 Genocide in Rwanda.* December 15, 1999. www.un.org/ Docs/journal/asp/ws.asp?m=S/1999/1257.

UN. *Implementation of the United Nations Millennium Declaration: Report of the Secretary-General.* A/57/270, July 31, 2002. www.un.org/ millenniumgoals/sgreport2002.pdf?OpenElement.

UN. *Human Rights Experts Issue Joint Report on Situation of Detainees in Guantanamo Bay.* Press Release. February 16, 2006. www.unhchr.ch/ huricane/huricane.nsf/view01/52e94fb9cbc7da10c1257117003517b3? opendocument.

UN. *The Millennium Development Goals Report 2008*. New York: UN Department of Economic and Social Affairs, 2008. www.un.org/ millenniumgoals/2008highlevel/pdf/newsroom/mdg%20reports/MDG_ Report_2008_ENGLISH.pdf

UN. *Millennium Development Goals Indicators.* UN, 2009. http://mdgs.un.org/ unsd/mdg/Data.aspx.

UN Department of Peacekeeping Operations. *UNAMIR Background Document.* n.d. www.un.org/Depts/dpko/dpko/co_mission/unamirS.htm.

UNDP (United Nations Development Programme). *Human Development Report 1994*. New York: Oxford University Press, 1994. http://hdr.undp. org/en/reports/global/hdr1994.

UNDP (United Nations Development Programme). *Human Development Report 1997*. New York: Oxford University Press, 1997. http://hdr.undp. org/en/reports/global/hdr1997/.

UNDP (United Nations Development Programme). *Human Development Report 1998*. New York: Oxford University Press, 1998. http://hdr.undp. org/en/reports/global/hdr1998/.

UNDP (United Nations Development Programme). *Human Development Report 2001*. New York: Oxford University Press, 2001. http://hdr.undp. org/en/reports/global/hdr2001/.

UNDP (United Nations Development Programme). *Human Development Report 2002*. New York: Oxford University Press, 2002. http://hdr.undp. org/en/reports/global/hdr2002/.

UNDP (United Nations Development Programme). *Human Development Report 2003*. New York: Oxford University Press. 2003. http://hdr.undp. org/en/reports/global/hdr2003/.

UNDP (United Nations Development Programme). *Human Development Report 2007/2008*. Basingstoke: Palgrave Macmillan, 2007. http://hdr.undp. org/en/reports/global/hdr2007-2008/.

UNESCO Institute for Statistics. "Literacy Topic." Dec. 1, 2008. www. uis.unesco.org/ev.php?URL_ID=6401&URL_DO=DO_TOPIC&URL_ SECTION=201.

UN General Assembly. *United Nations Millennium Declaration*. A/res/55/2, September 8, 2000. www.un.org/millennium/declaration/ares552e.htm.

UN-Habitat. *The Challenge of Slums: Global Report on Human Settlements 2003*. London: Earthscan, 2003. www.unhabitat.org/pmss/getPage.asp? page=bookView&book=1156.

UN-Habitat. "Urban Energy." n.d. www.unhabitat.org/content.asp?cid=288 4&catid=356&typeid=24&subMenuId=.

United States. "The National Security Strategy of the United States of America." September 2002. www.globalsecurity.org/military/library/policy/ national/nss-020920.pdf.

UN Millennium Declaration. General Assembly Resolution 55/2, 2000. www. un.org/millennium/declaration/ares552e.htm.

UN Population Division. *World Population Prospects: The 2008 Revision*. 2009. http://esa.un.org/unpp/index.asp?panel=2.

UNRISD (United Nations Research Institute for Social Development). *Gender Equality: Striving for Justice in an Unequal World.* Geneva: UNRISD/UN Publications, 2005. www.unrisd.org.

UN Security Council Resolutions. www.un.org/documents/scres.htm.

UNU-WIDER (United Nations University-World Institute for Development Economics Research). *World Income Inequality Database*, Version 2.0c, May 2008. www.wider.unu.edu/research/Database/en_GB/database.

Uranium Medical Research Center. *UMRC's Preliminary Findings from Afghanistan and Operation Enduring Freedom*. April 2003. www.umrc.net/ os/downloads/AfghanistanOEF.pdf.

Urbina, Ian. "UN Resolution: Dangerous Ambiguity." *Asian Times Online.* November 12, 2002. www.atimes.com/atimes/Middle_East/DK12Ak01.html.

USA Today. "Coalition Airstrike Kills 9 in Afghanistan." March 6, 2007. www.usatoday.com/printedition/news/20070306/a_wobs06.art.htm.

USDA (United States Department of Agriculture). *Thrifty Food Plan, 1999: Administrative Report.* Washington, DC: Center for Nutrition Policy and Promotion, USDA, 1999. www.cnpp.usda.gov/Publications/FoodPlans/MiscPubs/FoodPlans1999ThriftyFoodPlanAdminReport.pdf.

US Department of State. "Clinton Administration Policy on Reforming Multilateral Peace Operations" (PDD 25). February 22, 1996. www.fas.org/irp/offdocs/pdd25.htm.

Verkaik, Robert. "CIA Photos 'Show UK Guantanamo Detainee Was Tortured.'" *Independent.* December 10, 2007. news.independent.co.uk/world/americas/article3239372.ece.

Wantchekon, Leonard. "Why do Resource Dependent Countries Have Authoritarian Governments?" Working paper, Yale University, 1999. www.yale.edu/leitner/resources/docs/1999-11.pdf.

Warrick, Joby and Karen DeYoung. "Obama Reverses Bush Policies on Detention and Interrogation." *Washington Post.* January 23, 2009. www.washingtonpost.com/wp-dyn/content/article/2009/01/22/AR2009012201527.html.

Watal, Jayashree. "Access to Essential Medicines in Developing Countries: Does the WTO TRIPS Agreement Hinder It?" Science, Technology and Innovation Discussion Paper No. 8, Harvard Center for International Development, 2000.

Weale, Albert. "Democratic Legitimacy and the Constitution of Europe." In Richard Bellamy, Vittorio Bufacchi and Dario Castiglione, eds., *Democracy and Constitutional Culture in the Union of Europe.* London: Lothian Foundation Press, 1995.

Wenar, Leif. "Property Rights and the Resource Curse." *Philosophy and Public Affairs* 36 (2008): 2–32.

White House. "Bush Commemorates UN Day to Support Torture Victims." Press release, June 26, 2004. www.america.gov/st/washfile-english/2004/June/20040628140800LShsaN0.3632013.html/

WHO (World Health Organization). *The Global Burden of Disease: 2004 Update.* Geneva: WHO Publications, 2008. www.who.int/healthinfo/global_burden_disease/2004_report_update/en/index.html.

WHO and UNICEF (United Nations Children's Fund). *Progress on Drinking Water and Sanitation: Special Focus on Sanitation.* New York and Geneva: UNICEF and WHO, 2008. www.wssinfo.org/en/40_MDG2008.html.

Wilkinson, Marian. "Photos Show Dead Iraqis, Torture and Rape." *The Age.* May 14, 2004. www.theage.com.au/articles/2004/05/13/1084289818093.html.

Wilson, Nick A. and George Thomson. "Deaths from International Terrorism Compared with Road Crash Deaths in OECD Countries." *Injury*

Prevention, 11 (2005): 332–3. www.injuryprevention.bmj.com/content/11/6/332.full.

Wiser, Mike. "The Torture Question: Sidelining Geneva." *Frontline*. October 18, 2005. www.pbs.org/wgbh/pages/frontline/torture/themes/sideline.html.

World Bank. *World Development Report 1982*. New York: Oxford University Press, 1982. http://go.worldbank.org/O3Z20RVKJ0.

World Bank. *World Development Report 1999/2000*. New York: Oxford University Press, 1999. http://go.worldbank.org/YS1H0S2I20.

World Bank. *World Development Report 2000/2001*. New York: Oxford University Press, 2000. http://go.worldbank.org/L8RGH3WLI0.

World Bank. *World Development Report 2002*. New York: Oxford University Press, 2001. http://go.worldbank.org/YGBBFHL1Y0.

World Bank. *Global Economic Prospects 2002: And the Developing Countries*. Washington, DC: World Bank, 2002. http://go.worldbank.org/2HXB3JCLH0.

World Bank. *Globalization, Growth, and Poverty*. New York: Oxford University Press, 2002. http://econ.worldbank.org/prr/globalization/text-2857.

World Bank. *Cutting Agricultural Subsidies*. World Bank News and Broadcast, November 20, 2002. http://go.worldbank.org/E0MW6TEG81.

World Bank. *Global Economic Prospects 2004: Realizing the Development Promise of the Doha Agenda*. Washington, DC: World Bank, 2003. go.worldbank.org/QCUULNC2Y0.

World Bank. *World Development Report 2007*. Washington, DC: World Bank, 2006. www.worldbank.org/wdr2007.

World Bank. *Global Purchasing Power Parities and Real Expenditures: 2005 International Comparison Program*. Washington, DC: World Bank, 2008. http://siteresources.worldbank.org/ICPINT/Resources/icp-final.pdf

World Bank. *World Development Indicators 2008*. Washington, DC: World Bank Publications 2008. http://go.worldbank.org/XUR6QHSYJ0.

World Bank. *World Development Report 2009*. Washington, DC: World Bank, 2008. go.worldbank.org/O4MD5RGAF0.

World Bank. *PovcalNet*. 2009. go.worldbank.org/NT2A1XUWP0.

World Bank. *World Development Indicators 2009*. Washington, DC: World Bank Publications 2009. http://go.worldbank.org/U0FSM7AQ40.

World Bank. *World Development Indicators Online*. 2009. www.worldbank.org/data/onlinedatabases/onlinedatabases.html.

World Trade Organization. *TRIPS Material on the WTO Website*. n.d. www.wto.org/english/tratop_e/trips_e/trips_e.htm.

Yoo, John. Speech at a panel on "Human Rights, International Law, and the War on Terror." Institute of International Studies, University of California, Berkeley, May 2, 2005. webcast.berkeley.edu/event_details.php?webcastid=12285.

Zimmerman, Eilene. "Dining on a Dollar a Day." *Christian Science Monitor*, December 29, 2008. http://features.csmonitor.com/backstory/2008/12/29/dining-on-a-dollar-a-day.

Index